בס"ד

Why Open Orthodoxy Is Not Orthodox

David Rosenthal

With a Foreword by

HARAV AHARON FELDMAN

Yad Yosef Publications

Available from:

Amazon.com

www.createspace.com/6302233

NotOrthodox.blogspot.com

For questions and comments:

oobook18@gmail.com

In loving memory of
my grandmother

Shirley Rosenthal, ע"ה

An extraordinary woman
who is greatly missed

תנצב"ה

Contents

Foreword 9

Acknowledgments 15

Leaders of Open Orthodoxy 17

Chapter 1: What Is Orthodox? 19

Chapter 2: A New Movement 22

Chapter 3: Open Orthodox Ordination

    and Scholarship 46

Chapter 4: Torah as Divine and Eternal 81

Chapter 5: Values 112

Chapter 6: Homosexuality 135

Chapter 7: Women's Issues 159

Chapter 8: Ecumenicalism 196

Chapter 9: Biblical Interpretation 224

Chapter 10: Conclusion 239

Endnotes 247

Foreword

by Harav Aharon Feldman
Rosh HaYeshiva, Ner Israel Rabbinical College

Yeravam ben Nevat is the paradigm of the Jewish arch-sinner, the only leader in history described as a *chotey umachti es ha'am*— one who sinned and who brought the nation to sin. As the king of the secessionary tribe of Ephraim, he built two Temples in each of which he installed a golden calf which he encouraged his subjects to worship. Furthermore, he blocked the thrice-yearly pilgrimages to the *Beys Hamikdash* in Jerusalem. This would ensure that only his Temples, and not the *Beys Hamikdash*, would serve as the people's central places of worship. Not surprisingly he is listed in the Mishnah as one of those who have lost their share in the world-to-come.

Yet the Sages tell us that God Himself proposed to this arch-sinner that if he would repent, God would stroll together with him and Ben Yishai (King David) in the Garden of Eden (*Sanhedrin* 102a).

Yeravam must have been an outstanding sort of person to have been offered this proposition. And indeed the Sages relate that at one time Yeravam was the towering Torah scholar of his time next to whom the other scholars were like the "grass of the fields" (*ibid.* 101b). How, then, are we to understand that he could have fallen to such an irredeemable level of sin that he lost his share in the world-to-come?

One might conjecture that this outstandingly talented personality began his descent into his abyss with a rationalization. Building an alternative form of worship for the Jews, he argued, would actually be to their benefit. Too many Jews were worshipping idols in any event. The severe, uncompromising leadership of Yehuda believed that idolatry was anathema and they refused to tolerate it at all costs. As a result, those who worshipped idols—and there were many of them—felt like outcasts. Yeravam reasoned: Wouldn't it be better to have a supervised form of idolatry rather than have the people worship the idols of the nations of the world? Wouldn't building golden calves, a distinctly Jewish form of idol worship at the time of Moses, stem the tide of assimilation by making the Jews feel that they too were able to worship idols and did not need to join the other nations of the world in order to do so? And wouldn't keeping the populace from visiting Jerusalem's restrictive, critical ambience three times a year instill pride in them and give them a stronger Jewish identity? What better program could there be for saving the Jewish people from assimilation? Must the Jewish people always be mired in the immutable mold of the *mitzvos*? Didn't the time come for innovation?

But of course, Yeravam's argument was an exercise in self-deception. Idolatry is the antithesis of everything Judaism stands for. It is an absurdity to save the Jews by turning them to idol-worshippers; one cannot hope to save the Jewish people by undermining their very essence. An idolatrous Jewish nation is not a Jewish one.

What was Yeravam's true motivation? The conclusion of the above-cited Talmudic passage gives us a clue. After God proposed that Yeravam walk with Him and Ben Yishai in the Garden of Eden, Yeravam's response was: "Who will walk first?" When God answered, "Ben Yishai," Yeravam replied, "If so, I refuse" (*Sanhedrin ibid.*).

With this story, the Sages are telling tell us that the source of Yeravam's sin was that he could not abide that the dynasty of King David be recognized as supreme while his dynasty be known as second-best. It was this craving for power and recognition which kept him from the greatest imaginable human success—that of walking with God in Gan Eden, and which caused him to decide instead to make the worship of a golden calf his state religion.

In other words, Yeravam was indeed a great person with unusual blessings. But his downfall was that in his heart's heart he sought power and recognition. That is why, rather than walk second to Ben Yishai, he preferred not to walk at all with God.

One might say that the founders of Open Orthodoxy are reminiscent of Yeravam ben Nevat. Their early writings claim that their goal was to keep Jews from assimilation. Modern Orthodoxy, they claimed, had failed in its attempt to stem the tide of rejection of Torah by the youth. It had become stagnant and unyielding, and unwilling to bend to the winds of the times. Adjustments would have to be made to bring Orthodoxy in line with current morality and values or Judaism would be left behind in the swirling changes which were overtaking society. Jews were losing respect in the eyes of liberal America for their stances on feminism, gay marriage, and conversions. These would have to change if Jews were to survive.

But this was only self-deception. One might conjecture about the true motivation of Open Orthodoxy's founders. But it is difficult to avoid a conclusion that the motivation was a craving for recognition by the outside culture, a craving which made them ready to alter the Torah in order to gain that recognition. For this reason, from its inception, Open Orthodoxy began a downward slope which led it to reject the basic tenets of Jewish faith. What was once a program which professed an altruistic dedication to granting equal rights to women in the synagogue without explicitly overruling Halacha (e.g., leading the Friday night *kabbalas Shabbos* services), developed into a movement whose teachers and students blatantly rejected not only Halacha but the bedrock beliefs of Judaism, namely: that Torah is Divinely given; that *Torah She-be'al Peh* is the legitimate interpretation of the Torah; that *mitzvos* cannot be altered or rejected; and that sexual modesty is part of the fabric of Jewish culture.

In a remarkably short time, Open Orthodoxy was able to set up rabbinical seminaries for both men and women whose graduates' main efforts are directed toward spreading the beliefs—or anti-beliefs—of Open Orthodoxy and undermining the authority of Torah. One outrageous statement by Open Orthodox leaders, teachers or graduates follows on the heels of another: God was wrong in commanding Abraham in the *Akeidah*; the Forefathers were guilty of child-negligence, immorality, and sexism; Moshe Rabbeinu was an inadequate leader who erred in rejecting Korach; the Torah should be altered to align it with current social mores—and so forth. In short, Open Orthodoxy has become a vehicle for turning the Jewish people away from Torah—all of this purportedly to ensure its survival. Thus it is not far-fetched to accuse Open Orthodoxy of being a modern Yeravam ben Nevat, the quintessential *choteh u-machti es ha-am* whose goal is to turn the people away from Torah.

In what can only be described as a deliberate misleading of the public, Open Orthodoxy has preempted the name "Orthodox," despite the fact that it has rejected the bases upon which Orthodoxy stands. To our great misfortune, many communities, because of either ignorance or innocence, are not aware of this. Graduates of the Open Orthodox seminaries are being engaged throughout the country by Orthodox synagogues, university campuses and community centers under the presumption that they are Orthodox rabbis. This constitutes a serious threat to the continuity of authentic Torah in this land.

My student, Rabbi David (Shaul M.) Rosenthal, has thus made a notable contribution to our times by spending a year researching this topic thoroughly. Citing chapter and verse from statements of its leaders and graduates, he shows that

Open Orthodoxy has gone beyond the pale of Torah belief. This book demonstrates that Open Orthodoxy is a movement which poses as Orthodoxy, with teachers who pose as halachic authorities and with students who pose as Orthodox rabbis.

His presentation is well-documented and will compel anyone who reads this book to recognize that Open Orthodoxy is a dissident movement no different from Conservative and Reform Judaism, and one which has lulled the American public into accepting it as an authentic Torah voice.

I salute the indefatigable efforts and dedication which went into the writing of this book, and I fervently pray that Rabbi Rosenthal's efforts will have a deep impact on the public and help stem the tide of a spurious movement which threatens to engulf American Jewry with a sea of counterfeit Judaism.

Acknowledgments

I do not have the words to properly thank my Rebbe, Harav Aharon Feldman, *shlita*. I cannot begin to express my *hakaros hatov* for the years that he has shared with me his great Torah knowledge and sage counsel. It has been an honor to have a relationship with such a great man. In addition to providing the inspiration and encouragement to write this book, he guided me during its writing and was always available to answer any question that I had.

Anyone who derives any benefit from this book is indebted to Rabbi Avraham Gordimer. Many of the primary sources in this book were provided by him. For years, he has dedicated himself to exposing the truth about Open Orthodoxy. Despite many personal attacks against him, he continues in his mission. This book only became a reality because of his undying commitment and perseverance.

I would like to express my gratitude to Yeshivas Ner Yisroel where I have been blessed to learn for the past ten years. It is an unparalleled *makom Torah* filled with Torah giants whose only goal is to serve God in the fullest way possible.

I would also like to thank the many *talmidei chachamim* in Kollel Avodas Levi who took the time to review the manuscript and who shared their insight and great Torah knowledge. Specifically, I would like to recognize Rabbi Yosef Wagner whose extensive knowledge of *Shas* and *poskim* was vital to the writing of this book.

I would also like to thank Mrs. Libby Lazewnik whose editorial skill greatly enhanced the quality of this book and Mrs. Nechama Frand who carefully proofread the manuscript and provided valuable suggestions.

I wish to extend my thanks to Jeremy Staiman and his team at Staiman design for the beautiful cover.

Finally, I would like to express my love and gratitude to my parents, siblings, and grandfather. Without their support this book could never have become a reality.

Note to the Reader

Footnotes are marked with a superscript number. Only the relevant parts of quotations are cited in the text itself. The endnotes contain many of those quotes in greater detail, marked with a superscript capital letter.

Leaders of Open Orthodoxy

Rabbi Avi Weiss is the founder of Open Orthodoxy as well as its rabbinical school, Yeshivat Chovevei Torah (YCT) [1] and co-founder of Yeshivat Maharat,[2] an institution which trains women to be halachic decisors and spiritual leaders. He also helped establish the International Rabbinic Fellowship, the Open Orthodox rabbinic organization.[3]

Rabbi Asher Lopatin serves as the President of Yeshivat Chovevei Torah.

Rabbi Dov Linzer is the Rosh haYeshivah of Yeshivat Chovevei Torah.

Rabbi Ysoscher Katz is the Chair of the Department of Talmud and Director of the Lindenbaum Center for Halakhic Studies at Yeshivat Chovevei Torah.

---

1. http://www.yctorah.org/content/view/23/49. Retrieved August 28, 2015. All subsequent references to Yeshivat Chovevei Torah staff are taken from this website.
2. http://www.Yeshivatmaharat.org/faculty-and-staff. Retrieved August 28, 2015. All subsequent references to Yeshivat Maharat staff are taken from this website.
3. http://morethodoxy.org/2009/11/26/international-rabbinic-fellow-ship-press-release. Retrieved July 28, 2015.

Rabba Sara Hurwitz is the first female Orthodox rabbi ordained by Rabbis Avi Weiss and Daniel Sperber. She serves as the Dean of Yeshivat Maharat.

Rabbi Jeffrey Fox is the Rosh haYeshivah of Yeshivat Maharat and a 2004 graduate of Yeshivat Chovevei Torah.[4]

---

4. http://www.yctorah.org/content/view/44/84. Retrieved August 20, 2015. All subsequent references to YCT graduates are taken from this website.

1

What is Orthodox?

Orthodox or Torah Judaism is based on the belief that the Torah was given by God to the Jewish people on Mt. Sinai. This fact has been a mainstay of Jewish belief throughout all the thousands of years since Sinai. Orthodoxy maintains that the Torah is an eternal document and its commandments are forever binding.

The Written Torah was handed down along with its interpretation, known as the Oral Torah or *Torah she-be'al peh*. Without the Oral Torah, the Written Torah cannot be properly understood. This compendium contains, among other wisdoms, vital details and explanations for the *mitzvos* that appear in the Written Torah, such as *tefillin* or *shechitah*, whose exact parameters are unclear from the Written Torah alone. Without the Oral Tradition, it would be impossible to even read the text of the Torah, as the source of its vowelization is from this tradition. While other movements in our history have denied its veracity, Orthodoxy firmly believes that the Oral Torah is God given and unchanging. The Rambam writes in his introduction to *Mishneh Torah*, that the Talmud is the accurate and authoritative record of this tradition.

Halacha, or Jewish Law, is the practical application of the Written and Oral Tradition. Orthodoxy, as opposed to many other movements among Jews, maintains that Halacha is binding. It guides a Jew in his thoughts and actions in every area of his life. Everything from speaking, to eating, to marriage is an opportunity to serve God. A life guided by Halacha enables one to sanctify all areas of his existence by making his entire life an expression of God's will. Only the Jewish people, as the chosen nation of God, were given this special opportunity to achieve a unique closeness to Him through a meticulous observance of His law. Orthodox Jews have remained faithful to this commitment despite pogroms, holocausts, expulsions, intifadas, emancipations, and assimilation. That they have been able to maintain this depth of commitment despite these difficulties is perhaps the greatest evidence of its veracity. Only a commitment based on an historical fact could have been so tenaciously upheld.

Halacha does not change in response to pressure from outside society, but rather is determined by the rigorous and cumulative analysis of the Talmud and its accompanying literature.

In glaring contrast to the relativism of secular culture, Orthodox Judaism contends that there are certain absolute beliefs that are obligatory upon every Jew. These beliefs were codified by the Rambam in his *Mishneh Torah*[5] as well as in

---

5. *Hilchos Teshuvah*, Chapter 3.

his commentary to the tenth Chapter of *Sanhedrin*, where he lists his famous Thirteen Tenets of Faith. These principles were derived from the Oral Tradition. Among them are the belief that (a) God exists and is perfect; (b), that He has no body; (c) that the prophecy of Moses is unique and supreme above all other prophecies; (d) that the entire Written and Oral Torah were given by God; (e) that one cannot add or subtract from the Written or Oral Torah; (f) and that the Messiah will ultimately come.

In the course of this book, we will demonstrate that Open Orthodoxy unfortunately embraces many of the perspectives which the Rambam considers completely beyond the pale of accepted Jewish belief and therefore heretical. As a result, Open Orthodoxy cannot be considered Orthodox.

2

A New Movement

In 1997, Rabbi Avi Weiss coined the term "Open Orthodoxy."[6] Although his movement has been subjected to harsh criticism, it has burgeoned into a formidable force on the Jewish scene. Together with other Open Orthodox leaders, Rabbi Weiss established Yeshivat Chovevei Torah (YCT), which ordains Open Orthodox rabbis; Yeshivat Maharat, where women receive Orthodox *semichah* (ordination), and the International Rabbinic Fellowship (IRF), an Open Orthodox rabbinic organization.

Graduates of these institutions serve as Rabbis, Maharats, and Rabbas around the globe, in places as distant as Australia, Finland, and Kenya. They serve, or have served, across the United States in cities such as New York, Portland, Cleveland, Baltimore, Washington, D.C., St. Louis, Nashville, Los Angeles, Denver, Phoenix, and more. They hold positions as congregational rabbis, spiritual leaders, chaplains, campus rabbis, and teachers. Their presence is strongly felt in a number of major cities: as of the writing of this book, there were 22

---

6. Rabbi Avi Weiss. "Open Orthodoxy! A Modern Orthodox Rabbi's Creed" *Judaism* (Fall 1997): pp. 409-421.

YCT graduates serving in New York, seven in the Washington-Baltimore area, six in Chicago, six in Los Angeles and five in San Francisco. YCT alone has produced over 90 graduates, and in just eight years they predict that there will be another 60 in the field.[7] They preach their message to, and have the power to influence, thousands of Jews. As YCT Chairman Steve Lieberman boldly puts it:[8]

> The Modern Orthodox World is learning that it must get used to having YCT rabbis in leadership positions virtually in every place they look. And I have a message for those individuals who still haven't gotten used to this fact. You will have to get used to it or you will become completely irrelevant in the field of Modern Orthodoxy.

New movements are not new to the Jewish people. Many of them have come along over the course of our history, seeking to reshape Jewish life. Where Open Orthodoxy differs from those other movements is that its very name is fraudulent. While it claims to be Orthodox, in belief and in practice, as we will show, it is not.

This book will provide countless examples. It will show that the movement's anti-Orthodox views are pervasive and ubiquitous and in no way represent a minority opinion within the movement. We will provide extensive quotes from leaders of Open Orthodoxy as demonstrative of the movement's views. The

---

7. https://www.youtube.com/watch?v=Tfm_A7T-xWk. Retrieved July 31, 2015.
8. *Ibid.*

reader is encouraged to review the source material, for which extensive citation is provided in the footnotes and endnotes.

The most disturbing aspect of Open Orthodoxy is the fact that many of its leaders unabashedly make statements which are antithetical to Orthodox belief. Most basic of these is the denial, by some, of the Torah's divine origin.

The views of graduates of YCT and Yeshivat Maharat are also cited extensively in this book as evidence of Open Orthodoxy's non-Orthodox views. While some at YCT and Yeshivat Maharat may claim that the views of their students do not represent the views of Open Orthodoxy, the fact that similar views are held by the leadership, combined with the fact that YCT and Yeshivat Maharat rarely condemn the troublesome views of their graduates, is sufficient evidence that they approve of them.

While this book does cite the views of numerous YCT and Yeshivat Maharat alumni, quotations are not provided for every single graduate. However, each one of them may reasonably be suspected of harboring the problematic views of their mentors. They all spent years under their tutelage absorbing their teachings and worldview. Is it possible that they sat in classes imbibing these values for years and did not absorb them into their own philosophy of Judaism?

◆　◆　◆

Since its inception, the Reform movement has always been a reflection of the mores and morals of the society around it. In 1885, the Pittsburgh Platform declared that Reform Jews had no desire to return to Palestine.[9] After 1948 and the return of Jewish sovereignty to the land, Reform Jews became committed to the State of Israel and the movement currently encourages *aliyah*.[10] In 1985, the Reform movement issued a responsum stating that a rabbi could not participate in a same-sex wedding ceremony.[11] In 2000, as attitudes in America shifted, the Reform Movement reversed its position and permitted rabbis to officiate at such weddings.[12] This comes as no surprise, as the essence of the movement is to "reform" Judaism to bring it in line with the values of the day. Their policies therefore follow the current social preferences.

The Conservative movement has never been far behind Reform. In 1972, Sally Priesand became the first female Reform rabbi.[13] She was followed by Amy Eilberg in 1985, the first female rabbi of the Conservative Movement.[14] In 1990, the Reform Movement began accepting homosexual clergy.[15] In 2006 the Conservative movement did the same.[16] Each of these movements cite lengthy halachic responsa justifying these innovations, but it is clear from even a quick perusal of the

---

9. http://ccarnet.org/rabbis-speak/platforms/declaration-principles. Retrieved August 28, 2015.
10. http://ccarnet.org/rabbis-speak/platforms/statement-principles-reform-judaism. Retrieved August 28, 2015.
11. https://www.ccarnet.org/responsa/carr-297-298.
12. http://ccarnet.org/responsa/same-sex-marriage-kiddushin.
13. http://jwa.org/encyclopedia/article/priesand-sally-jane. Retrieved August 28, 2015.
14. http://jwa.org/encyclopedia/article/eilberg-amy. Retrieved August 28, 2015.
15. http://www.ccarnet.org/rabbis-speak/resolutions/2000/same-gender-officiation. Retrieved August 28, 2015.
16. http://www.nytimes.com/2006/12/07/us/07jews.html?pagewanted=all. Retrieved August 28, 2015.

literature that the logic is flawed and the sources misapplied. Like the famous archer who painted the targets after shooting the arrows,[17] they are ex post facto justifications for the acceptance into Judaism of foreign behaviors. What is all too clear is that the impetus for these innovations is not Halacha, but a desire to graft society's values onto the Torah. These movements have consistently followed the ebb and flow of the moral and social norms of the day. Neither movement believes in an absolute, God given Torah, but rather in, at most, a divinely-inspired set of guidelines which may be re-adjusted to fit the times.

Orthodoxy, on the other hand, has always rejected this view. The term "Orthodox" was originally coined by Reform leaders as a pejorative for the "unenlightened" Jews who stubbornly held fast to their ancient beliefs and practices, and was meant to imply that those who refuse to update their beliefs are relics of a bygone era.

For many years, it appeared that Orthodoxy in the United States was moribund. Reform and Conservative seemed poised to become the predominant form of Judaism in this country. However, the opposite has happened. Today, across the continent, Reform and Conservative synagogues are closing while new Orthodox *yeshivos* and synagogues are springing up in tens of communities. Once-vibrant Conservative Hebrew schools, which were, for the most part, "Bar Mitzvah factories" that teemed with children now stand empty. Where have their students and their students' children gone? They have totally assimilated.

---

17. This is in fact a metaphor used unabashedly by one of Open Orthodoxy's leading rabbis; see below.

Young people are attracted to integrity. Those ideas and movements which yield to current fads hold no attraction for them. Most would rather follow a movement which stubbornly remains steadfast in its beliefs despite social pressure to do otherwise. [18] For the same reason, non-Orthodox young men and women have been returning to Orthodoxy in droves. This is one reason why study after study has shown Orthodoxy is on the rise while the other movements are in decline.[19]

Orthodoxy maintains the core belief that the Torah is the ultimate truth and that God is the only arbiter of morality. It has withstood the test of time, guiding us as a nation from Egypt to Israel and then to Babylon, Rome, and beyond. The Torah's dictates have taught Jews how to live a moral and ethical life wherever they lived, which was in almost every culture on earth.

In contrast to remaining steadfast to Jewish beliefs, Rabbi Samuel Holdheim, an early Reform leader, said, "In the Talmudic age, the Talmud was right. In my age, I am right."[20] In today's secular society, the ultimate value is man's freedom to do as he pleases and satisfy his desires. Success is determined by the acquisition of wealth, power and fame. This attitude is behind most modern movements, most notably the modern

---

18. A poignant example: for thousands of years, humanity believed, like Aristotle, that the world was eternal. Jews never tried to reinterpret the verses in Genesis or held symposiums to discuss the validity of the Torah. Rather, they have maintained that the Torah is the literal word of God and it is in no need of reinterpretation. It is the popular world view that is in need of reinterpretation. In 1964, Arno Penzias and Robert Wilson discovered cosmic radiation from the Big Bang, which proved that the universe had a beginning. (https://cosmology. carnegiescience.edu/timeline/1964)

19. For example see http://www.pewforum.org/2015/08/26/a-portrait-of-american-orthodox-jews. Retrieved February 5, 2016.

20. Paul Johnson, *A History of the Jews* (New York: Harper and Row, 1987), p. 334.

feminist and gay-rights movements. What society once considered murder—abortion—is now permitted, because a woman has the right to do as she pleases with her body. In the same vein, those who have a same-sex attraction oblige society to legitimize this attraction by granting them the right to marry.

In truth, Jews are thankful to live in a society which holds personal autonomy as a core value. Such a value allows us the right to practice our religion freely and unmolested. However, Judaism's view of life is diametrically opposed to that of the surrounding culture. Judaism teaches that the purpose of life is to serve God and to forego one's own desires in carrying out that service. In the Jewish world, a hero is not the person who has achieved wealth, power or fame, but one who has overcome his drives and joyously submits to God's will.

From its embrace of society's values as sacred and its propensity to tailor the Torah to fit snugly around them, it is clear that Open Orthodoxy is a mere variant of the Reform and Conservative movements. And Open Orthodoxy is not shy about this. Rabbi Daniel Sperber, who serves on YCT and Yeshivat Maharat's advisory boards,[21] admits that many of Open Orthodoxy's actions seem non-Orthodox. In reference to ordaining women, he says:[22]

> Slowly but surely, it turns out that the entire status of women in Judaism is changing. Within this process there are several things that seem drastic, quasi-Conservative or neo-Reform....

---

21. http://www.yctorah.org/content/view/906/49. http://www.Yeshivat-maharat.org/advisory-board. Retrieved August 6, 2015.
22. http://www.haaretz.com/jewish/features/.premium-1.668002. Retrieved July 28, 2015.

He cautions:

> Until now, everything we've done was within legitimate halakhic parameters. We have to be careful not to cross the boundary, and the boundary is vague.

Rabbi Sperber cautions against crossing the elusive halachic boundary. However, if it was fealty to Halacha which motivated Open Orthodoxy, there should be no such fear. It is only because secular values drive Open Orthodoxy's agenda to uproot Halacha that this danger exists at all.

The movement's allegiance to society's values above those of the Torah's is abundantly clear from its members' writings. This is why, in 1997, when homosexuality was not yet widely accepted, Rabbi Weiss said that he opposed the Reform movement's liberal views on the issue[23]—yet in 2015 he openly supported the legalization of same sex marriage.[24]

As we will show, the theme that runs through their writings is consistent: "How do we adjust Halacha to fit society's morals?" It is not what the Torah wants that sets the agenda, but rather what the popular culture wants. For example:

- Society believes that destroying a nation is immoral; therefore the commandment to annihilate Amalek must be altered or erased.[25]
- Society believes that homosexuality is an acceptable lifestyle; therefore the Torah's attitude towards it must be changed. These Open Orthodox rabbis openly pray for the

---

23. Rabbi Avi Weiss, "Open Orthodoxy! A Modern Orthodox Rabbi's Creed" *Judaism* (Fall 1997): p. 416.
24. http://www.haaretz.com/opinion/1.666064. Retrieved July 20, 2015. See Chapter 6.
25. See Chapter 4.

passing of same-sex marriage legislation and pen pseudo-halachic arguments to legitimize homosexual relations.[26]

- Society believes that there is no halachic difference between men and women; therefore women can serve as rabbis and *poskim* and wear *tefillin*. Also, men must stop reciting the blessing of "*shelo asani isha*" if it does not fit into society's belief of egalitarianism.[27]

- Society believes in sexual liberation; therefore a Rosh haYeshivah at YCT can throw modesty to the wind by lecturing publicly about explicit sexual topics.[28]

- Society preaches that all religions are equal; therefore Orthodox leaders can attend a Jewish-Catholic conference where participants join together in prayer and dance in front of a golden statue of the Pope.[29]

The list goes on and on. In some cases, the views of certain Open Orthodox rabbis are more radical than their Reform and Conservative counterparts.[30] Subsequent chapters will deal with the above issues, and others, in great detail.

---

26. See Chapter 6.
27. See Chapter 7 why this blessing is recited.
28. *Ibid.*
29. See Chapter 8.
30. For example, Rabbi Shmuly Yanklowitz (YCT 2010) in an interview about conversion says that more converts are needed, as they will "expand the consciousness of the Jewish people." Contrary to the Talmudic position (*Yevamos* 47b) which does not favor encouraging conversion, he says, "For Judaism to survive in the 21st century and beyond it needs to be broad, and to not accept converts in the most inclusive way possible challenges that breadth and potentially narrows who we are." A Reform rabbi who was also interviewed did not share Rabbi Yanklowitz's view. She felt it was more important to focus our energies on people who are already Jewish. (https://www.youtube.com/watch?v=7obs7JwscC4. Retrieved August 12, 2015.)

The views of Open Orthodoxy are best summed up by one of their leaders. Rabbi Yosef Kanefsky is past president of the International Rabbinic Fellowship[31] and was a student of Rabbi Avi Weiss.[32] He is praised by Weiss as "one of the most articulate spokespersons of Modern Orthodoxy" and "one of the great rabbis in America."[33] Kanefsky writes in reference to a new halachic innovation, "In the end though, the halakhic scholarship simply paints a bull's eye around the target that I—and many others before me—had already identified."[34]

The process is a convenient one: first make the innovation, and only after fit the Halacha around it. This is the classic story of the man who wished to donate a covering for the synagogue's *Sefer Torah*. When the rabbi tried to put the covering on the Torah, he realized that it was too short. "I'm sorry, but it does not fit," the rabbi said. To which the man responded, "That's not a problem—just trim down the Torah and it will fit perfectly!"

That Open Orthodoxy seeks to find favor in the eyes of the world by emulating their values seems obvious. An example is a letter sent by Rabbi Shmuel Herzfeld and Maharat Ruth Balinsky Friedman (Yeshivat Maharat Class of 2013).[35] Rabbi Herzfeld is a student of Rabbi Avi Weiss,[36] an honorary alumnus

31. http://www.internationalrabbinicfellowship.org/leadership. Retrieved August 28, 2015.
32. http://morethodoxy.org/2014/03/17/my-teacher-and-my-mentor-a-tribute-to-rabbi-avi-weiss-by-yosef-kanefsky. Retrieved July 25 2015.
33. https://www.youtube.com/watch?v=_PUcfOoqmuI. Retrieved February 17, 2016.
34. Rabbi Yosef Kanefsky, "Follow-Up to the Blog Post: Adieu to "Thou Hast Not Made Me a Woman" *Keren* 2 (2014), p. 6.
35. http://www.Yeshivatmaharat.org/class-of-2013. Retrieved August 21, 2015. All subsequent references to Yeshivat Maharat graduates are taken from this website.
36. http://ostt.org/Rabbi_Herzfeld. Retrieved July 21, 2015.

of YCT,[37] and also serves on their Jewish leadership advisory board. [38] In the letter, they seek advice from Rabbi Jeffrey Fox, the Rosh haYeshivah of Yeshivat Maharat, regarding *mikveh* immersion standards for female converts. They state that many female converts are uncomfortable with current procedure, and then go on to offer another reason why the status quo should be changed:[39]

> …On top of that, here in DC the conversion process for women has become a mockery in the eyes of the world. The *Washington Post* published a lengthy article saying that the convert goes into the mikvah naked in front of male rabbis. This is in most cases not true, but the perception is very painful. What do you recommend in this difficult situation?

According to Herzfeld and Friedman, a critical and inaccurate article in the *Washington Post* constitutes a legitimate impetus for halachic change. In reality, however, this kind of motivation is neither valid nor compelling. Halacha should not be based on the whims of the editorial page, but rather on a sincere desire to know the will of God. Did Rabbi Moshe Feinstein decide halachic matters based on the *New York Times* or Rabbi Soloveitchik on the *Boston Globe*?

Why did its leaders decide to call their movement a form of Orthodoxy? The answer is that, today, the Conservative and

37. http://www.yctorah.org/index2.php?option=com_content&do_pdf=1&id=30. Retrieved August 30, 2015.

38. http://www.yctorah.org/content/view/906/49. Retrieved August 21, 2015.

39. ahttps://static.squarespace.com/static/5348363de4b0531dce75b-c53/t/546ce0d5e4b02e200e59ce8f/1416421589876/MaleBeitDinat-theImmersionofaFemaleConvert1.pdf. Retrieved July 30, 2015.

Reform sectors of Judaism are ideologically bankrupt, while the Orthodox brand has maintained its legitimacy. Calling a movement "Orthodox" latches onto brand recognition. They can claim the integrity of traditionalists while at the same time the status of enlightened progressives. In addition, some who grew up Orthodox may feel guilty about sharing the views of the Conservative movement. By calling themselves Orthodox, they can cling to their beliefs while retaining their native affiliation.

This is what is so insidious about Open Orthodoxy. When the Reform Movement came onto the scene in the nineteenth century, it was clear from its name exactly what it was: this was a group of people who sought to "reform" Judaism. By claiming to be Orthodox, Open Orthodoxy has duped many people into believing that its views are representative of Orthodox Judaism. While they have the legal right to preach their beliefs under any name, they do *not* have the moral right to call themselves something which they are not.

The obvious danger is that a synagogue may hire an Open Orthodox Rabbi, Rabba, or Maharat thinking that they are Orthodox. Many congregations may be seeking to hire an Orthodox rabbi but lack the background to differentiate between authentic Orthodoxy and dangerous imitations. Since Yeshivat Chovevei Torah is ostensibly an "Orthodox" institution, a synagogue may unwittingly hire one of its graduates for its pulpit. A dynamic young rabbi will make a charismatic speech and "wow" the congregation, although he may hold views that are antithetical to Orthodoxy and Jewish tradition. He may mislead his flock right into the abyss into which multitudes of Conservative and Reform Jews have disappeared.

Perhaps even more troubling is the fact that many Open Orthodox rabbis serve as teachers in high schools and on college campuses. In such positions, they have the potential to teach a non-Orthodox version of Torah to the next generation.

The following citations highlight the chilling similarities between Open Orthodoxy and the Reform and Conservative movements:

Mosaic Law

Pittsburg Platform Reform Movement (1885)[1]	Rabbi Ysoscher Katz
We recognize in the Mosaic legislation a system of training the Jewish people for its mission during its national life in Palestine, and today we accept as binding only its moral laws, and maintain only such ceremonies as elevate and sanctify our lives, but reject all such as are not adapted to the views and habits of modern civilization.	*(Chair of the Department of Talmud and Director of the Lindenbaum Center for Halakhic Studies at YCT)*[2] The Rabbis reject his [Moses] judicial views as conservative and archaic.

1. http://ccarnet.org/rabbis-speak/platforms/declaration-principles. Retrieved July 23, 2015.
2. https://www.facebook.com/ysoscher?fref=ts (February 25, 2015). Retrieved July 24, 2015.

Divinity of Torah

Rabbi Elliot Dorff (*Conservative Rabbi*)[3]	Rabbi Zev Farber (YCT 2006)[4]
In fact, the Torah contains many materials from widely different time periods and places, and that is why some of the laws and stories actually contradict each other.	The simplest explanation for these differences between the accounts in Exodus-Numbers and Deuteronomy is that they were penned by (at least) two different authors with different conceptions of the desert experience.

Morality of the Torah

Rabbi David Golinkin (*Conservative Rabbi*)[5]	Rabbi Zev Farber (YCT 2006)[6]
Finally, the Torah contains laws and stories which raise grave ethical problems.	The following are a few examples of ethically problematic laws. (Referring to explicit Torah commandments)

3. http://www.adath-shalom.ca/dorff59.htm. Retrieved August 28, 2015.
4. http://thetorah.com/devarim-recounting-different. Retrieved July 19, 2015.
5. http://www.responsafortoday.com/about/about.htm. Retrieved August 28, 2015.
6. http://thetorah.com/marrying-your-daughter-to-her-rapist. Retrieved August 22, 2015.

Bible Stories

Pittsburg Platform Reform Movement (1885)[7]	Rabbi Zev Farber (YCT 2006)[8]
We hold that the modern discoveries of scientific researches in the domain of nature and history are not antagonistic to the doctrines of Judaism, the Bible reflecting the primitive ideas of its own age, and at times clothing its conception of divine Providence and Justice dealing with men in miraculous narratives.	It began with the parts of the Torah which are clearly folkloristic or symbolic in character. The creation of the world in six days, the account of Adam and Eve in the garden, Noah's flood and the Tower of Babel—all of these were easily identified as ahistorical. These stories fit perfectly into the genre of folklore or allegory and each offers a simple narrative of intentionally fantastic character in order to explain some aspect of the world in which we live.

7. http://ccarnet.org/rabbis-speak/platforms/declaration-principles. Retrieved July 23, 2015.
8. http://thetorah.com/torah-history-judaism-part-5. Retrieved July 19, 2015.

Redemption

Pittsburg Platform Reform Movement (1885)[9]	Rabbi Shmuly Yanklowitz (YCT 2010)[10]
We consider ourselves no longer a nation, but a religious community, and therefore expect neither a return to Palestine, nor a sacrificial worship under the sons of Aaron, nor the restoration of any of the laws concerning the Jewish state.	My teacher Rabbi Dr. Nathan Lopes Cardozo once again hits a grand-slam reminding us to get our priorities straight as we approach Tisha B'Av. "Whether or not the Temple will be re-built is not our concern, nor is it our dream. It is of little importance. What we dream of is the day when we will be able to transform ourselves and reconstruct the Temple's message within our hearts."

9. http://ccarnet.org/rabbis-speak/platforms/declaration-principles. Retrieved July 23, 2015.
10. https://www.facebook.com/rshmuly.yanklowitz?fref=ts (July 23, 2015). Retrieved July 24, 2015.

Change

Zacharias Frankel	Dasi Fruchter
(*Early Conservative Leader*)[11]	(Student at Yeshivat Maharat)[12]
The means [of transformation] must be grasped with such care, thought through with such discretion, created always with such awareness of the moment in time, that the goal will be reached unnoticed, that the forward progress will seem inconsequential to the average eye.	There we are, day in and day out, a group of feminist scholars and leaders, in a movement seeking to change the gender landscape of Orthodox Jewish leadership.[13]

11. Michael A. Meyer, *Response to Modernity: A History of the Reform Movement in Judaism*. New York: Oxford University Press, (1988): p. 85. Cited by Rabbi Lawrence Kelemen: http://www.simpletoremember.com/articles/a/reformconservativeorthodox/#26.

12. http://www.buzzfeed.com/sigalsamuel/feminism-in-faith-orthodox-judaism#.bp4VMKKnn. Retrieved August 29, 2015.

13. http://lilith.org/blog/2013/07/can-we-speak-for-ourselves/#sthash.wVyBd6IU.dpuf. Retrieved August 29, 2015.

Women's Ordination

Rabbi Joel Roth	**Rabba Hurwitz**
(*Conservative Rabbi*)[14]	(*Dean Yeshivat Maharat*)[15]
In the final analysis, then, there is no legal objection to the technical granting of the title "rabbi" to a woman.	Hurwitz, speaking to the *Journal* from New York, said Yeshivat Maharat wants to "help the Orthodox community understand that it [ordaining women] is [halachically] permissible and something whose time has come."

14. http://www.jtsa.edu/prebuilt/women/roth.pdf. Roth is known for being a major influence in JTS's ordaining women.
15. http://www.jewishjournal.com/membership/article/orthodox_shul_ takes_first_step_to_hiring_female_clergy. Retrieved July 26, 2015.

Subjugation of Women

David Einhorn	Rabbi Yosef Kanefsky
(*American Reform Leader*)[16]	(Open Orthodox Rabbi Student of Rabbi Weiss)[17]
… Einhorn not only condemned the "gallery cage" but also brought women down from the gallery in his own synagogue.	And often she must content herself with *davening* in a cage in shul, from where her desire to say *kaddish* for a parent may or may not be tolerated.

16. Karla Goldman, *Beyond the Synagogue Gallery* (Cambridge, MA: Harvard University Press, 2009), p. 24.
17. Cited by http://www.lukeford.net/blog/?p=35831. Retrieved July 26, 2015.

Rabbi Pamela Barmash	Rabba Dr. Melanie Landau
(*Adopted by the Rabbinical Assembly [Conservative]*)[18]	(*Yeshivat Maharat Class of 2015*)[19]
Instead, women were excluded because they had subordinate status. They were exempted from the mitzvot that Jews are obligated to observe in the normal course of the day, week, and year because the essential ritual acts should be performed only by those of the highest social standing, those who were independent, those who were heads of their own households, not subordinate to anyone else.	I was viscerally feeling pain in my body because of the repression, exclusion and marginalization of the feminine in Jewish texts.

18. http://www.rabbinicalassembly.org/sites/default/files/public/hal-akhah/teshuvot/2011-2020/womenandhiyyuvfinal.pdf
19. http://www.jewishtelegraph.com/prof_191.html. Retrieved July 20, 2015.

Homosexuality

Rabbi Eliot Dorff	Rabbi Zev Farber
(*Conservative Rabbi*)[20]	(YCT 2006)[21]
These analogues in Jewish law, then, suggest that if homosexuality proves to be an orientation over which the individual has no choice, then the proper reading of Jewish law should be that homosexual acts, like heterosexual ones, should be regulated such that some of them are sanctified and others delegitimated—or perhaps even vilified as abominations.	I believe we must come to terms with the fact that, in the long run, Orthodox homosexual Jews really have no choice but to allow themselves to fulfill the intense desire for emotional and physical intimacy in the only way open to them.

20. https://www.rabbinicalassembly.org/sites/default/files/public/halakhah/teshuvot/19912000/dorff_homosexuality.pdf. Retrieved August 11, 2015.
21. http://morethodoxy.org/2012/01/11/homosexuals-in-the-orthodox-community-by-rabbi-zev-farber.

ReformJudaism.org[22]	Rabbi Dov Linzer
Reform Jews are also committed to the full participation of gays and lesbians in synagogue life as well as society at large.	(*Rosh haYeshivah YCT*)[23] This is one of the most challenging religious and halakhic questions that we are facing today, and I think that our focus has to be not on halakha, but on communal acceptance and on making gay men and women, and their spouses or partners, as well as their children, fully welcome and fully a part of our communities, synagogues, and schools.

22. http://www.reformjudaism.org/what-reform-judaism#st-hash.3LnuF9zJ.dpuf
23. https://www.jofa.org/blogcasts. Retrieved July 23, 2015.

Conservative Responsa adopted by the Rabbinical Assembly[24]	**Rabbi Ysoscher Katz** *(Chair of the Department of Talmud and Director of the Lindenbaum Center for Halakhic studies at YCT)*[25]
For homosexuals who are incapable of maintaining a heterosexual relationship, the rabbinic prohibitions that have been associated with other gay and lesbian intimate acts are superseded based upon the Talmudic principle of *kvod habriot*, our obligation to preserve the human dignity of all people.	The Torah makes clear that [intercourse] between two men is prohibited, but I like to talk about the 50 shades of gay, in other words, there are many other things they can do that are not expressly prohibited.

24. https://www.rabbinicalassembly.org/sites/default/files/public/hal-akhah/teshuvot/20052010/dorff_nevins_reisner_dignity.pdf
25. http://www.haaretz.com/beta/.premium-1.669680. Retrieved August 5, 2015.

Divorce

Rabbi Arnold Goodman	Rabbi Ysoscher Katz[27]
(Adopted by the Rabinical Assembly (Conservative))[26]	Leviticus 21:7. "They shall not marry a prostitute or a woman who has been defiled, neither shall they marry a woman divorced from her husband, for the priest is holy to his God." While not as challenging as Leviticus 18:22, it is still bothersome. It hurts seeing the divorcee compared to a prostitute.[28] Why should we ostracize someone whose sole crime is that their marriage dissolved? The fact that those divorcees are sometimes our sisters, moms, daughters, or ourselves makes the insult all the more painful אלי אלי למה עזבתני.
Divorce is viewed differently today. It is often an opportunity for a second chance, and our continued embrace of the Biblical prohibition of the marriage between a Kohen and a divorcee could reinforce the ancient prejudice against a divorced woman.	

26. http://www.rabbinicalassembly.org/sites/default/files/public/halakhah/teshuvot/19912000/goodman_marriagedivorcee.pdf. Retrieved July 23, 2015.
27. https://www.facebook.com/ysoscher (May 8, 2015). Retrieved July 16, 2015.
28. See Chapter 5 why it is inaccurate to say that the two are being compared.

3

Open Orthodox
Ordination and Scholarship

A video produced by Yeshivat Chovevei Torah,[40] entitled "Inside YCT's *Beit Midrash*,"[41] states that "the goal of the learning at Yeshivat Chovevei Torah is to create rabbis who are *talmidei chachamim* and *poskim* for their communities, and spiritual leaders for *Klal Yisrael*." Rabbi Linzer boasts that the, "Halacha learning at Chovevei is notable for both its intensity and its extensiveness." Let us take a moment to examine this claim.

Rabbi Linzer describes the curriculum at the yeshiva. A student will learn *Niddah, Shabbat, Kashrut, Geirut, Siddur Kiddushin,* and *Aveilut.* These topics are covered from "beginning to end" with *Gemara, Rishonim, poskim, Shulchan Aruch, Nosei Keilim,* and contemporary *teshuvot.* In addition, students will

---

40. This section will discuss Yeshivat Chovevei Torah's program for rabbinic ordination. Yeshivat Maharat's program will be discussed in Chapter 7.
41. https://www.youtube.com/watch?v=9LtaFnZv_nk. Retrieved July 15, 2015.

learn the laws of the *Beit Haknesset, Tzitzit, Tefillin, Mezuzah, Sefer Torah, Brit, Pidyon Haben,* Bar and Bat Mitzvah,[42] *Get,* divorce, adultery, *Bikkur Cholim, Kibud Av va-Em, Tanach,* and Jewish thought. Also, he says, the *Gemara* is studied with a classic *Brisker* approach as well as an academic one. Students take classes in pastoral counseling, homiletics, and pedagogy. In addition, they are required to do field work and yearlong internships.[43] The course work at YCT is enormous.

Any experienced yeshiva student can testify as to the difficulty involved in mastering a Talmudic text and the accompanying halachic literature. A brief explanation will enlighten the novice.

One begins by studying the relevant passage in the Talmud. This may be as brief as a few lines or as long as several pages. The text is impossible to grasp without the help of Rashi's commentary. Once a student has mastered the text with Rashi, he proceeds to Tosafos. The commentary of the Tosafists compares the passage at hand to other Talmudic texts. They often make vague references to such extraneous passages, with which the student may not be familiar. This makes it necessary for the student to study *those* texts, along with Rashi's commentary, in order to fully understand the comments of Tosafos.

After thoroughly familiarizing with Rashi and Tosafos, it is time to take a look at other commentaries, such as the Rashba, Ran, Rosh and the Rambam. Each of these commentators may explain the Talmudic text in a different way. Students must

---

42. It is unclear in which compendium of Jewish Law the laws of Bat Mitzvah are found.

43. http://www.yctorah.org/content/view/640/47/. Retrieved July 15, 2015.

review these commentaries several times in order to fully grasp their nuances and intricacies.

Often, the final Halacha is unclear from the Talmudic passage itself. Based on their interpretations, each commentator will write what he believes is the final legal ruling. There will frequently be several opinions as to the halachic conclusion.

After mastering the aforementioned material, the student is ready to proceed to the commentaries of the *Tur* and the *Beis Yosef*. The *Tur* is a medieval commentator who often summarizes the major halachic opinions, as well as offering his own interpretation. The *Beis Yosef*, written by Rabbi Yosef Karo, is a massive commentary on the *Tur* which summarizes the Talmudic passage and the relevant commentaries. It also cites more obscure commentaries which the student may not have seen. A diligent student will look up these commentaries at their source in order to acquire a clearer understanding of their opinions. In addition, the *Beis Yosef* adds his own approach as well as his interpretation of the other commentaries. After reading the *Beis Yosef*, many also study the other commentaries written on the *Tur*, such as the *Derishah, Perishah, Darchei Moshe,* and the *Bach*.

After studying several topics in this intensive manner, the student is ready to proceed to the *Shulchan Aruch*, the Code of Jewish Law. The *Shulchan Aruch* was written by Rabbi Yosef Karo, author of the *Beis Yosef*. In it, he summarizes his commentary on the *Tur* and records the final Halacha, or legal ruling. The Rema, printed as a gloss to the *Shulchan Aruch*, codifies the Ashkenazic view of the Halacha.

The *Nosei Keilim*, or commentaries on the *Shulchan Aruch*, are studied next. For example, this includes the *Taz* and *Shach* on *Yoreh Deah,* and the *Taz* and *Magen Avraham* on *Orach Chaim.* These commentaries are complex and quote a multitude of opinions. In *Orach Chaim,* students will also study the *Mishnah Berurah.*

All of the above is the required regimen for learning one small topic in Halacha.

In a classic yeshiva, a student learning the entire day, at a vigorous pace, can hope to complete the laws of meat and milk and the laws of forbidden mixtures in about a year. And this represents only a segment of the laws of *kashrus,* accounting for only 25 chapters in the *Shuchan Aruch!* (This is also while utilizing the classic *Brisker* approach alone.) To put this in perspective, the laws of *Niddah* comprise 18 chapters, the laws of *Aveilus* 62 chapters and the laws of *Shabbos* 123 chapters (excluding the laws of *Eruvin*). All of these topics, and more, are studied at YCT from "beginning to end" according to Rabbi Linzer.

Apparently, in four years, YCT students complete the laws of *Nidah, Shabbat, Kashrut, Geirut, Siddur Kiddushin,* and *Aveilut* along with all the aforementioned commentaries. And all this while studying with a classical *Brisker* approach as well as an academic approach. They also claim to learn the laws of *Beit haknesset, Tzitzit, Tefillin, Mezuzah, Sefer Torah, Brit, Pidyon Haben,* Bar and Bat Mitzvah, *Get,* divorce, adultery, *Bikkur Cholim, Kibud Av va-Em,* Jewish thought and *Tanach.* In addition they take classes in pastoral counseling, homiletics and pedagogy, with a yearlong internship. [44] This is quite a bold claim. The only reasonable conclusion to be drawn is that either

---

44. *Ibid.*

all these topics are not covered, or they are studied in a most superficial manner.

It is perhaps not surprising to find that the level of schooling required to gain admittance to YCT's *semichah* program is considerably lower than that of a traditional yeshiva. While prospective students are required to be able to "read and comprehend both Talmudic and Biblical sources with commentary," no official yeshiva education is mandatory for applicants. They are only required to have "completed two years of post-high school intensive study of rabbinic texts." Applicants are also required to have earned a Bachelor's degree.[45]

In fact, on YCT's alumni webpage, no previous full-time yeshiva education at all is listed for many of their graduates. For those who did study in yeshiva, many attended beginner programs where only the rudimentary basics of Talmud study are taught.

A list of the student body for the 2014-2015 academic year,[46] even lists six of the students as having previously attended the Jewish Theological Seminary or other Conservative institutions.[47] One student attended the Reform-affiliated Hebrew Union College. The only "yeshiva" education listed for eleven of the students is the Pardes Institute.[48] The Pardes Institute, according to its website, is "an open, co-ed and non-

---

45. http://www.yctorah.org/content/view/40/47. Retrieved August 25, 2015.

46. http://www.yctorah.org/images//about%20our%20students%20 2014-2015%20email.pdf. Retrieved August 26, 2015.

47. Two of those students are in the Beit Midrash program, which is a year-long preparatory program for those students not ready to enter the *semichah* program (http://www.yctorah.org/content/view/40/12), retrieved August 26, 2015.

48. One of these students is in the Beit Midrash Program.

denominational Jewish learning community, based in Jerusalem and with programs worldwide."[49]

In contrast, in a classic yeshiva, students begin studying the material for ordination after many years of full-time Talmud study. The vast majority of students have also studied Talmud in rigorous high-school programs so that, by the time they begin studying for ordination, they are already quite advanced.

Not only does Rabbi Linzer claim that his students study the extensive body of material required for ordination, he also claims that they are ready to serve as *poskim*, or decisors of Jewish law. A *posek* is someone who has completed all of the halachic material, has mastered it completely and knows the methodology of issuing a halachic ruling. Therefore, it is downright astonishing that Rabbi Linzer can confer upon his graduates "the authority to decide questions of Jewish law and practice."[50]

Deciding questions of Jewish law is not a theoretical issue. Many YCT graduates issue halachic rulings that have serious implications. No less than 35 YCT graduates signed a statement regarding the halachic definition of death.[51] It is amazing that with such little scholarship behind them, they feel confident in expressing their opinion on such a serious matter. From a halachic standpoint this is the equivalent of someone who took a biology class undertaking to perform open-heart surgery. Life and death issues are such a serious area of Halacha that even

---

49. http://www.pardes.org.il/about/pardes. Retrieved August 26, 2015.

50. https://www.youtube.com/watch?t=136&v=qEeZySSk2ss. Retrieved July 15, 2015.

51. http://organdonationstatement.blogspot.com. Retrieved January 19, 2016.

experienced Torah scholars hesitate before offering an opinion on them. Also, some YCT graduates have publicly stated their opinion regarding other controversial issues related to *gittin* (halachic divorce). This is another serious issue which has serious implications for the Jewish family and involves severe Torah prohibitions.[52]

A glitzy presentation and an exciting video may fool the layman into thinking that YCT's program is rigorous and its graduates qualified. Some of the unlettered and well-meaning Jews serving on synagogue boards will be duped into hiring a rabbi who is far from being a Torah scholar, unfit to issue a valid halachic ruling and unprepared to serve as a spiritual leader.

Scholarship of YCT and Yeshivat Maharat's Leaders

"There needs to be an emoticon called I am learning *hilchot niddah* and am displeased."[53]

This sentiment was expressed by a current student at Yeshivat Maharat who is studying for her *semichah* (ordination). While the standard *semichah* reads, "*yoreh yoreh ke-das u-ke-Torah*" or "Let him rule in accordance with the halachic tradition and the Torah,"[54] this student expresses her open displeasure with that tradition. It is not surprising that students at Open Orthodoxy's

---

52. http://jewishtimes.com/17945/kol-hakavod/opinion. Retrieved January 19, 2016.

53. https://www.facebook.com/chava.m.evans?fref=ts. (June 22, 2015) Retrieved August 6, 2015.

54. Rabbi Aharon Feldman, "The 'New Orthodoxy': Open to What?" *Dialogue: For Torah Issues and Ideas* 5 (2014), p. 15.

flagship schools express such views; as we will demonstrate, similar views are held by the leaders of these institutions.

This section will analyze the halachic scholarship of several leaders of Open Orthodox ordination programs. We will show that in their halachic positions, in addition to a lack of Torah scholarship, they display a lack of intellectual honesty. Sources are routinely misrepresented, misunderstood, and even mistranslated. Dissenting opinions are frequently suppressed and uncited to enable them to reach a desired halachic ruling.[55] They propose radical innovations without even consulting expert authorities. It is telling that none of their halachic innovations have been accepted by any mainstream Torah scholars.

We will examine the writings of Rabbi Dov Linzer, Rosh haYeshivah of Yeshivat Chovevei Torah; Rabbi Ysoscher Katz, Chair of the Department of Talmud and Director of the Lindenbaum Center for Halakhic Studies at YCT; Rabba Sara Hurwitz, Dean of Yeshivat Maharat; and Rabbi Jeffrey Fox, Rosh haYeshivah of Yeshivat Maharat.

We will also discuss the troubling *hashkafic* views of Rabbi Ysoscher Katz, including his startling negative views of God and the Rambam.

It is especially important to be made aware of the views and halachic methods of these leaders and teachers, as YCT and Yeshivat Maharat graduates spend (in most cases[56]) four years under their tutelage during which time they purportedly learn how to arrive at halachic decisions.

---

55. Another unfortunate example of this is Rabbi Zev Farber's responsum regarding homosexual relations. See Chapter 6 where we discuss this responsum at length.

56. In Chapter 7 we will discuss a program at Yeshivat Maharat where students can earn ordination in two years.

Rabbi Dov Linzer

Rabbi Linzer is the Rosh haYeshivah of Yeshivat Chovevei Torah.[57]

Rabbi Linzer penned a letter encouraging people to donate money to assist in the rebuilding of churches. On July 21, 2015, Rabbi Asher Lopatin, President of YCT, posted Linzer's letter on his Facebook page:[58]

> Given the recent horrific attack in Charleston and the terrible burnings of churches that has occurred in the last few days, I encourage all of you to show your support for those who have been attacked, and to act in a way *of kiddush shem Shamayim* to counteract these terrible hate crimes. One way you can do this is by donating money to help in the rebuilding of these churches.

The attack in Charleston was a horrific tragedy carried out by a white supremacist. No religious Jew anywhere would condone such vicious and violent conduct. At the same time, it is important to acknowledge that Judaism has major theological differences with Christianity. Christianity declares that the Torah

---

57. This book contains many of Rabbi Linzer's opinions. In Chapter 4 we will discuss his view that the Talmud should not be taught as absolute truth and that the rabbis "erased" the commandment to destroy Amalek. In Chapter 6, we will cite his opinion favoring homosexual couples living together. In Chapter 7, we will cite his egalitarian reforms for the Jewish wedding, and in Chapter 9 his critique of Moses' leadership and Abraham's parenting abilities.

58. https://m.facebook.com/story.php?story_fbid=10153301577356117&id=624706116. Retrieved July 21, 2015.

is irrelevant, the Talmud false, and the Jewish People no longer the chosen nation of God. It also teaches that God is corporeal. How can an Orthodox rabbi declare that it is a sanctification of God's name to donate money to an institution which denies the validity of basic Jewish beliefs? For thousands of years, Jews have given up their lives rather than accept Christianity as the true religion. Parents killed their own children rather than have them baptized. While thousands were martyred in the Crusades and Inquisition for not submitting to the cross, Linzer advocates donating money to promote those same beliefs.

To bolster his point, Rabbi Linzer cites a responsum by Rabbi Moshe Feinstein:[59]

> Relatedly, Rav Moshe (YD 1:68) ruled that an architect can draw up the plans for the construction of a church, and that *mi'ikar ha'din* [according to the strict letter of the law] it is permitted to actually participate in the building of a church (and this is even without the argument that it is not *avodah zarah* for them!).

Rabbi Feinstein writes that it is technically permitted to serve as an architect for a church—far from the implication given by Linzer that it is his opinion to allow a Jew to donate money to a church. Linzer neglects to cite where Rabbi Feinstein qualifies his ruling limiting it to situations where not to do such a job would entail a serious financial loss to the architect, or as pertains to the exigencies of a poor man's livelihood, or when not doing so would generate hatred. Linzer also neglects to mention that Rabbi Feinstein calls the practice "improper."

---

59. *Iggros Moshe* YD 1:68.

Moreover, Linzer omits mention of the fact that Rabbi Feinstein explicitly *forbids* donating money to a church in another responsum.[60] Rabbi Feinstein was asked about the permissibility of giving money to a Jewish Federation, when the funds would also be used to support Conservative and Reform institutions. In the course of his responsum, he makes reference to donating money to a church:

> It is probable that this [giving to a federation] is worse than giving money to non-Jews to help them build their house of worship. In that case, there is no issue of leading Jews astray, but rather a prohibition of putting a stumbling block before the blind....

While he deems giving to a church not as problematic as giving to a federation under the conditions cited above, Rabbi Feinstein clearly prohibits donating money to help build a church—a statement notably absent from Rabbi Linzer's letter. Clearly, Rabbi Linzer has engaged in what he in another place calls, "...bending the halakha to conform to our modern notions of egalitarianism."[61]

Rabbi Ysoscher Katz

Rabbi Ysoscher Katz is the Chair of the Department of Talmud and Director of the Lindenbaum Center for Halakhic Studies at YCT.[62]

---

60. *Iggros Moshe* YD: 1:149. See also, *Iggros Moshe* YD 3:34.
61. Rabbi Dov Linzer, "On the *Mitzvot* of Non-Jews: An Analysis of *Avodah Zarah* 2b-3a." *Beloved Words Milin Havivin* 1 (2006), p. 36.
62. This book will cite other un-Orthodox statements made by Rabbi Katz. For example, in Chapter 4, we cite his views that historical claims

Rabbi Ysoscher Katz permits women to nurse in synagogue. One of the issues he discusses is the prohibition of reciting words of sanctity before exposed nakedness. Such a prohibition would dictate that one may not recite words of sanctity in front of a woman who is nursing and thereby exposing herself. Katz argues that there is no such prohibition when the nakedness is revealed for a "purpose" and exposed for only a brief time. He quotes the Rosh (*Berachos* 3:52) as his source.

The cited Rosh explains why it is permissible for a *mohel* to recite the circumcision blessing even though the baby at that time is exposed. Katz writes:[63]

> The Rosh immediately adds another reason why there is no need to cover the nakedness: "it also appears that, since the *Mohel* is concentrating on the task of circumcision, the exposed penis is not a negation of the 'sacredness of your camp,' and there is no concern at in this brief period for 'nakedness shall not be seen.'"

Katz concludes:

> An analysis of the words of the Rosh shows that this latter reason is, in essence, a contraction or merging

---

regarding the Torah and God's authorship of it are unimportant, and that "troubling" Jewish texts should be excised. In Chapter 5, we will detail his view labeling the commandment pertaining to an *isha sotah* (a woman suspected of adultery) capricious and patriarchal, and the prohibition for a *kohen* (a member of the priestly caste in Judaism) to marry a divorcee an insult. In Chapter 6 we will touch on his sanctioning of certain homosexual relations.

63. http://www.yctorah.org/images/breastfeeding%20teshuva-english05.28.pdf. Retrieved January 27, 2016.

of two claims: 1) Since "the *Mohel* is preoccupied," this process would still fall under the appellation, "your camp shall be holy." 2) That the uncovering is merely "for a brief time" (literally, *le'sha'a*).

He also states:

> And regardless, we have the position of the Rosh, who tells us in his unequivocal position that there is no problem with fleeting exposure.

Katz claims that the Rosh is saying that there is no prohibition to recite words of sanctity in front of "purposeful" nakedness when it is only exposed for a brief moment.

However, this Rosh, upon which Katz bases his thesis, does not exist. This is the text of the Rosh:

וה"ר יונה ז"ל כתב דודאי בקטן כ"כ לא חשבינן ליה ערוה ואין צריך לכסותו בשעת הברכה. וגם נראה כיון דלתקוני המילה קאתי קרינן ביה שפיר והיה מחניך קדוש ואין בו באותו שעה משום לא יראה בך ערות דבר.

> And Rabeinu Yonah, z"l, writes that definitely for someone so young, it is not considered nakedness and it does not need to be covered at the time of the blessing. And also since he is performing a circumcision this is called "and your camp shall be holy" and at this moment there is no issue of "do not see nakedness."

To the last line which reads "…and at this moment there is no issue of 'do not see nakedness,'" Katz adds in the word "brief" which does not appear in the Rosh and is a total invention. The Rosh neither says the words "brief moment" and let alone does not permit the exposure of nakedness for this reason. But based on his contrivance, Katz claims there is no prohibition to say words of sanctity when nakedness is only visible for a brief moment.

To add insult to injury Katz argues that the case of a woman nursing is comparable to a *mohel* performing a circumcision:

> Here again, the exposure of the sex organ was done while the practitioner was preoccupied with "*tikkun*," and it is also only for short duration, a minute or two, for the purposes of nursing, and therefore, there is no problem according to halakha; this does not constitute halakhic gilu'i ervah.

Thus Katz argues that just like in a case of circumcision where it is permitted for a *mohel* to make the blessing in front of the child's uncovered body, so too regarding a woman who is nursing. It is an unwarranted leap of logic to compare performing a circumcision to nursing. The reason why a *mohel* can say the blessing is because he is "preoccupied." This only applies to the one performing the act. This would have no relevance to other people in the room who are not involved in the nursing or in the circumcision. Yet, Katz unequivocally states "...this does not constitute halakhic gilu'i ervah."

Katz proceeds to show that many halachic decisors side with the opinion of his invented Rosh. He concludes:

There is no doubt in my mind that all of these rabbinic decisors would say the same thing regarding breastfeeding. Even if the concern over the possibility of the [dadim] being revealed for a moment while the woman is preparing to nurse or after she has finished is valid and correct, as we have seen, it does not pose a problem of exposure of nudity, for that which was exposed during those few moments does not have the legal position of ervah at all.

Katz even claims the *Mishnah Berurah* supports his position:

A close reading of the Mishnah Berurah (75:3) would perhaps support this claim. He writes in the name of the Chayei Adam: "And therefore a woman must be careful at the time of nursing, when her [dadim] are exposed, that she should not speak any words of holiness at that point." The phrase "when her [dadim] are exposed" suggests that he is speaking of a situation in which the [dadim] are exposed for the duration of breastfeeding. But as in our case, the Chayei Adam and the Mishnah Berurah would agree that it is permissible for the mother and others to pray when the [dadim] are only exposed for a brief moment.

How does the phrase "when her [dadim] are exposed" imply that if she was exposed for a brief moment that it is permissible? There is no mention in these words as to the length of time in which the exposure took place. If anything it would imply that it is forbidden to speak words of sanctity even if they are exposed for a moment. Katz uses a citation which contradicts his own position, turns it on its head, and uses it as a proof text. The *Shulchan Aruch* there states (OC 75:1) "If a handbreadth of a woman's body is uncovered in a place that is usually covered, even his wife, it is forbidden to recite *Shema* opposite her." The *Mishnah Berurah* comments, "Therefore one needs to be careful when she is nursing and exposes her *dadim* to not speak words of holiness." Nowhere does the *Mishnah Berurah* differentiate between a long or short period of time. There could not be a more explicit statement contrary to Katz's position.

In conclusion, Rabbi Katz fabricates a Rosh by mistranslating his words. He then concludes that this is the final halachic position and misreads the *Mishnah Berurah*.

Despite Katz's errors he is very confident in his ability as a halachic authority. At a lecture in which he discussed the above responsum, he boasted:[64] A

So, in some ways it's pretty easy for me to write a *teshuva*. I can think of that Rosh I can think of that Rema, you know, and frankly if you read my *teshuva* I kind of knock a Rema and you know I have the *pai'ess* and I have the tradition so I can get away with it....

He might "get away with it" with unlearned audiences, but not with readers who can read the texts in their original.

---

64. Rabbi Ysoscher Katz, "Spiritual Explorers and their Discoveries." London, England. http://www.Yeshivatmaharat.org/audio-and-video-links. Retrieved January 19, 2016.

View of God

In a Facebook post from July 27, 2015, Rabbi Katz criticizes God in the form of a sarcastic "e-mail" blaming Him for the destruction of the Temple. In it, he refers to God as "sweetheart" and uses explicit sexual metaphors:[65]

Email to God; the day after Tisha b'Av
Subject: Friends?

Sweet Lord,
Oh my, God! (Literally) That was crazy. You really blew off some steam yesterday; dishes were flung, our home destroyed. Now that the dust has settled, hopefully You can listen to me. You were not talking but I think I can infer from Your behavior what You are trying to tell me: the constant intimacy does not work for You. Guess what, Sweetheart, מחמד ליבי, it does not work for me, either. I actually have a wild suggestion: You kicked me out of the house but apparently have no plans of ever giving me a *get* (Isaiah 50:1), in which case, why not be friends—with benefits! We will be friends with occasional moments of climactic intimacy. Here is how it'll work: You seem to crave intimacy during Shabbat and *chagim*. I'll try my best to be there for You during those times. In return, I want You to be there for me when I need You. During those occasional moments,

_____
65. https://www.facebook.com/ysoscher?fref=ufi&pnref=story (July 27, 2015).

when I drop You a note, shed a tear, promise that You will respond! (Isn't that how Your *niddah* thingy works; long periods of separation with occasional bouts of fiery intimacy?) The rest of the time, feel free to pursue Your other interests. (I am told that there is a huge Livyatan swimming in your fish tank with which You metaphorically play. (*Avodah Zara* 3:B) In the interim, I will just turn to Your books. Not sure you noticed, but in Your huff to leave You left behind Your library. You always struck me as the bookworm type. That is where I will look for You. Every time I desire Your embrace I'll just open Your books, to inhale Your scent and caress those beautiful, curvy letters. It will be as if we touched. And, by the way, that long and sensuous goodbye kiss You gave me yesterday was really nice. A little embarrassing (Yoma 54A), but really sweet. It penetrated my bones and will sustain me for the duration of our separation.

Lehitraot,

Your ex

Isru chag Tisha Be'av, 70 ce.

PS. Gotta run. At the Seforim Blog... and... are fighting, while over at Torah Musings... said some bold things about Maimonides. It's one thing to disagree with Rambam (I, too, dislike his theology), but to say that he does not matter is *narishkeiten.*

Jews are commanded to fear God to the extent that it is prohibited to even mention His name in vain. That Rabbi Katz would refer to God as "sweetheart," "a bookworm," and use phrases like "friends with benefits" in reference to the Almighty is astonishing—not to mention in extremely poor taste. That the Department Chair in Talmud at an institution that calls itself a yeshiva can write in this fashion speaks more loudly than any other words. In addition, this post was "liked" on Facebook by several YCT and Yeshivat Maharat students as well as by Dr. Erin Smokler, Yeshivat Maharat's Director of Spiritual Development.[66]

Rabbi Katz consistently speaks in gross anthropomorphic terms about God. In another Facebook post, he claims that a relationship with Him is "volatile." He says that while in the books of Exodus and Leviticus God was pursuing an intimate relationship with humanity, in the book of Deuteronomy, "...He acts like a jilted lover, ferociously angry and cursing uncontrollably." He says about God's behavior "it's a bit erratic."[67] [B] Trying to make sense of God's word is a legitimate and age-old Jewish pursuit. But this kind of language, reeking as it does of the most flippant kind of irreverence, has no place in Orthodoxy.

In another post, Katz quotes a portion of an article written by Joan Acocella, entitled "Is There Justice in the Book of Job?"[68] Katz calls this article "a must read." In the article, Acocella maintains the God is the "most troubling, least sympathetic character" in the book of Job. She claims that "he is not loving or fair."[69] [C]

---

66. http://www.yeshivatmaharat.org/faculty-and-staff.
67. https://www.facebook.com/ysoscher?fref=ts. (September 12, 2014). Retrieved August 31, 2015.
68. http://www.newyorker.com/magazine/2013/12/16/misery-3. Retrieved August 31, 2015.
69. https://www.facebook.com/ysoscher?fref=ts. (December 10, 2013). Retrieved August 31, 2015.

In describing how the Almighty did not permit Moses to enter Israel, Katz writes how "God harshly rejects Moshe's courtship." He describes how Moses was "drooling over the topographical beauty of Israel…" and that, "after pursuing God for many years, he was, so to speak, finally ready to move in." However, he claims that "God abhors intimacy" and after this rejection by Him, Moses experienced a "spiritual death." He concludes that the lesson of the story is that while humanity should not deviate from the path of God, they should also not get too close. He concludes, "Intimacy is not His thing."[70] D

In another troubling post, Katz describes a fictional conversation between physicist Stephen Hawking and God. He imagines that "God and Stephen Hawking walk into a bar" and have a conversation. Hawking says to God, "Science can prove that You don't exist." God replies, "I totally agree, Stephen. I NEVER existed, scientifically."[71] At the end of the post, Katz links to an article entitled, "Stephen Hawking Declares That Science Can Prove God Does Not Exist." Is this really what one would expect to see from a rabbi of the "Orthodox" persuasion?

View of the Rambam

In the above "e-mail" written to God, Katz states that he dislikes the Rambam's theology. It takes boldness to "dislike" the theology of one of the greatest sages in Jewish history; nevertheless it is

---

70. https://www.facebook.com/ysoscher?fref=ts. (August 10, 2014). Retrieved September 1, 2015.

71. https://www.facebook.com/ysoscher?fref=ts. (September 30, 2014). Retrieved September 1, 2015.

a tack he takes on many occasions. Katz consistently flaunts his displeasure with the Rambam and has no qualms venting his negative feelings towards him.[72] For example, he writes:

Personally, my rejection of the Maimonidean ethos and realization of the degree to which Chassidut can speak to the modern searcher was a long and arduous process. It came about as a result of a deep sense of betrayal by Maimonides, the champion of Rationalist Judaism. I, for many years, was the object and fool of Maimonides' "the seventh reason," as presented in his introduction to the *Guide* by not seeing his philosophic views. In that passage, Maimonides condones misleading the masses for their greater good, even to the point of advocating contradictory ideas for different audiences and then obscuring those contradictions. Growing up in Satmar and then Brisk, I was oblivious to his non-halakhic writings and led to believe that he fully and literally believed every word he wrote in the *Yad*. I was exposed to his other writings only later and when I did I felt cheated. I was part of that the masses, whom he thought could not handle his unconventional approach to theology and tradition. As much as I have read about him, I personally have not managed to reconcile his two sides.

---

72. https://kavvanah.wordpress.com/2015/05/31/torat-chaim-veahavat-chesed-rabbi-ysoscher-katz. Retrieved July 30, 2015.

The passage in the *Guide for the Perplexed*[73] to which Katz refers speaks about concealing exceedingly deep matters from the layman. This is not a unique idea. The Rabbis of the Talmud often disguised their more esoteric messages in the form of parables. The reason for this was to prevent the unlettered from misinterpreting and misapplying their teachings. The Rambam[74] explains the purpose of concealing the inner meanings of *aggadata*:

> ...also to blind the eyes of those fools who do not restrain [the desires of] their hearts, and who, if the full force of truth were revealed to them, would reject it because of their character deficiencies.

---

73. Hebrew text reads as follows:

והסיבה השביעית הכרת הדברים בעניינים עמוקים מאוד, שצריך להסתיר מקצת ענייניהם ולגלות מקצתן. ופעמים גורם הדוחק בדבר מסוים להמשיך את הדברים בו לפי הנחת הקדמה מסוימת, ויגרום הדוחק במקום אחר להמשיך הדברים בו לפי הנחת הקדמה הסותרת לראשונה. וצריך שלא ירגיש ההמון כלל את מקום הסתירה שביניהם. ויש שמערים המחבר להסתיר את הדבר בכל אופן. (תרגום רב קאפח http://www.daat.ac.il/daat/mahshevt/more/ a2-2.htm#3)

The seventh reason [for contradictions in various writings] is [that there are] some exceedingly deep matters, parts of which need to be hidden and parts of which need to revealed [since the unlearned will not be able to understand them and will misinterpret them]. Sometimes the necessity in a particular matter causes its ideas to be drawn out in accordance with a particular premise and necessity in another place will cause its ideas to be drawn out in accordance with a premise contradictory to the first. [They only appear contradictory because the hidden parts of the idea cannot be revealed since the unlearned would be unable to understand them, but are really not contradictory]. It is necessary that the masses should not at all become aware of the contradiction between them [lest they conclude that there is a contradiction between the matters]. At times an author will conceal such matters completely.

74. From his introduction to the *Mishnah*.

Katz, however, somehow extrapolates this to indicate that the Rambam did not mean what he wrote in his halachic work, *Mishneh Torah*—a trumped-up conclusion that, Katz says, caused him to feel fooled and betrayed by the Rambam. This is quite a logical leap!

Katz even blames the Rambam for Modern Orthodox children leaving the fold:[75]

> The skyrocketing attrition rate in Modern Orthodoxy has absolutely nothing to do with Open Orthodoxy. The reason so many of our youth are leaving MO is because of the rabid Maimonideism of its standard bearers, not because of Partnership Minyanim.

Much of Jewish law and thought is gleaned directly from the teachings of the Rambam. It is disconcerting that the head of the Talmud department at YCT feels "a deep sense of betrayal by Maimonides," believes that he did not mean what he wrote, and is convinced that he has contributed to Modern Orthodox assimilation. In sad truth, it is not only the Rambam with whom Katz so confidently disagrees. In a February 6, 2015 Facebook post, he begins, "Rashi got it wrong...."[76] E

---

75. https://www.facebook.com/ysoscher?fref=ts. (March 4, 2014). Retrieved September 1, 2015.
76. https://www.facebook.com/ysoscher?fref=ts. (February 6, 2015). Retrieved September 16, 2015.

Rabba Sara Hurwitz

Rabba Hurwitz[77] serves as the Dean of Yeshivat Maharat[78] and is recognized as the first female Orthodox rabbi.[79]

Rabba Hurwitz proposes an approach to conversion which runs counter to that of the Talmud. She believes that the convert should not be discouraged from joining the Jewish people. She writes, "The initial rabbinic response should not be to push away a convert, but to embrace and empower him or her."[80]

However, the Talmud is clear that one is supposed to discourage a convert. The *Gemara* in *Yevamos* (47b) says:

אמר מר גר שבא להתגייר אומרים לו מה ראית שבאת להתגייר ומודיעים אותו מקצת מצות קלות ומקצת מצות חמורות מ"ט דאי פריש נפרוש דא"ר חלבו קשים גרים לישראל כספחת דכתיב ונלוה הגר עליהם ונספחו על בית יעקב

We were taught above: A convert who wants to convert, we say to him, "What did you see that you want to

---

77. This book contains many of Rabba Hurwitz's opinions. For example, in Chapter 7, this book will detail her claim that a *get* (halachic divorce) was orchestrated by the Rabbis and oppresses women; and her opinion that there is no Halacha preventing women from wearing *tefillin* or serving as rabbis. Her approval of radical reforms to solve the *agunah* issue will be mentioned there as well. Also discussed in Chapter 9, is her criticism of Abraham for following God's command in binding Isaac.

78. http://www.yeshivatmaharat.org/faculty-and-staff. Retrieved August 26, 2015.

79. http://www.tabletmag.com/jewish-life-and-religion/134369/orthodox-women-ordained. Retrieved August 26, 2015.

80. http://hosted-p0.vresp.com/1015677/8ea250b637/ARCHIVE. Retrieved August 7, 2015.

convert?" We tell him some of the minor and serious commandments. What is the reason? So that if he changes his mind, let him do so. For Rav Chelbo said that converts are harmful to Israel like a sore, as it says, "...the convert will join them and be [ונספחו] attached to the house of Jacob"[81]

While Rabba Hurwitz does acknowledge that some "traditional sources" can be interpreted as a policy to discourage conversion, she has a novel interpretation for this, as follows:[82]

Yet, many of the traditional sources can be interpreted as encouraging Rabbis to initially reject any potential convert. There is a tradition to send a potential convert away three times before beginning a conversation with him or her. At first glance, this appears to be an orientation to reject the convert. However, the origin of this practice was not because we automatically suspect every candidate's motivation, but rather to help converts understand that historically Jews were persecuted.

According to Hurwitz, discouraging a convert is actually intended to help him or her understand Jewish suffering. Hurwitz rejects the reason given by the Talmud and in its place adopts a novel explanation of her own.

---

81. See also 47a for other things that are said to try to discourage conversion. See also *Aruch ha-Shulchan* (YD 268:5).
82. http://hosted-p0.vresp.com/1015677/8ea250b637/ARCHIVE. Retrieved August 7, 2015.

Rabbi Jeffrey Fox

Rabbi Jeffrey Fox is the Rosh haYeshivah of Yeshivat Maharat, as well as a 2004 graduate of YCT.[83]

Rabbi Fox was asked his opinion regarding a male rabbinical court observing a female immerse in the *mikveh* for conversion. According to Jewish law, a rabbinical court is required to witness the conversion process, which includes immersion in the *mikveh*. The question was posed by Rabbi Shmuel Herzfeld and Maharat Ruth Balinsky Friedman (Yeshivat Maharat Class of 2013). They state that potential female converts are upset that a male rabbinical court must enter the *mikveh* room for a moment and see their heads submerge under water. They state:[84]

> We were shocked by the fact that most of the women responded to us with tears in their eyes and shaky voices, explaining that this would not only be embarrassing, but difficult. We will always remember their tears. On top of that, here in DC the conversion process for women has become a mockery in the eyes of the world. The *Washington Post* published a lengthy article saying that the convert goes into the mikveh naked in front of male rabbis. This is in most cases not true, but the perception is very painful.

---

83. http://www.Yeshivatmaharat.org/faculty-and-staff. Retrieved August 26, 2015.

84. https://static.squarespace.com/static/5348363de4b0531dce75b-c53/t/546ce0d5e4b02e200e59ce8f/1416421589876/MaleBeitDinat-theImmersionofaFemaleConvert1.pdf. Retrieved July 30, 2015.

It is certainly important to be sensitive to the potential convert's feelings. However, should a negative and inaccurate article by the *Washington Post* be an impetus for halachic change?

Rabbi Fox attempts to prove that according to Jewish law, a rabbinical court is not required to be in the room or see the immersion. He maintains that it is sufficient for them to merely hear the splash of the water. In the summary of his piece, Rabbi Fox concludes:[85]

> Since there is no requirement to enter the room, it should therefore be the policy of all conversion courts to stand outside the door. Some may choose to leave the door open enough to see the back of the convert's head while she immerses in a robe; others may leave the door open just a crack or closed entirely and insure that sound can reach them.

However, he reaches this conclusion through a misinterpretation and a misrepresentation of sources. The *Shulchan Aruch* (YD 268:2) rules that required practice is to have a rabbinical court witness a female convert immerse in the *mikveh*. The next Halacha (YD 268:3), discusses a situation where procedure was not followed and a woman immersed with no rabbinical court present. Is the conversion valid *after the fact*? The *Shulchan Aruch* cites two opinions. The first opinion is that of Tosafos and the Rosh that the conversion is valid *after the fact* and the second opinion is that of the Rif and the Rambam that the conversion is invalid.

---

85. http://static1.squarespace.com/static/5348363de4b0531dce75bc53/t/
546ce2e4e4b03a986e5c7094/1416422116144/MaleRabbinicCourtinF
emaleConversion-Summary.pdf. Retrieved July 30, 2015.

Fox contends that even though the *Shulchan Aruch* cites both opinions, his final opinion is according to the lenient view that it is valid. The general rule is that when the *Shulchan Aruch* cites two halachic opinions, the Halacha is in accordance with the first opinion.

He also states that Rabbi Ovadia Yosef[86] is "so upset" with this lenient interpretation of the *Shulchan Aruch* that he reads it against its "plain meaning." He implies that Rabbi Yosef's opinion is a deviant approach. However, Rabbi Yosef lists no less than four others who also interpret the *Shulchan Aruch* as siding with the stringent opinion that immersion after the fact is invalid—contrary to Fox.[87]

Fox also omits the numerous other *poskim* cited by Rabbi Yosef who explain that although the *Shulchan Aruch* usually sides with the first opinion he cites, this rule does not apply if the second opinion is that of the Rambam and the Rif (as in this case). It is interesting that Fox omits this, as he himself states that it is "somewhat surprising" that the *Shulchan Aruch* rules against the Rambam and the Rif.[88] In fact, this is not surprising at all given Rabbi Yosef's explanation.

Fox also omits Rabbi Yosef's other argument, that since the Ramban, Rashba, Ritva, *Nemukei Yosef*, and *Smag* also rule stringently, the Halacha is in accordance with the stringent opinion. This is all conspicuously missing from Fox's responsum.

---

86. *Yabia Omer* YD 1:19.

87. He lists the *Nahar Mitzrayim* (Laws of Converts 5), *Kiryas Chana Dovid* (YD 2:15), *She'eris Yehudah* (YD 9), and *Prach Mateh Aharon* (2:51).

88. "It is somewhat surprising that the מחבר in this instance is deciding in accordance with ש"ראand תוספות and against his two other עמודי הוראה, the רי"ף and רמב"ם."

It appears that Fox seeks to marginalize the approach of Rabbi Yosef, one which is actually championed by many Torah scholars by omitting his arguments and implying that his is a deviant approach.

Fox spends a good portion of his article trying to prove that an immersion where no rabbinical court is in the room is valid *after the fact*. However, this point is actually irrelevant. As stated above, the *Shulchan Aruch*, in the previous law (268:2), clearly states that the initial required procedure is for the rabbinical court to witness the immersion:

> She sits in the water and after *immerses in front of them,* they then turn around and leave so she can come out of the water without them seeing her....

It is clear from the *Shulchan Aruch* that the preferred approach is to have the rabbis see the immersion in the *mikveh*. The Halacha which Fox discusses addresses only a situation in which the conversion *already took place* when no court was present. This point is not lost on Rabbi Fox, who defends his thesis by claiming that the *Shulchan Aruch* rejects its own statement! He writes that even though the *Shulchan Aruch* cites the opinion of the Rambam (268:2) which requires the rabbis to see the immersion, the *Shulchan Aruch* rejects this in the very next Halacha (268:3) by siding with Tosafos. He says about this Halacha (268:2):[89]

---

89. https://static.squarespace.com/static/5348363de4b0531dce75b-c53/t/546ce0d5e4b02e200e59ce8f/1416421589876/MaleBeitDinat-theImmersionofaFemaleConvert1.pdf. Retrieved July 30, 2015.

This is consistent with the opinion of the רמב"ם that the
מחבר quotes in סעיף ג which requires the presence of
the בית דין. However, the מחבר means to *pasken* against
the רמב"ם in this area. Therefore, the מחבר must also
presume that when we *pasken* like the סתם position of
Tosafot in סעיף ג that the language of the רמב"ם from
סעיף ב is also implicitly rejected.

Rabbi Fox is convinced by his own argument. He contends
that the *Shulchan Aruch* did not actually mean what he wrote
in this Halacha! He maintains that the *Shulchan Aruch* quotes
the opinion of the Rambam in Halacha 2, only to reject it in
Halacha 3. This is absurd. The obvious fact that 268:2 refers to a
preferred practice and 268:3 is referring to a ruling *after* the fact
seems not to matter a whit to Rabbi Fox.[90]

---

90. Fox also tries to show why his case should be considered "after the
fact." Since this is a time of pressing need, he says, it is inappropriate to
follow the Shulchan Aruch's preferred approach of having the rabbinical
court witness the immersion.

He cites the principle that שעת הדחק כדיעבד דמי, that a time of pressing
need is as if it already happened, and therefore the preferred method is
not to have the rabbinical court in the room at all. He writes:

> Rav Sternbuch does not offer a conceptual analysis but seems
> to just take for granted that we hold like רמב"ם over תוס' such
> that there is no room for debate. In the current climate this is
> a powerful example of חומרא האתי לידי קולא. Both the Jewish
> and non-Jewish community have been shocked by the notion
> of men "witnessing" naked women. This has led to a terrible
> embarrassment and suspicion of leading and well-respected
> rabbanim. While Rav Sternbuch may not accept my argument
> on a לכתחילה level, I think that he would have to accept the
> possibility to be lenient based on שעת הדחק כדיעבד דמי (Ibid.).

Fox also omits important relevant information that is contrary to his position. Rabbi Fox mentions Rabbi Ovadia Yosef's final halachic opinion only in passing. He neglects to quote Rabbi Yosef's conclusion, in which he vehemently opposes Fox's reforms. In the same responsum that Fox himself quotes, Rabbi Yosef writes:[91]

> This is the conclusion, to not be lenient initially in this law. The judges need to enter the room to see the immersion with their eyes... to be lenient and immerse not in front of the court is not correct at all. And it is incumbent upon the court to stand against the modern reformers with all their strength. And God should send his holy help to those who go in the proper path. And God is with the judge and his feet should not falter.

Rabbi Yosef clearly is of the opinion that the rabbinical court needs to be in the room to see the immersion. Yet this statement is missing from Fox's responsum. Also, earlier, Rabbi Yosef even criticized certain "modern people" who claimed that it was immodest to have a rabbinical court enter the room when the woman immersed. Again, the irony is that Rabbi Fox cited

---

It is disingenuous to claim that modern society is more sensitive to modesty, and therefore this situation should have the status of שעת הדחק. It is interesting that Open Orthodox rabbis are not sensitive to the laws of modesty in other areas (see Chapter 7). See below what we have cited from the responsum of Rabbi Ovadiah Yosef regarding this attitude. Also, the fact that people mistakenly believe that the rabbis witness naked women should not impact Halacha.

91. *Yabia Omer* YD 1:19.

this same responsum! Rabbi Yosef writes about opposition he personally faced when he instituted a policy requiring the rabbinical court to be in the room:[92]

> …even though there were many modern people (who were wise in their own eyes) who opposed this practice with all their might. They came with the complaint that it was not proper for the rabbinical court to enter the woman's *mikveh* room at all when there was a woman in the *mikveh*. ((According to them) only an immodest doctor is "permitted" to check a naked woman for any minor medical issue, but not so for a modest Torah scholar. This is the "Torah" of the modern people. This is the opposite of our holy Torah, which differentiates between proper people and immodest people in the opposite way regarding the laws of seclusion. The straight ones, they bend. Should not our complete Torah be more significant than their idle chatter?…)

This harsh criticism was directed at those who made arguments similar to Rabbi Fox, yet it is absent from his piece. It is clear that Fox saw this responsum, as he quotes from a different part of it. Either Rabbi Fox did not read the entire text, or he deliberately left out information that was contrary to his position.[93]

---

92. *Ibid.*

93. Rabbi Yosef mentions the hypocrisy of certain people who claim that the immersion procedure is immodest, yet do not exhibit the same sensitivity to modesty in other areas. In one such example, Rabbi Ysoscher Katz writes in a concurring opinion to Fox that requiring the rabbinical court in the room at the time of immersion, even after the fact, is immodest: "In terms of law that is put into actual practice

In the same responsum, Rabbi Yosef also offers other suggestions that would be sensitive to modesty and fulfill all halachic requirements. Some of the methods currently used are: wearing a loose garment or an umbrella-like covering that sits over the neck or covering the surface of the water with a tarp.

In conclusion, based on a spurious logical claim, a misapplication of the *Shulchan Aruch*, Fox has proposed a new halachic innovation. He partially quotes Rabbi Yosef's responsum but neglects to cite relevant information which is contrary to his own opinion. It is clear from Fox's writing that he had a halachic goal in mind. As Rabbi Yosef Kanefsky so succinctly puts it, he painted the bullseye around the target.[94]

It is important to note that this opinion is not only theoretical but one put into action. Rabbi Ysoscher Katz who wrote a concurring opinion[95] to that of Rabbi Fox, has overseen at least two conversions where the rabbinical court was not in

---

there is a dispute, as there are those who are stringent and mandate the presence of males at the immersion even after the fact or *ex post facto* (something that is, as I have emphasized, an appalling breach of the fences of modesty)....." However, Katz's sensitivity to modesty apparently does not extend to what he posts online. On July 28, 2014, he posted an article which contained a picture of a woman dressed in only a *tallis*. Apparently, it is only traditional immersion procedures that, in his view, represent "an appalling breach of the fences of modesty." (http://www.yctorah.org/images//katz%20mikvah%20teshuvah%20-%20english%20version.pdf. Retrieved September 2, 2015.) (https://www.facebook.com/ysoscher/posts/10152218137433639. (July 28, 2014) Retrieved September 1, 2015.)

94. Rabbi Yosef Kanefsky, "Follow-Up to the Blog Post: Adieu to 'Thou Hast Not Made Me a Woman.'" *Keren* 2 (2014), p. 6.

95. http://www.yctorah.org/images//katz%20mikvah%20teshuvah%20-%20english%20version.pdf.

the room.[96] Such a conversion is, according to most opinions, invalid. As the Sages say:[97]

רבים—חללים רבים הפילה—"she has caused many fallen victims"—this refers to those who have not acquired the ability to rule and who nevertheless rule.

Rabbi Dov Lerea

Rabbi Lerea is the Dean and *mashgiach ruchani* at YCT. While this book does not cite any controversial statements from Rabbi Lerea, it is telling that while he did receive ordination from Yeshiva University, he also received ordination, as well as a Doctorate of Education, Jewish Education, and a Master of Arts in Jewish Studies from the Jewish Theological Seminary (Conservative).[98]

♦ ♦ ♦

As mentioned before, the classic rabbinic ordination reads "*yoreh yoreh ke-das u-ke-Torah*" or "Let him rule in accordance with the halachic tradition and the Torah."[99] Yet, YCT and Yeshivat Maharat's leaders show their disregard for the halachic process by their lack of scholarship and misrepresentation of

---

96. Rabbi Ysoscher Katz, "Spiritual Explorers and their Discoveries." London, England. http://www.yeshivatmaharat.org/audio-and-video-links. Retrieved January 19, 2016.

97. *Avodah Zarah* 19b.

98. http://www.jtsa.edu/The_Davidson_School/Rabbi_Dov_Lerea. xml?ss=print. Retrieved July 31, 2015.

99. Harav Aharon Feldman, "The 'New Orthodoxy': Open to What?" *Dialogue: For Torah Issues and Ideas* 5 (2014), p. 15.

sources. As will be shown in Chapter 5, Open Orthodoxy shows contempt for the halachic tradition in general. The following chapters will cite many more deviant statements from these leaders. Obviously if these are the opinions of their teachers, the graduates cannot be far behind. It is impossible for them not to have absorbed the teachings of their mentors. Indeed, in subsequent chapters we will cite many examples of how the graduates of these institutions have integrated the teachings of their masters into their *weltanschauung*.

4

Torah as Divine and Eternal

For over 3000 years, the Jew has viewed Torah as an eternal, unchanging document given by God at Sinai. He has delved into its intricacies, working tirelessly to understand its laws and its nuances. As the Torah itself states numerous times, it is an eternal covenant.

The Rambam, in his explanation of the Mishnah,[100] details 13 principles which derive from the Written and Oral Law which every Jew must believe. These principles have always been at the core of Orthodoxy. Among them is the belief that the Torah was given by God to Moses, and that it is unchanging:[101]

> The Eighth Principle: to believe that the Torah is from heaven and that this Torah was given through Moses; that it is all from the Almighty—that is to say, that it reached us in its entirety from God....

> The Ninth Principle: that this Torah is from God and no other. And it cannot be added to or subtracted from, as

---

100. *Sanhedrin*, Chapter 10.
101. See also *Mishneh Torah, Hilchos Teshuvah* 3:8.

it says, *You shall not add to that which I command you, and you shall not subtract from it...* (Deuteronomy 13:1).

The centrality of the Revelation at Sinai is also described by the Rambam in his *Mishneh Torah.* He writes that a Jew's unquestionable faith in the prophecy of Moses derives from the experience at Mount Sinai. It is through the experience at Sinai alone that a Jew has complete faith in the prophecy of Moses— that is, in the divinity of the holy Torah.[102 A]

Once one does not believe in a Divinely-given Torah, there is no limit to the deviations which may emerge. Commandments are seen as immoral, the Torah becomes misogynistic and revered Biblical figures stagger under the weight of their flaws. A rejection of the God-given nature of Torah is the source of all these, and many other, misinterpretations.

Unfortunately, many Open Orthodox leaders espouse beliefs that are contrary to the ideas delineated by the Rambam. Some say that commandments have been abrogated; some declare the unimportance of the Revelation at Sinai; others teach that the Torah was written by humans and that its stories are fictional.

For example, Rabbi Dov Linzer, Rosh haYeshivah of YCT, takes issue with the commandment to destroy Amalek:[103]

What possible message can we learn from this mitzvah? God is a vengeful God. Violence must be met with violence. Even innocents—the infants and the future

---

102. *Hilchos Yesodei ha-Torah* 8:1.
103. http://rabbidovlinzer.blogspot.com/2013_02_17_archive.html. Retrieved July 19, 2015.

descendants of the original nation—can be slaughtered by the hand of Israel when Israel is following God's command and is the agent of God's justice. Is this the message of Amalek? Is this the story that we tell? We know that it is not. It is not the story that we as a people have told. Having as a people been persecuted and slaughtered in the name of religion, and as witness today to the evils that can be perpetrated by a murderous, fundamentalist religious belief—this also is not the story that we can ever tell.

He goes on to stipulate that, because of the immoral nature of this commandment, the rabbis have sought to erase it:[104]

This story can be heard in the writings of all those halakhic authorities who, through various halakhic devices, make the mitzvah to destroy Amalek moot. From Rambam's claim that if they accept the Noachide laws they are not to be destroyed, to the consensus amongst *poskim* that such a people can no longer be identified, this mitzvah has effectively been erased. We have erased not Amalek, but the mitzvah to destroy them….

The Torah clearly states, *and you shall not subtract from it [the Torah]* (Deuteronomy 13:1), yet Rabbi Linzer claims the Rabbis have erased the mitzvah to destroy Amalek. While he concedes that others will not agree with his interpretation and

---

104. *Ibid.*

will read the commandment literally, he dismisses them as fundamentalist and extremist:[105]

> But we cannot lose sight that there are others who hear other voices. Others for whom the fundamentalist and extremist voices are the most attractive. Others who are more prepared to hear the mitzvah of *mechiyah* and *milchamah,* of war and destruction.

Not only has Linzer erased a commandment in the Torah, but he also accuses those who believe in the literal word of the Torah of being extremist and fundamentalist.

Rabbi Linzer claims that the mitzvah to destroy Amalek is immoral and therefore the rabbis sought to erase it. This claim has no basis, because to say that a mitzvah is immoral is illogical. If God commands something, it is by definition moral. God created humanity, and He declared that there is a nation so evil that it deserves to be annihilated. When Amalek rebelled against God by attacking the Jewish people, it forfeited its right to live. The nation of Amalek epitomizes a culture in opposition to God. *For the hand is on the throne of God; God maintains a war against Amalek, from generation to generation* (Exodus 17:16). Rashi comments that the name and throne of God are not complete until the name of Amalek is erased. King Saul lost the monarchy because he failed to fulfill the Divine command to destroy Amalek. We can no longer perform this commandment since we do not know which nation is Amalek, but claiming that the Rabbis purposefully erased this commandment is incorrect. Even more, it is inconceivable to an Orthodox Jew.

---

105. *Ibid.*

Linzer's view of the Oral Torah is also apparent from his writing. He views Rabbis, the ones who bear the tradition of the interpretations of the written Torah, as social reformers who modify the written law to suit modern sensibilities.[106]

The leadership of Open Orthodoxy has not only expressed the view that certain commandments no longer apply, some have even questioned the Torah's divine nature in its entirety.

Every believing Jew knows that the Torah was given before millions of people at Mount Sinai. God spoke to the people in a national revelation that has never been repeated in all of world history. He said, *I am the Lord your God who has taken you out of the land of Egypt, from the house of slavery. You shall have no other gods before Me* (Exodus 20:1). No religion in the history of mankind ever even laid claim to such a revelation. The centrality of this event in Jewish history cannot be overstated.

However, to some Open Orthodox leaders, whether the Torah was actually written by God or events in the Torah actually happened is irrelevant. On July 27, 2015, Rabbi Ysoscher Katz engaged in a heated exchange regarding a provocative statement which he posted on Facebook. In response to the post, someone suggested that perhaps the Torah was not written by God. Katz responded:[107]

I absolutely BELIEVE that He wrote it, so whether He FACTUALLY wrote [it] is immaterial.

---

106. See Chapter 5 for a further discussion of this topic.
107. https://www.facebook.com/ysoscher?fref=ts. (Comment made July 28, 2015 to a post from July 27, 2015) Retrieved August 2, 2015.

When asked to clarify this evasive language, he responded:[108]

> ...are you telling me what I mean? I mean what I said, I BELIEVE. Facts are immaterial because it's a faith claim, not a scientific postulate.

Astonishingly, Rabbi Katz declares that the "fact" of whether or not God wrote the Torah is immaterial.

Katz also seems to be of the opinion that there is no rational way to explain religion. In another Facebook post, he writes:[109]

> There is no proof that God exists, that He gave the Torah, etc. It is precisely this sense of illogicality which makes it a religious exercise.

He declares that there is no proof for God's existence or whether He gave the Torah. In fact, this view seems to have led him to propose that a new concept of faith should be taught, since he feels that the classic notion of faith does not resonate with many people:[110 B]

> Our new model should be: BELIEF in a God you doubt or believe no longer exists; and, along those lines, BELIEF in a Maamad Har Sinai moment that you no longer accept as factual.

---

108. *Ibid.*
109. https://www.facebook.com/ysoscher?fref=ts (November 18, 2013). Retrieved August 31, 2015.
110. https://www.facebook.com/ysoscher?fref=ts (April 2, 2014). Retrieved August 31, 2015.

Paradoxically, Katz proposes that one should believe in a God that one does not believe exists!

In another circuitous statement, Katz reacts to an article which cites archeological proofs that validates the historical accuracy of the Exodus. Katz downplays the importance of this find and concludes that the Exodus story happened "in the Torah," implying that it may not have historically taken place at all.[111] C

In a similar vein, Katz in an April 3, 2015 Facebook post declares:[112]

Biblical Fiction. According to the Rabbis, the retelling of the Exodus story is fiction. It is a record of God's conversation with fictionalized characters. He is dialoguing with four recalcitrant and doubting young male archetypes.

It is unclear why Rabbi Katz believes that because the story of the Exodus is later retold to these archetypical characters, it means that it is fiction.

This attitude is not only reserved for the story of the Exodus. In another post Katz labels those who read the story of Noah literally as "extremists."[113]

111. https://www.facebook.com/photo.php?fbid=10152659216583639 &set=a.10151170390208639.451104.509528638&type=1&theater (March 2, 2015). Retrieved July 30, 2015.

112. https://www.facebook.com/ysoscher?fref=ufi&pnref=story (April 3, 2015). Retrieved July 30, 2015.

113. https://www.facebook.com/ysoscher?fref=ufi&pnref=story (April 9, 2014). Retrieved January 23, 2016.

Katz goes even further and proposes that certain "troubling" parts of Jewish texts, including *Tanach*, should be erased. In a conversation on Facebook he writes:[114]

> Chassidic and kabbalistic racism and misogyny is deeply problematic, and, of course, troubles me a lot, but the problem is intrinsic to Jewish texts in general, not just to mystical texts. It's true for the Tanach, Chazal, Rishonim and Achronim. Texts are products of their times, strongly influenced by the contemporary social reality. As time goes by, we learn to adapt those texts to our new reality, excising or updating the troubling parts or reapplying them in new ways.

After accusing the Bible and subsequent Jewish texts of being misogynist and racist, he contends that the offensive parts should simply be excised or updated.

In Chapter 3, we discussed Rabbi Katz's "dislike" of the Rambam. Another of his Facebook posts describes how he rejects the Rambam's Eighth Principle of Faith which stipulates that one must believe that the Torah was given by God. He argues that such a belief is not obligatory.

He writes, "Likewise, I don't accept the Divinity of the Torah because of Maimonides' Eighth Principle." He concludes, "My beliefs are volitional, not obligatory; a mental choice, not necessarily an intellectual conviction."[115] D Contrary to the

114. https://www.facebook.com/ysoscher?fref=ts. (June 9, 2015 comment to a post from June 1, 2015). Retrieved August 26, 2015.
115. https://www.facebook.com/ysoscher?fref=ts. (September 4, 2014). Retrieved August 31, 2015.

Rambam, Katz believes that a Jew is not required to believe that the Torah is Divine.

Many students at YCT share Rabbi Katz's views. Rabbi David Almog is a 2005 graduate. Interestingly, in 2010, he began studying for a doctorate at the Jewish Theological Seminary (Conservative) where he also studied as an undergraduate student.[116] In an essay, he discusses the ramifications of not believing in a Sinaitic Revelation:[117]

> Whether or not the specific event of Sinai happened does not undermine my own experiences of the sweetness and goodness of Torah, or my sense of their prophetic nature.

The Rambam writes that the event of Sinai is the only true source of faith in the prophecy of Moses, yet Rabbi Almog begs to differ. He believes that whether or not it happened is simply—irrelevant!

Some YCT graduates have been even more radical in their views.

Rabbi Dr. Zev Farber is a 2006 graduate of YCT. He holds a standard *Yoreh Yoreh* ordination, as well as a *Yadin Yadin* ordination (both from YCT) which qualifies him to be a Rabbinical Judge.[118] He is heavily involved in Open Orthodox institutions. Farber is a founding member of the

---

116. http://www.yctorah.org/content/view/44/84. Retrieved August 10, 2015.
117. http://thetorah.com/ask-a-rabbi/experiencing-faith. Retrieved August 18, 2015.
118. http://www.yctorah.org/content/view/44/84. Retrieved August 26, 2015.

International Rabbinic Fellowship (IRF), Open Orthodoxy's rabbinic organization.[119] He also served as chairman of the IRF's conversion committee[120] and currently serves on Yeshivat Maharat's advisory board.[121] In 2014, he published a 65-page article in their Torah journal.[122] In addition, he edited the IRF's book which deals with the halachic definition of death.[123]

In an essay, he discusses several apparent contradictions between the book of Deuteronomy and other books of the Torah. So-called contradictions are the basis of much Bible criticism, an endeavor launched by the Reform Movement many years ago. It is based on the assumption that the Torah was written by man. However, the basis of Judaism is that it is God-given. Based on this assumption, there are explanations for all seeming contradictions; the Oral Torah solves them all. To be properly understood, each aspect of a mitzvah must be seen in the context in which it appears. The words of the Torah are *nitnu me-Roeh echod*, "given from one Shepherd" (*Chagigah* 3b).

However, Farber proposes a different approach to such apparent contradictions:[124]

---

119. *Ibid.*
120. http://internationalrabbinicfellowship.org/news/rabbi-yair-silver-man-serve-coordinator-irf-vaad-hagiyur. Retrieved August 2, 2015.
121. http://www.Yeshivatmaharat.org/advisory-board. Retrieved August 19, 2015.
122. Rabbi Zev Farber, "The Creation Blessings and the Morning Blessings: A Case Study in the Fluidity of Liturgy and Its Practical Applications." *Keren* 2 (2014), p. 12.
123. http://www.cjnews.com/books-and-authors/book-debates-halach-ic-debate-brain-death. Retrieved September 2, 2015.
124. http://thetorah.com/devarim-recounting-different. Retrieved July 19, 2015.

The simplest explanation for these differences between the accounts in Exodus-Numbers and Deuteronomy is that they were penned by (at least) two different authors with different conceptions of the desert experience.

In the summary of the same piece, he writes:[125]

Despite sharing many details with the desert story as told in Exodus and Numbers, there appears to be no way to make the two versions work with each other without unreasonably stretching the meaning of the texts. The simplest literary approach is the academic one which posits multiple authors with multiple traditions. How such an approach meshes with traditionalist belief requires serious thought but it is necessary to start by recognizing the simplicity and straightforwardness of the academic approach.

He also writes:[126]

.... the Torah seems to have evident signs of being an edited work which makes use of multiple sources and contains layers of redaction.... Second, religious practices as well as aspects of the Jewish belief system have changed and developed over the generations. The Oral Torah explanation proffered by the rabbis, i.e. that all of the practices not found in the Bible were

125. *Ibid.*
126. http://thetorah.com/torah-history-judaism-part-4. Retrieved July 19, 2015.

either told to Moses directly at Sinai or are derived from midrashic reading of text, does not even begin to realistically address the religious changes Judaism has gone through in a believable way.

Rabbi Farber clearly and unabashedly expresses the view that the Torah is not God-given. That a basic tenet of faith held across the millennia by all Orthodox Jews should be rejected by a supposed Orthodox rabbi and rabbinical judge is, at the very least, extremely jarring. Even more disturbing is the fact that the same person served as Chairman for the conversion committee of the IRF and still is listed as an advisor at Yeshivat Maharat.

In addition, Farber contends that figures that appear in the Torah did not actually exist:[127]

Abraham and Sarah are folkloristic characters; factually speaking, they are not my ancestors or anyone else's.

Describing the biblical narratives, Farber writes:[128]

It began with the parts of the Torah which are clearly folkloristic or symbolic in character. The creation of the world in six days, the account of Adam and Eve in the garden, Noah's flood[129] and the Tower of Babel—all of

---

127. http://thetorah.com/torah-history-judaism-conclusion. Retrieved July 19, 2015.
128. http://thetorah.com/torah-history-judaism-part-5. Retrieved July 19, 2015.
129. Farber suggests that the flood of Noah was not an actual event. Even from an academic perspective, this is a ridiculous claim. The fact that dozens of cultures, from every continent, have a flood narrative

these were easily identified as ahistorical. These stories fit perfectly into the genre of folklore or allegory and each offers a simple narrative of intentionally fantastic character in order to explain some aspect of the world in which we live.

He continues:[130]

The idea that the twelve tribes of Israel were formed by the twelve sons of Jacob has all the appearances of a schematic attempt of Israelites to explain themselves to themselves: "We are all one family because we are all children of the same father." These Torah stories are not history, the recording of past events, they are mnemohistory, the construction of shared cultural-memory through narratives about the past.

Also:[131]

---

in their heritage indicates that the flood was a historical event. Is it more likely that people had a compulsion to write fictional flood narratives? Especially striking are the similarities between some of the narratives and the story in Genesis. While a Jew believes in Torah because of a tradition that his ancestors heard the word of God, it is interesting that even from an academic perspective, which Farber seems to champion, the evidence points to a historical flood. (http://www.talkorigins.org/faqs/flood-myths.html Retrieved January 27, 2016.) See also Rabbi Moshe Meiselman, *Torah, Chazal, and Science.* Israel Bookshop Publications, 2013. Section 7.

130. http://thetorah.com/torah-history-judaism-part-5. Retrieved July 19, 2015.

131. *Ibid.*

Given the data to which modern historians have access, it is impossible to regard the accounts of mass Exodus from Egypt, the wilderness experience or the coordinated, swift and complete conquest of the entire land of Canaan under Joshua as historical.

One would expect YCT to vehemently condemn comments which deny basic tenets of Orthodox Judaism. However, such a condemnation never came. Farber's views evince no more than a mild statement from YCT's President, Rabbi Asher Lopatin in July of 2013. While he does state that YCT is committed to a belief in *Torah min ha-Shamyim*, he actually praises Farber and contends that his views fall within the bounds of Orthodoxy:[132] E

> Some *talmidim* are in the midst of theological work to uphold Orthodoxy in a way they find intellectually honest. One recent example is Rav Zev Farber, whose journey has taken him to the outer boundaries of Orthodox thinking on this subject. Rav Zev is thinking honestly and personally, but his ideas are different from, and in some ways contradictory to, what we teach and ask our students to believe at YCT.

As for his protestation that Open Orthodoxy believes in *Torah min ha-Shamyim*, he consistently praises those who deny this belief. While Farber openly states that the Torah is fiction, Rabbi Lopatin is comfortable declaring that Farber's views fall within the bounds of Orthodoxy, and commends his honest thinking.

132. http://morethodoxy.org/2013/07/26/revelation-and-the-education-of-modern-orthodox-rabbis. Retrieved August 18, 2015.

One wonders if, should the Secretary of State suddenly declare his support for Communism, the President would commend his honest thinking and say that his views are demonstrative of American capitalism. The fact that Farber's views have not elicited condemnation from YCT or Open Orthodoxy, coupled with the fact that Rabbi Farber still serves as a rabbinic advisor to Yeshivat Maharat, are indicative of the movement's embrace of these non-Orthodox ideas. In fact, as we have shown, some Open Orthodox leaders have themselves aired views similar to Farber's.[133]

Farber continues to be praised for his work by YCT's president. On July 9, 2015 Rabbi Asher Lopatin wrote the following on Rabbi Shmuel Herzfeld's Facebook page:[134]

> During the Three Weeks, I suggest we refrain from theological warfare. We are proud of the work Rabbi Zev Farber is doing to bring many many Jews closer to the Divine Torah.

Lopatin is proud of the work Rabbi Farber is doing to "bring many many Jews closer to the Divine Torah." He seems unaware of the irony of his statement, since Farber himself writes that the Torah was not written by God.

The Orthodox world has not remained silent in the face of YCT's lack of condemnation of Rabbi Farber. Rabbi David

---

133. Rabbi Katz suggests that whether or not biblical events factually happened is irrelevant, and both Linzer and Katz advocate erasing or excising parts of Torah which they deem offensive. (See above.)
134. https://www.facebook.com/shmuel.herzfeld?fref=ts. (Comment on July 9, 2015 to a post of the same day). Retrieved August 20, 2015.

Berger, in a July 15, 2015 article for the *Jewish Link of New Jersey* criticized YCT for neglecting to take a stand against Farber's views.[135] Rabbi Ysoscher Katz responded to Rabbi Berger by claiming that for Modern [i.e., Open] Orthodoxy to develop a proper response to heresy will require a great deal of time. On August 20, 2015, he wrote:[136] F

> YCT will, of course, make a judicial decision about those students who have unfortunately espoused heretical views, but that decision will be distinct from its predecessors. It will also take time to produce. Those who clamor for resolution will have to wait.

He assures us that YCT will—eventually—respond appropriately to its students who espouse heretical views. He says that it will take time to develop such a response. However, Katz wrote nearly the same thing nearly *two years* earlier. On October 28, 2013 he wrote on Facebook:[137] G

> There is no doubt that one can raise legitimate critiques of YCT. (I'm the first one to admit that there are many.) Addressing them, however, requires knowledge, nuance and sophistication, something that's sorely missing in

135. http://jewishlinknj.com/index.php?option=com_content&view=article&id=8820%3Athe-rabbinical-council-of-america-and-Yeshivat-chovevei-torah-a-response-to-rabbis-avi-weiss-and-asher-lopatin. Retrieved September 1, 2015.

136. http://www.jewishlinknj.com/index.php?option=com_content&view=article&id=9252%3Aresponse-to-dean-david-berger-on-open-orthodoxy&catid=150%3Anews&Itemid=562. Retrieved September 1, 2015.

137. https://www.facebook.com/ysoscher?fref=ts. (October 28, 2013). Retrieved September 1, 2015.

these columns and blog posts. Heresy is one of the most complex questions in Halacha, something we at Chovevei have been debating for years... נצחיות התורה makes us confident that we will eventually figure this out, but it will take time, nuance, knowledge and sophistication, not loud voiced newspaper columns, to get there.

How much time, one wonders, does it take to develop a response to heresy? Perhaps, by brushing the issue under the rug, they hope that it will simply go away.

Students at YCT continue to espouse views similar to those of Rabbi Farber. Daniel Ross Goodman, a student at the yeshiva,[138] and editor of YCT's Torah Journal *Milin Havivin* (volume 7)[139] writes:[140]

[T]he Bible is also not a work of "philosophy" or "theology" because the biblical writers were similarly unfamiliar with such logical, systematic disciplines; to impose our familiarity with these disciplines upon the biblical writers is to commit an anachronism... one may still acknowledge the evolutionary nature of the Bible's composition, and one may still recognize the archeological, philological, historical and ethnological findings that indicate the Pentateuch's multiple authorship, while still believing (in a theological sense) in the divine unity of the Torah....

---

138. http://www.yctorah.org/images//about%20our%20students%20 2014-2015%20email.pdf. Retrieved August 26, 2015.

139. http://www.yctorah.org/images/milin%20havivin%202013-2014%20-%2012.18.14.pdf. Retrieved January 19, 2016.

140. Daniel Goodman, "Sacred Scriptures, Secular Interpretations: The Bible as an Anthology of Philosophy, Psychology, Literature, and Religion." *Religious Studies Review* 39:4, p. 231.

He refers to the "multiple authorship" of the Torah and the "biblical writers," completely abandoning the belief in a God-given Torah, the central tenet of Jewish faith. After public pressure was applied to YCT regarding their student's non-Orthodox views,[141] Goodman recanted two days before his ordination in 2016.[142] In another article, Goodman writes:[143]

> Religion cannot, nor should it, attempt to explain how the world was created, nor should it attempt to explain how the universe works. Science, not religion, possesses the answers to these questions.

Given Goodman's belief that religion cannot and should not explain the creation of the world, it is unclear how he would interpret the first chapter of Genesis.

In another display of Open Orthodoxy's view of Torah, Yoram Hazony describes a program at an Open Orthodox synagogue where Bible academics discussed topics such as the gradual revelation of Torah and the ahistorical nature of some biblical stories. He recalls that, when an older man in the congregation pointed out that such views run contrary to Jewish tradition, he was promptly silenced. He relates the reaction of the congregation's rabbi:[144]

> Here in our synagogue we advocate what we call Open Orthodoxy. What we mean by that is that unlike

---

141. http://haemtza.blogspot.com/2016/03/yct-statement-on-belief.html. http://www.cross-currents.com/archives/2016/03/10/the-upcoming-ordination-imbroglio/. Retrieved June 6, 2016.

142. http://blogs.timesofisrael.com/guest-blog-religious-maturation-publicly-refining-our-theological-positions/. Retrieved June 6, 2016.

143. http://www.thepublicdiscourse.com/2014/06/13167.

144. http://www.torahmusings.com/2014/05/open-orthodoxy.

others who avoid dealing with the issues presented by modernity and academic thought, we want to confront issues like this by meeting them head-on, presenting the scholarship here in the synagogue so that we can wrestle with the hard issues instead of avoiding them.

While theological discussions are important, the views of Bible critics should not be held sacred while those of Torah Judaism are silenced.

The list of Open Orthodox leaders who espouse these troublesome views seems endless. Rabbi Herzl Hefter is a defender of Open Orthodox reforms and lectures at YCT.[145] He also serves on YCT's Jewish leadership advisory board.[146] He does not understand Divine Revelation in the classic Orthodox way:[147]

It is possible, then, to accept that the Torah in its current form is the product of historical circumstance and a prolonged editorial process while simultaneously stubbornly asserting the *religious belief* that it none-theless enshrouds Divine revelation.

According to Hefter, rather than being dictated by God to Moses, the Torah was a product of a "prolonged editorial

145. https://www.facebook.com/asher.lopatin/posts/10153338401851117?pnref–story. (July 19, 2015) Retrieved July 29, 2015.

146. http://www.yctorah.org/content/view/906/49. Retrieved January 19, 2016.

147. http://morethodoxy.org/2013/09/16/guest-post-by-rabbi-her-zl-hefter-the-challenge-of-biblical-criticism-dogma-vs-faith. Retrieved August 29, 2015.

process." Rabbi Hefter has also tried to re-interpret Divine revelation in other unique ways. In an essay, he seeks to justify women's ordination based on such an interpretation. Utilizing Chasidic as well as Christian sources, he redefines revelation. After denigrating those who believe in absolute, God-given truth as "adolescent," he goes on to propose a new theology:[148]

> We need a contemporary theology which expresses the authentic ethos of Jewish tradition lived fully within a context of *Yirat Shamayim, Ahavat Yisrael* and *Kevod HaAdam*. I propose such a theology predicated upon the following two principles: Humility: We do not have access to certainty or objective truth. Humans are created in God's image, which means that human consciousness is the instrument of divine revelation. Since God is revealed through human consciousness, our refined moral convictions and religious sensibilities may be considered a form of divine revelation.

Rabbi Hefter contends that human beings do not have access to God-given truth. This is quite a remarkable claim. The Jewish people believe that God revealed himself to the Jewish people on Mount Sinai. Revelation means that God Himself spoke to the nation and declared His will to them. How is it possible to assert that God does not reveal absolute truth?

Hefter's second contention is also quite creative. In order to solve the dilemma experienced by Open Orthodox rabbis

---

148. http://blogs.timesofisrael.com/why-i-ordained-women. Retrieved July 29, 2015.

surrounding the clash between secular values and the Torah, he maintains that it is actually people's own "moral convictions and religious sensibilities" which constitute divine revelation. In other words, that which I think is right, God must think is right. Hefter has effectively turned man into God.

This second article became the object of praise by YCT's president. Rabbi Asher Lopatin posted it on his Facebook page along with the following comment:[149]

> Rav Herzl Hefter is thoughtful and brave and a first rate *talmid chacham*. I view this article—and even his bold act of ordaining Orthodox women rabbis—as the continuation of a process started at Sinai of understanding Torah and our relationship to revelation and Hashem's word. This is not the end of the conversation. In fact, Rav Hefter writes this powerful piece to involve us all in this important discussion. I am so happy our students at YCT get an opportunity each year to learn from this great man.

Not only does YCT's president not condemn Rabbi Zev Farber's opinion that Torah was written by man, but he goes on to label Rabbi Hefter—who also denies the Orthodox view of divine revelation—a "great man." Rabbi Elliot Kaplowitz (YCT 2007) also called Hefter's article a "wonderful articulation of Modern Orthodox theology."[150]

---

149. https://www.facebook.com/asher.lopatin/posts/10153338401851117?pnref=story. (July 19, 2015). Retrieved July 29, 2015.

150. https://twitter.com/rabbikap (July 19, 2015).

In a sentiment similar to Rabbi Hefter's, Rabbi Ysoscher Katz diminishes the importance of teaching Torah as objective truth: [151] [H]

> We live in a post-modern world where objective truth is rejected and absolute claims are frowned upon. I would go as far as to say that rationalism (in the general and colloquial sense) as a source for *Emunah* is bankrupt, it increasingly speaks to fewer people. It, therefore, behooves us to come up with alternative models.

He continues and explains that *"Chasidut"* is the proper theology to embrace. However, he has a novel interpretation of *Chasidut*:[152]

> The Torah for Chassidim is there to teach us how to live life and serve God; the narrative *qua* narrative (the origin story) is mere background music. The narration parts of the Torah are, therefore, not of much theological significance to them. They are a-historical.

Katz advocates teaching a theology which does not value truth and which views biblical accounts as "a-historical"—that is, not necessarily connected with factual history. This is consistent with Katz's other statements, which we cited earlier, asserting that the factual accuracy of events described in the Torah is irrelevant.

---

151. https://kavvanah.wordpress.com/2015/05/31/torat-chaim-veaha-vat-chesed-rabbi-ysoscher-katz. Retrieved July 29, 2015.
152. *Ibid.*

Others at YCT concede that the Torah is divine, yet argue that Jews are no longer bound by it. Rabbi Yitzchak Greenberg is a member of YCT's adjunct faculty[153] and its Jewish leadership advisory board.[154] He makes the illogical claim that God has to do "*teshuvah*" for the Holocaust:[155]

> Therefore, morally speaking, God must repent of the covenant, i.e., do teshuvah for having given his chosen people a task that was unbearably cruel and dangerous without having provided for their protection.

He continues that Jews are no longer bound by the covenant:[156]

> Morally speaking, then, God can have no claims on the Jews by dint of the covenant. The fundamental shift in the nature of the covenant can be put yet another way. It can no longer be commanded.

He writes further:[157]

> What then happened to the covenant? I submit that its authority was broken but the Jewish people released from its obligations, chose voluntarily to take it on again. We are living in the age of the renewal of the

---

153. http://www.yctorah.org/content/view/911/49.

154. http://www.yctorah.org/content/view/906/49/

155. Rabbi Irving (Yitzchak) Greenberg, "Voluntary Covenant." *Wrestling with God: Jewish Theological Responses during and after the Holocaust.* Ed. Steven Katz, Shlomo Biderman, and Gershon Greenberg (New York: Oxford University Press, 2007), p. 545.

156. *Ibid.*

157. *Ibid* p. 546.

covenant. God was no longer in a position to command, but the Jewish people was so in love with the dream of redemption that it volunteered to carry on its mission.

Rabbi Greenberg believes that due to the suffering of the Jewish people during the Holocaust the covenant between them and God was broken. The Jews then "voluntarily" accepted it upon themselves again. Contrary to Greenberg's claim, the Torah states countless times that God made an "eternal covenant" with the Jewish people and that the commandments are eternally binding.[158] The Torah also states:[159]

> But despite this, while they are in the land of their enemies, I will not have been revolted by them nor will I have rejected them for I am Hashem, their God. I will remember for them the covenant of the ancients, those for whom I have taken out of the land of Egypt before the eyes of the nation, to be a God unto them, I am Hashem.

While the Holocaust was a time of unspeakable horror for the Jewish people, the covenant was never abrogated.

It is not only the Written Torah which Open Orthodox rabbis question; the Oral Torah is afforded the same treatment. The Rambam writes that someone who denies the explanation of the Torah, i.e., the Oral Law is considered a *kofer* (heretic).[160] The Talmud is the record of that oral transmission explaining the

---

158. For example see Genesis (17:13, 19), Exodus (12:17, 27:21), Leviticus (23:14, 21, 31), Numbers (15:15, 18:23).
159. Leviticus (26:44-45). Translation from ArtScroll Stone Chumash.
160. *Hilchos Teshuvah* 3:8.

Torah, given by God at Mount Sinai. Through the self-sacrifice and integrity of the Sages, that tradition has reached us in the present day. The Talmud is its accurate and authoritative record. As the Rambam writes in his introduction to *Mishneh Torah*:

> … everything in the Babylonian Talmud, all of the Jewish people are required to follow. And we should compel every city and every country to act according to its customs, to enact all of its decrees and follow all of its ordinances.

However, not everyone at YCT agrees with this approach. Referring to a comment by a friend, cited by him, Rabbi Linzer approvingly writes: [161]

> She said to me, "It is not your job to defend the Talmud. The Talmud says what it says. It is your job to take responsibility for how it is taught, if it is taught as unquestionable, God-given truth, or if it is taught with an acknowledgment of its problems and challenges." This is what it means to take the Torah out of heaven and bring it to the earth. This is the Torah that we must teach and represent.

Rabbi Linzer advocates teaching the Talmud not as unquestionable truth, but rather with an acknowledgment of its problems and challenges. Rabbi Katz similarly asks:[162] I

---

161. http://rabbidovlinzer.blogspot.com/2014/05/message-from-rosh-haYeshiva_30.html. Retrieved July 19, 2015.

162. https://www.facebook.com/ysoscher?fref=ts. (December 3, 2014). Retrieved September 1, 2015.

What is the role of the Talmud in MO *pesikah*; does it have legal weight and halakhic authority, or did *chasimas ha'talmud* rob it of halakhic significance?

For the head of YCT's Talmud department to question whether the Talmud has halachic significance is disturbing, to say the least.

While claiming to be Orthodox, Open Orthodoxy's leaders consistently make statements that are antagonistic to Orthodoxy. In declaring the Torah to be the product of human writers, in theorizing that commandments have been erased and that the events and characters in the Torah are fabrications, they have jettisoned any semblance of Orthodox belief. As we have shown, the leaders of Open Orthodoxy, who are training the next generation of rabbis, espouse these views. Their students echo their beliefs and are, in some cases, even more outspoken.

Outside the Pale

Principle 3

The Rambam's Third Principle of Faith posits that one must believe that God has no physical characteristics. Any reference to God's physicality in the Torah is only meant as a metaphor to help people understand His nature. [163]]

The Rambam, in the first chapter of *Hilchos Yesodei ha-Torah* ("Laws of the Fundamentals of Torah"), expands on this concept. The accepted view, as expressed by him, is that God

---

163. Explanation of the Mishnah, *Sanhedrin*, Chapter 10.

has no physicality or emotions, and that any reference to these things in the Torah is meant only as a metaphor.[164] [K]

A famous example of the use of metaphor to describe God touches on the holiday of *Shemini Atzeres*. Rashi writes that the idea of the final day of *Sukkos*, known as *Shemini Atzeres* (literally, "the eighth day of the festival") is comparable to a king who invites his children for a feast. When the children are about to leave, the king says, "Please stay for one more day, as your departure is difficult for me." [165] Rashi relates a parable which expresses God's love for the Jewish people. This is consistent with the Rambam's opinion that notions of physicality are used only as metaphor when describing God.

However, Rabbi David Kalb, a member of Yeshivat Maharat's advisory board,[166] has a different interpretation:[167]

You know what is also interesting about this reading of Shemini Atzeret? God's loneliness. What Rashi is really saying is that God wants *us* ; God needs *us*. It's funny to talk about God's wants and needs… But that's clearly what we want to say as a community about God: God has *issues,* like all of us…. There's something very compelling about God having issues. Yes, we need God on these holidays, but God needs us, too.

---

164. *Hilchos Yesodei ha-Torah* 1:11.
165. Leviticus 23:36.
166. http://www.yeshivatmaharat.org/advisory-board. Retrieved August 19, 2015.
167. http://forward.com/wondering-jew/207476/left-out-then-lingering-hoshana-rabba-and-shemini/#ixzz3jHuBUS9B. Retrieved August 19, 2015. He also serves as the Director of Learning and Innovation at a Reform synagogue. *Ibid.*

Rabbi Kalb claims that God is "lonely" and "has issues." He maintains that God has wants and needs—a view utterly rejected by the Rambam.

Dr. Erin Smokler Yeshivat Maharat's Director of Spiritual Development[168] goes a step further and claims that humans have the ability to teach God:[169]

> In the Talmudic imagination, between the two clauses of our verse (Ex. 3:14), Moshe taught God (whom he had only just met) a profound lesson about humanity. He taught God that there exists an important, necessary gap between who God is and who we need God to be.[170]

Principle 12

Jews have yearned for the Messiah for 2000 years to rebuild the Temple in Jerusalem. Orthodox Jews pray three times a day: *May it be your will, Hashem, our God, that you rebuild the Temple speedily in our day.* As Jews entered the gas chambers in Aushwitz they sang the *Ani Ma'amin* fervently, hoping with their last, dying breath that the Messiah would arrive. This concept is twelfth in the Rambam's Thirteen Principles of Faith.[171 L]

---

168. http://www.Yeshivatmaharat.org/faculty-and-staff/
169. http://hosted-p0.vresp.com/1015677/c789d064da/ARCHIVE. Retrieved January 18, 2016.
170. See Chapter 9 where we cite Dr. Smokler's view that God failed the test of the *Akeidah.*
171. Explanation of the Mishnah, *Sanhedrin* Chapter 10.

In addition to declaring that it is a principle of faith to believe that the Messiah will come, the Rambam writes that one who "belittles the Messiah's arrival denies the authority of Torah."[172]

Rabbi Dr. Shmuly Yanklowitz,[173] a 2010 graduate of YCT and the executive director of the Valley Beit Midrash in Phoenix Arizona, teaches the ideas behind Tisha B'av: [174]

---

172. *Ibid.*

173. Rabbi Dr. Shmuly Yanklowitz is an outspoken proponent for many Open Orthodox reforms. He is closely associated with YCT and Open Orthodox leaders:

- He co-founded *Uri L'tzedek*, a social justice organization with Rabbi Ari Hart, YCT's former Director of Admissions. The organization is praised by leaders of Open Orthodoxy such as Rabbi Avi Weiss, Rabbi Asher Lopatin, Rabbi Nathaniel Helfgot, former Chair, Departments of Bible and Jewish Thought and Director of Continuing Rabbinic Education at YCT, Rabbi Yaakov Love, former Chair, Department of Halakha, at YCT, Rabba Sara Hurwitz, Rabbi Jeffrey S. Fox, Rabbi Adam Mintz, professor of Talmud at Yeshivat Maharat, Rabbi Yosef Kanefsky, and Rabbi Jason Herman, Executive Director of the International Rabbinic Fellowship. (http://utzedek.org/about-us/supporters/rabbis/)
- Rabbis Avi Weiss and Asher Lopatin serve on the advisory board of the Valley *Beit Midrash* where Yanklowitz serves as Executive Director. (https://www.valleybeitmidrash.org/about-us/leadership. Retrieved August 25, 2015.)
- In addition, Rabbis Avi Weiss, Haggai Resnikoff, Rebbe at YCT, Daniel Sperber, and Steven Exler (YCT 2009) lecture at Yanklowitz's Valley Beit Midrash. (https://www.facebook.com/rshmuly.yanklowitz?fref=ts (August 2015). Retrieved August 25, 2015.)
- Also several articles written by Yanklowitz are featured on YCT's webpage and newsletter. (http://www.yctorah.org/content/view/32/11/. Retrieved August 5, 2015.)
- YCT's alumni page does not record any previous yeshiva education for Yanklowitz.

174. https://www.facebook.com/rshmuly.yanklowitz?fref=ts. (July 23, 2015). Retrieved July 24, 2015.

My teacher, Rabbi Dr. Nathan Lopes Cardozo, once again hits a grand-slam reminding us to get our priorities straight as we approach Tisha B'Av. "Whether or not the Temple will be re-built is not our concern, nor is it our dream. It is of little importance. What we dream of is the day when we will be able to transform ourselves and reconstruct the Temple's message within our hearts."

He contends that the rebuilding of the Temple is unimportant. In a similar vein, he discusses why the Jewish people are actually better off in exile. In an article entitled "Was the Destruction of the Temple good for the Jews? A Tisha B'Av Reflection," he writes: [175]

> The fantasy of returning to one centralized monolithic form of Judaism is not only wishful thinking. It's also dismissive of two of the most important aspects of modern Jewish life: diversity and adaptability. Further, in any centralized system of authority, abuses of power and limits of transparency and empowerment have proven to be inevitable. The new paradigm that the Temple's destruction and exile from Israel enabled is one that says, Bring God into your hearts and into the wide world every day and in every way; the Temple was a vehicle for this once, now we have so much more.

---

175. http://blogs.timesofisrael.com/also-have-trouble-mourning-on-tisha-bav. Retrieved July 29, 2015.

TORAH AS DIVINE AND ETERNAL

He also states:[176]

> We have made too many mistakes throughout history, thinking that the Messiah is a person or event. They are called Bar Kochva, Abulafia, Shabbatai Zvi, Jacob Frank, and certain Chassidic rebbes. It was Christian influence that helped further this idea of the single divine human. The Jewish notion, preceding that, suggested that all people are imbued with Divinity (*Tzelim Elokim*). At the end of the day, I would like to suggest that we are Moshiach—we are the ones we have been waiting for.

Contrary to Yanklowitz's view, Judaism views the Messiah as a singular person. As the Rambam writes:[177]

> The King Messiah will establish and return the Davidic Kingship to its previous rule and build the Temple and gather the banished of Israel.

However, to Yanklowitz, the Messiah is not a person, and whether or not the Jewish people ever rebuild the Temple is supremely unimportant.

Open Orthodoxy's leaders consistently and unabashedly express beliefs that profoundly contradict basic tenets of Judaism. That their views are outside the pale of accepted belief is troubling enough; what is more shocking is that they claim that these views are Orthodox.

---

176. http://www.thejewishweek.com/features/street_torah/most_important_and_dangerous_jewish_value_messianic_impulse. Retrieved July 21, 2015.
177. Laws of Kings (11:1).

5

Values

Orthodox Jews believe in a God given Torah. That the Creator of the world charged the Jewish people with carrying out His will in this world is the fundamental tenet of our faith. When a conflict arises between one's own values and those of the Torah, it is the mission of the Jew to nullify his own will in favor of the Almighty's. While it is no easy task to forego one's desires, this unwavering commitment to God has sustained us throughout our history.

However, Open Orthodox rabbis do the opposite. When a conflict arises between their own values and those of the Torah, it is the Torah and the Halacha which must be altered. They treat society's morals as sacred while eschewing those of the Torah.

This approach has led many of its proponents to criticize the Torah itself when its values conflict with their own. Many at YCT have expressed the opinion that certain biblical commandments and Jewish practices are immoral. They then go a step further, claiming that the Rabbis of the Talmud also viewed Torah laws as immoral and tried to "fix" these laws in order to make them fit better into the framework of society's values.

What arises from this approach is a perverted view of the halachic process. Not only do they not subjugate their own beliefs to Halacha, but they state that values external to Torah should actually determine halachic rulings. Just as the Sages "fixed" certain Torah commandments to fit their own personal definition of morality, so, too, should current Halacha and Jewish practice be altered to conform to modern ethical norms.

Torah Under Attack

Jewish tradition is constantly under attack by Open Orthodoxy.[178]

In a straightforward declaration, Rabbi Shmuly Yanklowitz (YCT 2010) writes, "There are teachings from our tradition that are evil."[179]

It is not surprising that a graduate of YCT makes such an unorthodox statement, when one of its most prominent leaders has also criticized and expressed his moral discomfort with commandments in the Torah. On Facebook, Rabbi Ysoscher Katz criticizes the Torah's law prohibiting a *kohen* from marrying a divorcee. He writes:[180]

Leviticus 21:7. They shall not marry a prostitute or a woman who has been defiled, neither shall they marry

---

178. For example, in Chapter 7 we will show that many Open Orthodox leaders believe that Jewish tradition is sexist and was formed by misogynistic rabbis.
179. https://www.facebook.com/rshmuly.yanklowitz/posts/ 10153019106696307?pnref=story. (November 3, 2015). Retrieved January 18, 2016.
180. https://www.facebook.com/ysoscher (May 8, 2015). Retrieved July 16, 2015.

a woman divorced from her husband, for the priest is holy to his God. While not as challenging as Leviticus 18:22, it is still bothersome. It hurts seeing the divorcee compared to a prostitute. Why should we ostracize someone whose sole crime is that their marriage dissolved? The fact that those divorcees are sometimes our sisters, moms, daughters or ourselves makes the insult all the more painful. אלי אלי למה עזבתני.

Orthodox Jews have always strived to understand God's commandments to the best of their ability. They have not described the commandments as "challenging," "bothersome" or an "insult." Contrary to Katz's contention, there is no comparison in the verse of a divorcee to a prostitute. If in the same sentence one says that apples and oranges are forbidden, does that mean they are prohibited for the same reason? To add insult to injury, Katz concludes with the verse in Psalms (22:1), *"My God My G–d why have you forsaken me?"* to indicate his displeasure with the Torah.[181]

In another post, he mentions his son's reaction when informed that some authorities differentiate between Jews and Gentiles with regard to the laws of purity of a corpse. Katz mentions his son's discomfort with this non-egalitarian ideal. He bemoans the fact that his son will one day have to confront "the terror of religiosity" and remarks that parts of the Torah require us to "suspend our moral compass."[182] The "terror of religiosity" is not a phrase commonly heard from the chairman

---

181. This post was "liked" by several of Rabbi Katz's students at YCT.
182. *Ibid* (June 26, 2015). Retrieved July 15, 2015.

of a yeshiva's Talmudic department. Katz seems to view the Torah as something to battle against and overcome. In his vision, there is a competition between the Torah on one side, and one's personal moral compass on the other.

In reality, contrary to Katz's view, one need not suspend one's moral compass to understand the laws of purity. The Torah calls the Jewish people a *"goy kadosh,"* a holy nation.[183] As the chosen people of God, the Jewish nation has a heightened level of holiness. In general, as many commentaries have explained, spiritual impurity results from the void resulting from the absence of a prior holiness. It is therefore understandable, that because a Jew's level of holiness was greater than that of a non-Jew during his lifetime, when he dies, his body is invested with more impurity.

Katz further demonstrates his displeasure with parts of the Torah in his descriptions of circumcision and the episode of Abraham's binding of Isaac. After pontificating about what it will be like for his son to learn about these aspects of Judaism, he goes on to describe how one must tolerate these biblical stories: [184]

Reading and tolerating these stories is an endurance test. Many pass the test (albeit emotionally bruised and spiritually battered) and manage to stay, while many others find these stories offensive and disturbing and, therefore, choose to chuck the system and drop out. Sadly, either choice, to stay or to leave, can scar us,

---

183. Exodus (19:6).
184. https://www.facebook.com/ysoscher?fref=ts. (November 6, 2014). Retrieved September 1, 2015.

forcing us to constantly grapple with the emotional consequences of the option we chose. God Almighty: why does loving (or rejecting) You have to be so hard?!

Apparently, stories which form the foundation of Judaism can cause Katz scarring and emotional pain. And loving God—a fundamental commandment in the Torah and the essence of our relationship with Him—is so terribly "hard."

Rabbi Zev Farber (YCT 2006) follows in the path of Rabbi Katz by criticizing a number of the Torah's commandments. Before listing several divine laws which he finds immoral, he writes, "The following are a few examples of ethically problematic laws." [185]

Can something written by God, the source of all good and justice, be considered "evil" or "ethically problematic"?

Among the laws which Farber cites is the commandment to destroy Amalek, a popular target of Open Orthodox rabbis. Rabbi Farber writes:[186]

Certain enemies of Israel, like the seven Canaanite nations or the Amalekites, must be slaughtered, man, woman and child (Deut. 20:16-18, 25:19). In other words, the Torah commands their genocide, an act that any ethical person today must abhor.

Thus, Rabbi Farber maintains that an ethical person must "abhor" a commandment in the Torah. Later in his article, he

185. http://thetorah.com/marrying-your-daughter-to-her-rapist. Retrieved August 22, 2015.
186. *Ibid.*

even suggests that the rabbis altered the commandments through the same mechanisms suggested by his Rosh haYeshivah, Rabbi Linzer (see Chapter 4). As we explained earlier (*Ibid.*), while it is of course immoral to murder, if God Himself, the Creator of humanity and of morality, declares that Amalek must be annihilated because of their wickedness, it is an absurdity to claim that this commandment is ethically problematic.

Rabbi Farber does not limit his critique of Torah to the commandment to destroy Amalek. He also feels that the laws of a rebellious son are immoral:[187]

> A son who is a glutton and a drunk, and who speaks rudely to his parents, should be stoned to death (Deut 21:18-21). No one nowadays could possibly advocate for such a punishment.

Contrary to what Farber may believe, God, the Creator of the world and of humans said that there is something called an evil seed. A child can be so wicked that it is better that he not mature into adulthood. Of course only the all-knowing God can make such a declaration.[188]

Farber goes on to list more commandments which he deems "immoral" because they violate the principle of religious freedom:[189]

> Anyone who worships idols (Deut 13:7-12), or practices any form of witchcraft or sorcery (Exod 22:17; Lev 20:27), must be put to death. Entire cities that worship

---

187. *Ibid.*
188. See *Sanhedrin* 71a.
189. *Ibid.*

idols must be destroyed entirely (Deut 13:13-19). In modern times, freedom of religion is one of our most sacred principles, and witch-hunting is synonymous with barbaric and primitive behavior. In the U.S., we remember the Salem witch trials with shame.

Monotheism is the core belief of Judaism. The purpose of the world is for humanity to come to the recognition that there is one God. Idolatry, a belief in polytheism, fundamentally undermines this goal. Therefore, God has declared that idolatry is an evil which must be eradicated. For this reason, the Torah commands the execution of idolaters and the destruction of idolatrous cities. They undermine the foundation of Judaism and God's plans for the world. This, too, is the reason why witchcraft is forbidden. Witchcraft, whose ancient practitioners were able to control certain aspects of nature to a limited degree, gave the appearance that a force exists in the world other than God. Similar to idolaters, its practitioners were subject to the death penalty for the same reason. The fact that certain Christian zealots in seventeenth-century Massachusetts falsely accused innocent men and women of this practice is entirely irrelevant to this commandment.

Especially ironic is his reference to the "sacred" principle of religious freedom. In the same breath, he is able to denigrate the dictates of God as immoral while terming an accepted societal value "sacred."

The function of a rabbi should be to engage in teaching and spreading Torah. But in Open Orthodoxy the Torah is routinely attacked and denigrated. Members of this group exhibit total allegiance to their own value system, and when the dictates of the Torah conflict with that system, the Torah and Jewish tradition are decried as "evil" and "ethically problematic." Thus in this warped view, it is not society which must be adjusted, but the Torah itself.

The Sages: The First Open Orthodox Rabbis?

It is not enough that Open Orthodoxy attacks the Torah, but its rabbis go further and ascribe their own views to the Sages of the Talmud. In their view, the Sages were aware of supposed immoral passages in the Torah, and attempted to rectify them through reinterpretation.

The Oral Tradition has its origins at Sinai. Without the Oral Torah, it is impossible to understand the Written Torah. One would not know how to make *tefillin* or slaughter an animal. Even more so, the Torah would also be impossible to read without the Oral Tradition, for that tradition is the source of the pronunciation of its vowels. It is only through the Oral Tradition and its vowelization that Jews know that it is forbidden to cook meat with milk (חָלָב—*chalav*) together, but not meat with fat (חֵלֶב—*cheilev*). The rabbis of each generation selflessly toil to ensure the accurate transmission of the Oral Torah. They act with no bias other than to ensure the Torah's continuity. This is apparent to any student of Talmud who has witnessed their integrity and their honest commitment to maintaining and strengthening that tradition.

In contrast, Open Orthodox leaders attest that the Oral Law is a later creation which seeks to rectify the mistakes of

WHY OPEN ORTHODOXY IS NOT ORTHODOX

the Written Law. They view the Rabbis of the Talmud as social crusaders who adjusted the Torah to fit the societal values of their times. The natural extension of this belief is that we should do the same thing today to rectify the parts of Torah which are, in their view, "immoral." This is based on the misguided idea that the Torah should be altered to conform with modern man's notions of morality.

Rabbi Ysoscher Katz, in a May 29, 2015 Facebook post, describes his view of the Sages:[190] A

> Chazal were the R. Riskin's of their time. They too were committed to creating a Yiddishkeit which is in constant dialogue with their ethical sensibilities. They read Torah with a critical lens and whenever they encountered a perceived injustice they did whatever they could (within legitimate boundaries) to undo the challenging misread.

Katz not only subscribes to the absurdity that something commanded by God Himself can be immoral; he also believes that the Sages did "whatever they could" to correct it. In this manner, he claims, *Chazal* "revised" the mitzvah of *sotah*:

> This week's *parsha* is a perfect example. Simply read, the biblical *sotah* procedure seems capricious and patriarchal. The rabbis, incorporating Divinely ordained hermeneutics, drastically revised the procedure.

190. https://www.facebook.com/ysoscher?fref=ts. Retrieved July 16, 2015.

The result: a process that is sensitive and somewhat egalitarian. They were the progressives of their time, and, relative to their milieu, quite radical. They too were vilified, but in the end they prevailed.

According to Katz, God's command in the Torah seems "capricious and patriarchal." Therefore, he says, the Rabbis radically reinterpreted it to suit their ethical sensibilities.

Katz further expresses his views in another Facebook post. Responding to an article dealing with apparent textual difficulties in the Torah, he claims that the Rabbis saw "...a built-in amorphousness that allows for and perhaps even demands perpetual reinterpretation."[191] Rabbi Katz views *Chazal* not as men charged with explaining and elucidating the Law as it was given at Sinai, but as innovators who constantly re-evaluate and reinterpret that Law.

In an even more radical approach, Rabbi Zev Farber claims that the Rabbis of the Talmud reinterpreted ethically problematic Torah laws on their own, and then falsely claimed it as the Torah's original meaning:[192] B

In other words, *Chazal* avoided the problem by reinterpreting the laws and presenting their interpretation as the Torah's original intent.

191. https://www.facebook.com/photo.php?fbid=10152288757453639& set=a.10151170390208639.451104.509528638&type=1. (September 2, 2014). Retrieved July 15, 2015.
192. http://thetorah.com/marrying-your-daughter-to-her-rapist. Retrieved August 22, 2005.

Contrary to Katz and Farber's contention, however, the explanation of the Rabbis, as presented in the Oral Law, is the only one that the Jewish people have. It has never been re-interpreted; it is the *only* interpretation. There is absolutely no evidence that there was ever another explanation which underwent re-interpretation. This total baseless conjecture is enough for them to conclude that the Rabbis did not accurately transmit Torah, but instead radically altered it.

As cited above, Rabbi Dov Linzer feels that the commandment to destroy Amalek is immoral. It is important to cite this example again because it also demonstrates Open Orthodoxy's view of the role of the Rabbis. [193] Linzer claims that the Rabbis actively tried to abrogate the commandment through different halachic techniques: "This story can be heard in the writings of all those halakhic authorities who, through various halakhic devices, make the mitzvah to destroy Amalek moot." He concludes, "We have erased not Amalek, but the *mitzvah* to destroy them."[194] Linzer makes the baseless claim that the Rabbis viewed this commandment as immoral and therefore erased it.

Rabbi Shmuly Yanklowitz (YCT 2010) has learned from his Rebbe, Rabbi Linzer. On Facebook, he lists several Jewish traditions which he finds "evil," including what he calls the

---

193. However, Rabbi Linzer does not always view the Rabbis in a positive moral light. Linzer dismisses the Tosefta's description of Rabban Gamaliel and the Sages studying Torah on Passover as elitist. (http://rabbidovlinzer.blogspot.com/2015/04/a-thought-on-pesach.html. Retrieved July 21, 2015.)

194. http://rabbidovlinzer.blogspot.com/2013_02_17_archive.html. Retrieved July 19, 2015.

"genocides."[195] In an article, he performs halachic gymnastics in order to alter this "evil" commandment:[196]

In the Guide for the Perplexed, Maimonides explains further that the command to wipe out Amalek isn't based on hatred, but on removing Amalek-like behavior from the world (3:41). For Maimonides, then, the commandment is not necessarily fulfilled through killing; it can be fulfilled through moral influence and education.

Based on the reasoning for the commandment, Yanklowitz deduces that it is not necessarily fulfilled through killing. However the Rambam states, "We are commanded to destroy the seed of Amalek ([though] not other descendants of Eisav), men, women, young and old." [197] Contrary to Yanklowitz's claim, the Rambam never mentions that this commandment is fulfilled through education.[198] Based on his own view of right and wrong, Yanklowitz has brazenly altered a commandment in the Torah.

---

195. https://www.facebook.com/rshmuly.yanklowitz/posts/ 10153019106696307?pnref=story. (November 3, 2015). Retrieved January 18, 2016.
196. http://www.myjewishlearning.com/article/genocide-in-the-torah/3/.
197. Positive Commandment 188.
198. Destroying Amalek is not the only Jewish practice that Yanklowitz finds immoral. He also takes issue with *shechitah* practices and opposes the use of chickens for *kapparos*. (http://www.wsj.com/ articles/shmuly-yanklowitz-why-this-rabbi-is-swearing-off-kosher-meat-1401404939. http://www.shamayimvaretz.org/kaparot.html. Retrieved August 6, 2015.)

Rabbi Ari Hart is an alumnus of Yeshivat Chovevei Torah (Class of 2012). He also served as Director of Recruitment and Admissions and is currently the Associate Rabbi at the Hebrew Institute of Riverdale.[199] In a blog post for the *Times of Israel*, entitled, "Can Orthodox Jews Support the Legalization of Same-Sex Marriage in America?" Rabbi Hart writes:[200]

> The rabbis of the Talmud famously wrestled with texts they found morally challenging, like the commandment to kill a wayward and rebellious son or the commandment to destroy an idolatrous city. Yaakov was called Yisrael because he wrestled with God.

How and why Rabbi Hart came to the conclusion that the Rabbis of the Talmud found the commandment to kill a wayward son and to destroy an idolatrous city "morally challenging" is anyone's guess. Hart's claim that the Rabbis found any part of the Torah less than moral is baseless in addition to being a logical absurdity. As stated, something written by God cannot be immoral. Moreover, contrary to what Hart says, there is no source that the Rabbis "wrestled" with these "immoral" God-authored texts. Hart and his like have transformed the Sages from transmitters and elucidators of Torah into correctors and censors of Torah.

In the same vein, YCT rabbis routinely view *Chazal* as men who sought to advance social justice. Rabbi Katz claims that the

---

199. http://www.yctorah.org/content/view/44/84/. Retrieved July 15, 2015.
200. http://blogs.timesofisrael.com/can-orthodox-jews-support-the-legalization-of-same-sex-marriage-in-america. Retrieved July 15, 2015.

Rabbis "feminized" the commandment of Shabbos despite the sexism of the day. In a July 10, 2015 Facebook post he writes:[201]

> Shabbos is the only mitzvah the Rabbis gendered. Feminizing a mitzvah must have been anathema to the contemporary ear. (It was "their generation's *mechitzah*") And yet, in hindsight, we have come to appreciate their courage. Instead of demeaning the day, it ended up enriching it.

Katz has transformed the holy Sages into feminist crusaders the likes of Betty Friedan and Gloria Steinem.

We have shown that the leaders of Open Orthodoxy subscribe to the oxymoronic belief that a commandment written by God can be immoral. They also believe that the Sages of the Talmud sought to readjust these immoral sections of Torah to suit the social norms and values of the day. The extension to this philosophy is obvious. If the Rabbis of the Talmud corrected God's mistakes, certainly we can correct the Rabbis' mistakes.

Open Orthodox Halacha

The goal in determining Halacha is to understand how God wants us to act. Just as the Sages sought to accurately transmit Torah, so, too, must we do our best to come to honest halachic conclusions.

---

201. https://www.facebook.com/ysoscher?fref=ufi&pnref=story. (July 10, 2015) Retrieved July 30, 2015.

When a halachic conclusion comes into conflict with our own set of values, feelings, or beliefs, it is our responsibility to remain loyal to Halacha despite any personal desire to the contrary.

It goes without saying that one's personal set of values or beliefs should not be a factor in determining Halacha. However, such an approach is actually championed and embraced by Open Orthodoxy. In their view, the Halacha does not dictate how one should act; rather, how one acts determines the Halacha!

They erroneously—and brazenly—perceive this approach to Halacha as a continuation of the work of the Sages. After commenting that parts of Jewish tradition are "evil," Rabbi Shmuly Yanklowitz (YCT 2010) declares:[202]

> The nuanced teachings were progressive in their time but our sacred responsibility is now to reinterpret them (as our Sages have always done) to be moral lights in our time. Within Jewish law, the principles, not the rules, are eternal.

He proposes a "reinterpretation" of Jewish tradition so that we may become "moral lights in our time." In other words, Jewish law and tradition should be reinterpreted in order to fit with the values of the day.

Rabbi Yosef Kanefsky, in an article for *Keren*, Yeshivat Maharat's Torah journal, says that he has stopped saying the blessing of "*shelo asani isha*," thanking God for not making him a woman. He describes how he was criticized for not backing

---

202. https://www.facebook.com/rshmuly.yanklowitz/posts/10153019106696307?pnref=story (November 3, 2015).

up this practice with halachic evidence. As stated above, he says that the halachic scholarship justifying his innovation only "paints a bull's eye around the target." In other words, after the goal was identified, it was backed up with halachic justification.[203]

Rabbi Kanefsky succinctly summarizes the views of Open Orthodoxy: man's values stand at the center and the Torah is meant to fit around them. To achieve a desired result, all one has to do is:

1) Choose the desired innovation based on one's personal set of values.
2) Defend the innovation with creative "halachic" reasoning.

Open Orthodoxy exhibits an unyielding loyalty to society's current values. It is no surprise that this attitude affects their approach to Halacha. Rabbi Ysoscher Katz asks:[204] C

> How do we deal with a halakhic requirement that no longer conforms with contemporary notions of ethics and morality?

To an Orthodox Jew, the answer to this question is obvious. Where Halacha and contemporary ethics conflict, one must remain faithful to Halacha and question contemporary morality. In another article, however, Katz offers a very different answer:[205]

---

203. Rabbi Yosef Kanefsky, "Follow-Up to the Blog Post:Adieu to 'Thou Hast Not Made Me a Woman'" *Keren* 2 (2014): p. 6.
204. https://www.facebook.com/ysoscher?fref=ts. (December 3, 2014). Retrieved September, 1 2015.
205. https://kavvanah.wordpress.com/2015/05/31/torat-chaim-veahavat-chesed-rabbi-ysoscher-katz. Retrieved July 29, 2015.

One of the most pressing tensions in the community is how to reconcile our values with our convictions; what to do when halakha points us in one direction and our values in another direction. We are tempted to follow our values but pulled to abide by our halakhic commitments. A proper resolution requires an emboldened stance towards tradition, one that allows us to cajole the tradition to reconcile itself with our modern sensibilities. [Using, of course, legitimate halakhic mechanisms developed by our predecessors when they were confronted with similar challenges.]

Rabbi Katz says that we should "cajole the tradition to reconcile itself with our modern sensibilities." Instead of man subordinating himself to Halacha, Katz favors the opposite: Halacha should be "cajoled" to fit modernity. These sorts of statements are repeated so often they have become the mantra of Open Orthodoxy. It is not coincidental that that the demand that the Torah be adjusted and reinterpreted to fit with the times, is also the basis of Reform and Conservative Judaism. As stated above, Open Orthodoxy has the same agenda as these movements.

◆ ◆ ◆

There are many values which motivate Open Orthodox rabbis to alter the Halacha. One of their sacred cows is egalitarianism. As mentioned earlier, Rabbi Dov Linzer questions whether we should be "bending the Halacha" in order to fit with egalitarian values.[206] According to Linzer, it appears that if society holds egalitarianism as sacred, the Halacha must be adjusted to fit that ideal.

In Chapter 3 we mentioned Rabbi Linzer's view that one is obligated to donate money to a church, a practice which is clearly against Halacha. Other egalitarian innovations will be discussed in Chapter 7, such as the ordaining of women, the deletion of the blessing *shelo asani isha*, egalitarian additions to the wedding ceremony and others. In Chapter 8 we will discuss Rabbi Avi Weiss's view that non-Orthodox movements in Israel should be granted the right to perform weddings and conversions. The common denominator in all these innovations is that Halacha is altered by the set of values held by the surrounding society.

Linzer even claims, with no basis, that *poskim* (halachic decisors) of the past purposefully misinterpreted texts in order to achieve an egalitarian goal. There is a dispute amongst many *poskim* regarding the meaning of a certain Tosafos. Many interpret this Tosafos as saying that a non-Jew does not violate the prohibition of idolatry if he holds the beliefs of a certain religious group. Linzer claims this interpretation is "a total misunderstanding of what Tosafos is saying." [207] He goes on to

---

206. Rabbi Dov Linzer, "On the *Mitzvot* of Non-Jews: An Analysis of *Avodah Zarah* 2b-3a." *Beloved Words Milin Havivin* 1 (2006): p. 36.
207. Rabbi Dov Linzer, "Being an American Jew: Orthodoxy Confronts the Holiday Season." Chicago, Illinois. November 2006. (http://www.yctorah.org/component/option,com_docman/task,cat_view/gid,78/Itemid,13.)

say that the reason this interpretation took root was because, "… besides that it allows more latitude in halachic areas, I think it really resonates to a developing, modern, more tolerant, and even pluralistic approach." Amazingly, Linzer is saying that the *poskim* deliberately misinterpreted Tosafos in order to achieve a pluralistic goal. Without a shred of evidence he has convicted them of intellectual dishonesty.

There is no proof that the motivation of these *poskim* was to achieve a more pluralistic Judaism, and not that they were engaged in an honest analysis of the text. One might venture to say that it is not surprising that Linzer accuses earlier *poskim* of misrepresenting texts to achieve a desired goal, since he himself does the same thing (see Chapter 3).

Rabbi Linzer also proposes accomplishing the "bending" of Halacha by "finding within the Talmud voices that articulate those same values that are driving us."[208] [209] This is echoed by

---

208. Rabbi Dov Linzer, "On the *Mitzvot* of Non-Jews: An Analysis of *Avodah Zarah* 2b-3a." *Beloved Words Milin Havivin* 1 (2006): p. 36.

209. In a lecture, Rabbi Avi Weiss describes how the Modern Orthodox approach to Halacha differs from that of the Conservative movement. He explains that the practice of the Conservative movement is to adopt an opinion of the Talmud even if it has not been accepted into halachic practice, "In other words if there was a *deah* in the *Gemara* that never really took hold, but if there is such a *deah*, that would be enough to lean on. Conservatism therefore remains free to select whichever position within the prior legal history that appeals to it." (https://www.youtube.com/watch?v=_PUcfOoqmuI. Retrieved February 17, 2016.)

His description of the Conservative approach to Halacha is nearly identical to what Rabbi Linzer advocates in "finding within the Talmud voices that articulate those same values that are driving us." In both cases, a non-authoritative opinion is adopted in order to advance an agenda.

Rabbi Katz, who claims that "halakhic mechanisms"[210] are used to help the Torah conform to man's values. In other words, the halachic system itself is manipulated to reach a desired goal. As we have shown, their own halachic writings suffer from this identical fault (see Chapter 3).

The practice of manipulating Halacha to reach a desired goal is apparently taught to their students. Rabbi Nissan Antine (YCT 2006 and President of the International Rabbinic Fellowship[211]) was quoted in an article when he was a student at YCT:[212]

> ... my immediate goal for my years in Rabbinical School is to acquire the tools that are necessary to overcome the *halakhic* and social impediments to change.

According to Antine, Halacha is an "impediment," and his goal at YCT was to acquire the tools necessary to overcome it. In a classic yeshiva, students dedicate themselves to learning the halachic system, while at YCT they learn how to overcome it.

Often, the drive to seek alterations to Halacha is not based on any moral compass but simply on a desire to be accepted by the surrounding culture. In Chapter 3, we explored Rabbi Fox's responsum in which he sought to relax certain conversion standards. We showed that the desire for change was partially

210. https://kavvanah.wordpress.com/2015/05/31/torat-chaim-veahavat-chesed-rabbi-ysoscher-katz. Retrieved July 29, 2015.
211. http://www.internationalrabbinicfellowship.org/leadership. Retrieved August 19, 2015.
212. http://www.yctorah.org/component/option,com_docman/task,doc_view/gid,97. Retrieved February 14, 2016.

motivated by a negative article in the *Washington Post*. Approval by the paper's editorial page is apparently more important to him than an unbiased commitment to Jewish Law.

Not only do external values influence Open Orthodox rabbis' halachic decisions; even emotional arguments trump Halacha. Rabbi Akiva Herzfeld, a 2007 graduate of YCT and former Rabbi of the Shaarey Tphiloh Congregation of Portland, Maine, writes that he changed his views on same-sex marriage because of conversations with friends:[213]

> The truth of their hearts helped me overcome my wall of religious textual evidence that helped justify arguments for the other side. Now I know with complete faith that the love of homosexuals should be respected as equal by society.

The truth of Rabbi Herzfeld's friends' hearts, he says, has helped him overcome his "wall of religious textual evidence." Torah is viewed as a "wall" which must be broken down and overcome and the feelings in his friends' hearts are the battering ram that helps him do it. Herzfeld has allowed an emotional argument to trump the clear and unequivocal fact that homosexual relations is prohibited by the Torah. Here again, Open Orthodoxy views societal norms as binding while the Torah's values are to be relegated to the dustbin. Stated in other words, emotional appeals and social fads are more compelling to the Open Orthodox rabbi than explicit verses in the Torah.

---

213. http://www.pressherald.com/2012/12/12/at-hanukkah-rejoicing-over-peaceful-victory-for-same-sex-marriage_2012-12-12.

While most Open Orthodox rabbis at least claim that they are remaining faithful to Halacha, it is not unusual to find that some have abandoned it completely when it conflicts with their own values. In the introduction to her book, Rabba Dr. Melanie Landau (Class of 2015) writes:[214]

> In truth, this book also reflects my ambivalence about the binding nature of the tradition and the extent to which I would follow traditional norms where they conflict with other values that I hold.

Open Orthodoxy's warped view of the halachic system has led to radical changes in Jewish law and tradition.

In Chapter 6 we will discuss how some Open Orthodox rabbis have legitimized homosexual relations and many support same-sex marriage reflecting society's attitude towards homosexuality.

In Chapter 7, we will discuss Open Orthodox positions on women's issues which are heavily influenced by secular feminist ideals.

To any experienced Torah scholar, it is obvious that Halacha is determined through rigorous and objective analysis. There is no motivation other than to know the will of God. External values have no place in the halachic process. If Halacha conflicts with one of these values, it means that it is not a value shared by Judaism.

---

214. Melanie Landau, *Tradition and Equality in Jewish Marriage: Beyond the Sanctification of Subordination* (New York: Bloomsbury Publishing, 2012), p. 3.

Unfortunately, Open Orthodoxy has rejected this approach and has incorporated extraneous societal values into the halachic process itself. This allegiance to foreign ideals is the basis for many of the halachic and theological ideas espoused by Open Orthodoxy.

6

Homosexuality

This Chapter should never have needed to be written. The Torah states, *You shall not lie with a man as one does with a woman; it is an abomination* (Leviticus 18:22). The Torah unambiguously forbids the homosexual act.

Leading a life committed to Torah while having a same-sex attraction is no easy task. However, the Torah demands that a Jew try his hardest to live according to all of its dictates.[215]

215. So what is the Orthodox homosexual to do? While it is no longer acceptable in American society to suggest that a homosexual can change his orientation, many individuals have achieved success in this area. (For a discussion of this topic, see Dr. Benzion Sorotzkin, (Psy.D.) "SSA: Beyond the Rhetoric." *Dialogue: For Torah Issues and Ideas* 4, p. 218). In situations where this is impossible, Harav Aharon Feldman, in *The Eye of the Storm*, writes that a homosexual can live a celibate and fulfilling life. A homosexual who is not burdened by familial responsibilities is more able to dedicate his life to the Jewish people. Harav Feldman relates the story of a rabbi who was not able to get married. Since he was not responsible for a family, he was able to have a major impact in a far-flung Jewish community. To these Jews Rabbi Feldman applies the verses in Isaiah (Chapter 58). *Let not the saris [who is physically unable to have children] say 'I am a dried-up tree.' For so says G-d to the sarisim who keep My Sabbath, who choose what I desire, and who keep my covenant: I shall make*

In contrast, YCT's faculty and alumni condone homosexuality, proactively lobby for the legalization of same-sex marriage, and in some cases permit homosexual acts. Some have even compared homosexuals' struggle to the suffering of the Jews in Egypt,[216] and the passage of same-sex marriage legislation to the victory of the Maccabees.[217]

As we mentioned in Chapter 2, Rabbi Avi Weiss, the founder of Open Orthodoxy, supports the legalization of same-sex marriage. He maintains that civil law should not reflect religious law. However, he goes even further:[218] A

> Over the years, I have met countless gay people and gay couples who live loving, exemplary lives.... But as an Open Orthodox rabbi, I refuse to reject the person who seeks to lead a life of same-sex love.

A person who struggles with same-sex attraction should be embraced and supported by his rabbi and community. But Rabbi Weiss is referring to a person who consciously chooses to embrace a lifestyle that stands in violation of the Torah, by seeking "to lead a life of same-sex love." Rabbi Weiss also

---

them a monument, a shrine, in My house and within My walls, better than sons and daughters. I shall make their name everlasting, one which will never be forgotten. An Orthodox homosexual can lead a spiritually fulfilling life while observing all of the commandments. (Harav Aharon Feldman, *The Eye of the Storm* [Jerusalem: Yad Yosef Publications, 2009], p. 236.)

216. http://www.nola.com/opinions/index.ssf/2015/04/religious_freedom_louisiana.html. Retrieved July 29, 2015.

217. http://www.pressherald.com/2012/12/12/at-hanukkah-rejoicing-over-peaceful-victory-for-same-sex-marriage_2012-12-12. Retrieved July 16, 2015.

218. http://www.haaretz.com/opinion/1.666064. Retrieved July 20, 2015.

claims, "If I welcome with open arms those who do not observe Sabbath, Kashrut or family purity laws, I must welcome, even more so, homosexual Jews, as they are born with their orientation." However, there is no comparison. He fails to make the distinction between behavior which is not according to Halacha and flaunting an ideology which is against the Torah. For example, if a group of Shabbos desecrators would proclaim that they proudly violate the Shabbos laws, belong to a *chillul* Shabbos society, and declare that they have no intent to change their behavior, would Rabbi Weiss not reject them?

Interestingly, in 1997, when homosexuality was much less accepted in American society,[219] Rabbi Weiss wrote:[220]

> I do not view Reform and Conservative Judaism as being correct on a whole variety of issues, from *Torah mi-Sinai* to patrilineal descent to acceptance of homosexuality, to their approach to Halacha.

It would appear that Rabbi Weiss's opinions are not the product of independent halachic analysis, but rather the result of societal influence.

---

219. For example, according to Gallup, in 1996, only 27% of Americans felt same-sex marriage should be legal, while in 2015, 58% supported legalization. (http://www.gallup.com/poll/1651/gay-lesbian-rights. aspx. Retrieved July 21, 2015.) Also in 1997, no states permitted same sex marriage and 25 had laws forbidding it. In addition, the Defense of Marriage Act (DOMA) was in effect, a law signed by Democratic President Bill Clinton which defined marriage for federal purposes as the union between a man and a woman. (http://gaymarriage. procon.org/view.resource.php?resourceID=004857. Retrieved July 21, 2015.)

220. Rabbi Avi Weiss, "Open Orthodoxy! A Modern Orthodox Rabbi's Creed." *Judaism* (Fall 1997), p. 416.

In 2010, Rabbi Asher Lopatin, President of YCT, participated in the LGBT change prayer breakfast in Chicago, Illinois. "The focus of the event was to unite local faith-based leaders in a rare gathering that galvanized renewed support and affirmation from the faith community for same-sex civil unions and equality for LGBT people."[221] Rabbi Lopatin[222] delivered the following message:[223]

> *Ribbono shel Olam*, Master of the Universe, you instructed us in your wisdom and your understanding in the Torah, in the book of Genesis, "*lo tov heyot hadam lvado*," it is not good and it is not right for a human being to have to live a life alone. God, in Your mercy you told us we have to establish a society and a community in a way that allows for a person to find a life partner to live a life of companionship and love, with equality and without discrimination. So, God, please bless our public servants to find that life filled with love for themselves and to be able to work hard to make sure that our state and our community lives up to God's merciful and just standards to make sure that everyone has a right to seek out that life partner and to live and love together with full right with that person. "*Lo tov heyot hadam lvado.*" Every person has a right to togetherness and a life filled with love. A life of love blessed by God, our state, and our society. Amen.

---

221. https://www.youtube.com/playlist?list=PL41E52D7CB02C1EEB.
222. He is also seen seated at the dais while Cantor Aviva Katzman sings a song. https://www.youtube.com/watch?v=oOh7yXeYPTM&index-=8&list=PL41E52D7CB02C1EEB.
223. https://www.youtube.com/watch?v=794gdsKd9Us.

Rabbi Lopatin was successful in his efforts. In 2013, Illinois passed the Religious Freedom and Marriage Fairness Act guaranteeing the right of same-sex couples to marry.[224] In a joint statement with a Reform and Conservative Rabbi, Rabbi Lopatin advocated for the bill's passage. The statement begins:[225] B

> As rabbis, parents, and citizens of Illinois, we want to offer all loving and committed couples in our community the support and protections of having the state recognize their marriage.

The statement continues, implying that the Torah itself actually favors homosexual marriage. It declares:

> The best way to offer these protections is through the passage of the marriage bill in the Illinois legislature as it not only supports loving couples, but allows clergy to make their own decisions about whether to officiate. The words of Psalm 89 resonate deeply with us, "This world will be built on love... Righteousness and justice are the foundation of God's throne, compassion and truth go forth from it." We find compassion in our tradition as the Torah commands us to treat everyone with dignity for humankind was created in God's image.

---

224. http://patch.com/illinois/palatine/religious-freedom-and-marriage-fairness-act-signed-into-law. Retrieved August 26, 2015.
225. http://www.aclu-il.org/wp-content/uploads/2013/01/Written-Testimony-Rabbis-Conover-Lopatin-and-Siegel.pdf. Retrieved July 16, 2015.

The Rabbis seek to appeal to one's sense of justice and righteousness by citing this verse. The statement continues that the Torah commands us to treat everyone with dignity, and that we are obligated to "build this world on love." The way to strengthen this love is by insuring that all couples can obtain Illinois marriage licenses.

The statement also argues that Jewish tradition "...commands us to not discriminate against anyone including couples who deserve the rights and protections of a marriage recognized by the state." However, one suspects that homosexual couples would find the commandment in Leviticus discriminatory. That an Orthodox rabbi advocates for same-sex marriage is troubling enough; that he uses the Torah itself to support his claim is even more disturbing.

Rabbi Daniel Sperber goes a step further than YCT's founder and president by entertaining the possibility that Orthodox rabbis may perform same-sex marriages. He maintains that the only problem would be calling it "marriage." As *Haaretz* reported:[226]

> As liberal as they become, (Rabbi Ysoscher) Katz does not believe that Orthodox rabbis will ever agree to perform same-sex marriages, though Sperber thinks there may be a way around this. "The problem is with the word 'marriage,'" he notes. "Perhaps they can call it something else like a 'partnership.'"

---

226. http://www.haaretz.com/beta/.premium-1.669680. Retrieved August 5, 2015.

Even the Rosh haYeshivah of YCT feels it is acceptable for homosexuals to live together. Rabbi Dov Linzer, in a blog cast, is asked: "Is there any hope for a gay man to live a meaningful sexual and romantic life with another man within halakhah?" He responds:[227]

> Regarding halakhah, as I am sure you are aware, there is a Biblical prohibition for two men to have [intercourse] with one another. This does not necessarily mean that two men cannot, within halakhah, live in the same home, have a committed, loving relationship, and raise children (if they choose) together as a family.

While, he does note that the *Shulchan Aruch*[228] states two men should not be secluded together if there is a fear that they will have relations, he does not seem to take it too seriously, for he maintains that two gay men may live together in a committed relationship. Is it advisable for two people who are sexually attracted to each other to live together, when the Torah imposes such a harsh penalty for violating this law? Could a heterosexual man dream of overcoming such a test while living with a woman he is attracted to? The Torah says... *do not stray after your hearts and after your eyes* (Numbers 15:39). It is forbidden to incite within oneself a desire to transgress a commandment.[229] Every morning, Jews pray to not be challenged with tests—yet Rabbi Linzer essentially advocates walking right into the lion's den.

---

227. https://www.replyall.me/jofas-cast/fireside-chat-with-rabbi-dov-linzer/. Retrieved July 23, 2015.
228. EH 24.
229. See also *Shulchan Aruch* EH 24, Gra.

YCT and the Jewish Orthodox Feminist Alliance (JOFA) sponsor a series of podcasts called the "Joy of Text" about Judaism and Sexuality.[230] Sexual topics are discussed by Rabbi Dov Linzer and Dr. Bat Sheva Marcus, a founding member of JOFA.[231]

Featured at one event was Miryam Kabakov, the Executive Director of Eshel,[232] an organization that seeks "...acceptance for lesbian, gay, bisexual, and transgender Jews and their families in Orthodox communities."[233] Kabakov is openly lesbian and describes herself as "disobedient Orthodox."[234] At the program, she lamented the lack of halachic guidelines for Orthodox homosexual couples that are dating, such as laws regarding touching and being secluded together. She also minimized the prohibition of male homosexuality.[235] C With baseless optimism, she blithely predicted that the rabbis will eventually stop focusing on the God-given Torah prohibition of homosexuality. Her comments elicited no condemnation from Rabbi Linzer.[236]

On June 26, 2015, the Supreme Court of the United States ruled, in a 5-4 decision, that same sex couples have the right to

230. http://jpmedia.co/podcasts/joy-of-text. Retrieved August 20, 2015.
231. https://www.linkedin.com/in/bat-sheva-marcus-9a420b13. Retrieved February 21, 2016.
232. http://www.eshelonline.org/about-new/meet-our-team. Retrieved August 28, 2015.
233. http://www.eshelonline.org/about-new/our-mission. Retrieved August 11, 2015.
234. http://jpmedia.co/does-sexting-lead-to-mixed-dancing-and-more. Retrieved August 19, 2015.
235. *Ibid.*
236. *Ibid.*

marry. Open Orthodox reaction to the decision was swift. On the day of the decision, Rabbi Ari Hart (YCT 2012) commented on his Facebook page:[237]

> It is not good for a person to be alone. Genesis 2:8. Mazel tov, America.

In a blog post for *The Times of Israel* entitled, "Can Orthodox Jews Support the Legalization of Same Sex Marriage in America?" Rabbi Hart also wrote:[238]

> We can celebrate with the families that many of us know with committed, loving, same-sex parents, some in our own Orthodox community. These families, committed to Torah, *tefillah* and *mitzvot*, to sending their Jewish kids to Day Schools, will not have to worry about a spouse not able to be with a partner on a death bed. We can celebrate for their children who will be raised in loving homes without legal question.

Hart, calls the Supreme court decision something to celebrate. Furthermore, he refers to those living openly in homosexual relationships as "committed to Torah." Hart concludes:[239]

> These issues are complicated, and require further study, thought and struggle. But as we wrestle with these and

---

237. https://www.facebook.com/ari.hart (June 26, 2015). Retrieved August 11, 2015.
238. http://blogs.timesofisrael.com/can-orthodox-jews-support-the-legalization-of-same-sex-marriage-in-america. Retrieved July 15, 2015.
239. *Ibid.*

so many other issues, issues that force us to ask the big questions: What is good, and what does God truly want from us, we can turn towards today's *haftorah* from the book of Micah for a way forward. What is good, and what does God want from you? To do justice, to love kindness, and to walk humbly with your God.

He says this complicated issue forces us to ask the big questions—*what is good and what does God truly want from us.* To an Orthodox Jew, the answer to this question is actually quite simple. Goodness and what God truly wants are *one and the same.* And how has the Orthodox Jew historically determined what "God truly wants?" He has looked in the Torah.

In contrast to Open Orthodoxy, other Orthodox organizations have strongly opposed the Supreme Court's recognition of same-sex marriage. On June 26, 2015, the Rabbinical Council of America issued a statement in response to the decision.[240]

The RCA stated their concern over the Supreme Court's redefinition of marriage, and expressed the need to guarantee protection to religious groups. This is what one expects to hear from a group of Orthodox rabbis. However, Rabbi Ysoscher Katz, condemned the RCA statement. He claimed that it was too "simplistic." On June 28, he commented on his Facebook page:[241]

---

240. http://www.rabbis.org/news/article.cfm?id=105821. Retrieved July 15, 2015.

241. https://www.facebook.com/ysoscher?fref=nf (June 30, 2015). Retrieved July 15, 2015.

Every MO rabbi who doesn't denounce the offensive RCA statement is complicit in this tragedy. אם החרש נחריש בעת הזאת רוח והצלה יעמוד ליהודים ממקום אחר ואנו ובית אבינו נאבד; vibrant MO will write itself out of the parshah.

Rabbi Katz finds the RCA's statement offensive. He exhorts Modern Orthodox rabbis to denounce the statement and expresses the dire urgency of his suggestion by issuing a warning in the words which Mordechai said to Esther when she was initially reluctant to plead on behalf of the Jewish people prophesying that salvation for the danger to the Jewish people would come from some other source.

In a similar reaction to the RCA statement, Ben Greenfield, a student at YCT,[242] responded:[243]

> *Teshuvot* and *Peirushim* (and RCA announcements) are far less significant than FB Photo streams. In the Modern Orthodox world, *Mishkav Zakhar* is now *muttar*. Time to deal with it.

Thus, according to Greenfield, homosexual relations are now permitted in the Modern Orthodox world. Rabbi Katz responds:[244]

---

242. http://www.yctorah.org/images//about%20our%20students%20 2014-2015%20email.pdf. Retrieved August 26, 2015.

243. https://www.facebook.com/benzgreenfield/posts/ 10154024876366686?fref=nf&pnref=story. (June 28, 2015) Retrieved July 16, 2015.

244. https://www.facebook.com/ysoscher?hc_location=ufi (June 28, 2015). Retrieved July 15, 2015.

Thank you, Ben Greenfield, for succinctly (albeit somewhat convolutedly) expressing the debilitating dissonance we are forced to grapple with at this pivotal historical moment: Theologically, we accept the *issur* of homosexual sex, while sociologically we support and embrace those in our midst who struggle with this issue. There is a glaring disconnect between what we think and what we do. We believe it is *assur* but we live as if it is *muttar*.

Following a method of reasoning by which contradictions co-exist (see Chapter 4)[245] he concludes that we believe homosexuality is forbidden but act as if it is permitted. One would hope that believing something is forbidden would stop them from acting differently.

In an article for the *Forward*, Rabbi Katz further explains his views:[246]

The legalistic voice has dominated the Orthodox public sphere — but our gay brothers and sisters deserve to have the harshness of moral certitude dulled by the tenderness of spiritually infused pastoral care. History will determine how the journey of Orthodox homosexuality will turn out.

---

245. There we cited such paradoxical statements such as, "Our new model should be: BELIEF in a God you doubt or believe no longer exists."
246. http://forward.com/opinion/311475/weve-heard-enough-rabbis-on-gay-marriage-ruling-now-we-need-a-rebbe. Retrieved July 15, 2015.

With a flourish of his pen, Rabbi Katz calls for the "dulling of the harshness of moral certitude." In essence, he is calling for the dulling of the moral view espoused by the Torah. He states that moral certitude should be dulled by the tenderness of spiritually infused pastoral care. One fails to see the connection between objective morality and pastoral care and how pastoral care is supposed to dull it. On the contrary, pastoral care should serve to bolster one's morality as defined by the Torah. For the Orthodox homosexual who strives to fulfill *all* of God's commandments, the "tenderness of pastoral care" should serve to strengthen his commitment to Torah. The rabbi should assist the Orthodox homosexual in conquering his drives and remaining a committed Jew.

Rabbi Shmuly Yanklowitz (Class of 2010) has also published on this issue. On December 19, 2013 he wrote a blog for the *Huffington Post*, entitled, "5 Reasons Being an Orthodox Rabbi Compelled Me to Support Gay Marriage." The article begins: [247]

> I am coming out of the closet. I am an Orthodox rabbi and an advocate for gay marriage.

In a video posted on the blog, an interviewer asks Rabbi Yanklowitz, "Why did you post this blog?" Sitting in front of shelves of Hebrew *sefarim* he begins, "You know, it really comes from a deep place of belief in God, in the Torah, in the Hebrew Bible...." According to Yanklowitz, not only does the Torah not oppose gay marriage, it actually favors it. The interviewer, a

---

247. http://www.huffingtonpost.com/rabbi-shmuly-yanklowitz/ortho-dox-rabbi-gay-marriage_b_4452154.html. Retrieved July 16, 2015.

non-Jew asks Yanklowitz how he would respond to those who argue that the verse in Leviticus means that we are doctrinally charged *not* to favor same sex marriage. Yanklowitz gives an answer, but the interviewer is not satisfied. At the end of the interview, he seems perplexed about how an Orthodox rabbi could favor same-sex marriage. He says that he has to ask again, and push back a little bit: "Can you do that and say you are Orthodox? Might it be simpler to say I am no longer Orthodox?" Apparently, a non-Jewish reporter has a better grasp of the views of Orthodox Judaism than an Open Orthodox rabbi.

In the interview, Rabbi Yanklowitz also says:

> I really believe religion in this country will become irrelevant if religious leaders stand on the wrong side of justice. And I am proud of my fellow religious leaders who stood beside Mandela, who stood with MLK and other causes of civil rights. Today is another time to stand up.

Appealing to Americans' love of justice and civil rights, Yanklowitz places himself among such reformers as Nelson Mandela and Martin Luther King. He invokes the names of these social heroes to find favor in the world's eyes. He also says, "I don't have all the religious problems resolved." He treats the values of the world as sacred and the Torah as a problem which must be overcome. Ironically, he also writes:[248]

---

248. *Ibid.*

I believe the essence of religious conviction is that we must do what is right, not what is popular.

The clamor by Open Orthodox rabbis to legalize gay marriage just happens to coincide with its acceptance in society at large. While portraying himself as a maverick going against the establishment, Yankowitz actually embraces it. Supporting gay marriage has never been more popular. It is actually those Orthodox Jews who oppose same-sex marriage despite societal pressure who are doing what is right rather than what is popular.

He also writes, that "Fifteen states and counting have formally approved marriage equality. It's time that traditional faith leaders stand for gay rights, including the right to marriage." In other words, society has accepted homosexuality; therefore, Orthodox Jewry cannot be left behind. It is clear that the motivation is not one of objective Torah analysis, but rather of doing what is popular in order to curry favor with society's non-Jewish population.

More recently, Yanklowitz praised the Boy Scouts of America for their acceptance of gay adult leaders.[249] D

Open Orthodox rabbis around the country share these views. Rabbi Benjamin Greenberg is a 2009 Graduate of YCT and a board member of the International Rabbinic Fellowship.[250] He formerly served as rabbi of the BMH-BJ congregation in Denver, Colorado. He proudly declares that his synagogue was the first Orthodox congregation to host a Keshet training

---

249. https://www.facebook.com/rshmuly.yanklowitz?fref=ts. (July 28, 2015) Retrieved July 28, 2015.

250. http://www.internationalrabbinicfellowship.org/leadership. Retrieved August 19, 2015.

program. Keshet is an organization which, according to its website, is "working for the full equality and inclusion of lesbian, gay, bisexual, and transgender Jews in Jewish life."[251] Greenberg compares his actions to that of a previous rabbi of his congregation who saw the need to give his sermon in English as opposed to Yiddish in order to be inclusive. [252]

Rabbi Akiva Herzfeld is a 2007 graduate of YCT and former Rabbi of the Shaarey Tphiloh congregation in Portland, Maine.[253] He compares the miracle of Chanukah to the "miracle" of passing same-sex marriage legislation in Maine:[254]

> We Jews are now celebrating Hanukkah. Long ago in ancient Israel, a small band of Jews fought against a much larger Greek army and the Jews won…. We light Hanukkah candles each year to remember the ancient miracle. The menorah of Hanukkah shows that God's miraculous light can shine in the world. This Hanukkah, I celebrate the past and the present. With my very own eyes, I have seen a great miracle this year, right here in Maine. A small group of people, homosexuals and their

251. http://www.keshetonline.org. Retrieved July 16, 2015. They also state, "However long it takes Keshet will work for a day in which Jews of all sexual orientations and gender identities can live fully integrated Jewish lives."

252. http://www.myjewishlearning.com/keshet/living-inclusion-why-our-orthodox-synagogue-hosted-an-lgbt-training-institute/2. Retrieved July 16, 2015.

253. http://www.yctorah.org/content/view/44/84. Retrieved August 26, 2015.

254. http://www.pressherald.com/2012/12/12/at-hanukkah-rejoicing-over-peaceful-victory-for-same-sex-marriage_2012-12-12. Retrieved July 16, 2015.

supporters, stood up for their equal rights in marriage. They fought to convince the American people that they are human beings just like the rest of us in our great country. They said that homosexuals should be allowed to celebrate love in marriage, just like the rest of us. Vast numbers of people stood against them. A few years ago, the gay-rights supporters were defeated at the polls in Maine, and the sacred ground of their pure hearts was crushed. They continued to fight because they knew that justice was on their side. This year they overcame the odds, and finally won.

In a role reversal, Rabbi Herzfeld compares this group to the Maccabees, who were victorious against a larger enemy in defending observance of the Torah. In another comparison, Rabbi Gabriel Greenberg (YCT 2012), a rabbi in Louisiana, believes that the slavery of Egypt should teach us how to behave toward homosexuals:[255]

Throughout our Biblical and later rabbinic texts, the experience of oppression in Egypt serves as an imperative reminder to take care of those in our own day and age who endure oppression, who live on the margins of our own society. Commandments such as the following in *Deuteronomy* 10:19 are common in the Bible: *Remember the stranger, for you were strangers in the Land of Egypt*. It is, therefore, quite disconcerting

255. http://www.nola.com/opinions/index.ssf/2015/04/religious_free-dom_louisiana.html. Retrieved July 29, 2015.

to watch Gov. Bobby Jindal's recent foray into the "religious liberty" fight, in his outspoken support for House Bill 707, the "Marriage and Conscience Act." Jindal stated in his *New York Times* op-ed that the bill does not "create a right to discriminate against, or generally refuse service to, gay men or lesbians."

His statement is a reaction to Louisiana Governor Bobby Jindal's attempt to pass legislation that would protect religious individuals from negative consequences if they would deny services to homosexuals based on their religious beliefs. Greenberg opposes the bill:[256]

> As an Orthodox Jewish man and a rabbi, I find Jindal's pursuit of this bill's passage to be sacrilegious and offensive.

A bill meant to safeguard religious liberty is considered "sacrilegious" and "offensive" to an Open Orthodox rabbi.

Rabbi Avi Orlow, a 2004 YCT graduate, is troubled when reading the prohibition against homosexuality during the *Mincha* service of Yom Kippur:[257]

> Why would we read the primary religious source used to substantiate homophobia on our most holy day of the year? While I might not have an answer to this question, I do feel that silence on this issue is its own sin.

---

256. *Ibid.*
257. http://www.huffingtonpost.com/avi-orlow/if-i-have-gay-children-_b_5923490.html. Retrieved July 23, 2015.

Rabbi Zev Farber (YCT 2006) goes even further than his mentors and colleagues and attempts to blunt the prohibition of homosexuality by applying the concept of *oness rachmana patrei* (that when one is forced to sin, he is not punished).[258] He also claims that rabbis should not urge homosexual Jews to remain celibate:[259]

> However, no Orthodox rabbi should feel duty-bound to urge homosexual Jews to be celibate. This is not a practical option for most people, and advocating this will only cause that person intense pain and guilt. In short, there should be no social penalty in the Orthodox world for being a non-celibate homosexual Jew.

Rabbi Farber writes that a Rabbi (whose job it is to guide his congregation in the ways of the Torah) should not feel "duty bound" to instruct congregants from refraining from the homosexual act which the Torah explicitly forbids. He concludes:

> Homosexual congress is not a moral violation; it is purely a violation of a religious prohibition, one that is the inevitable consequence of the person's psychological and even biological makeup. If God overlooks the inevitable, so should we.

---

258. The details of his argument will be discussed in the next section.
259. http://morethodoxy.org/2012/01/11/homosexuals-in-the-ortho-dox-community-by-rabbi-zev-farber. Retrieved July 24, 2015.

Rabbi Farber's belief that God overlooks the homosexual act is surprising, given that He Himself wrote, *You shall not lie with a man as one does with a woman it is an abomination* (Leviticus 18:22).

Same-Sex Relations

Some at YCT claim that certain homosexual acts are actually permitted. Rabbi Ysoscher Katz was quoted in an article:[260]

> The Torah makes clear that [intercourse] between two men is prohibited, but I like to talk about the 50 shades of gay, in other words, there are many other things they can do that are not expressly prohibited.

Contrary to Katz's contention, the "other things" are in fact included under the prohibition of, *you shall not come close to uncover nakedness* (Leviticus 18:6). Also, it is prohibited to spill seed in vain (*Shulchan Aruch* EH Chapter 23), and the Torah forbids one to incite his evil inclination, as it says... *do not stray after your hearts and after your eyes* (Numbers 15:39). Coincidentally, the official position of the Conservative movement is to prohibit the homosexual act itself, yet permit other intimate acts.[261]

While Katz states that the actual act of homosexuality is prohibited, others at YCT are more liberal. Rabbi Zev Farber

---

260. http://www.haaretz.com/beta/.premium-1.669680. Retrieved August 5, 2015.

261. https://www.rabbinicalassembly.org/sites/default/files/public/halakhah/teshuvot/20052010/dorff_nevins_reisner_dignity.pdf. See Chapter 2.

(YCT 2006) attempts to apply the principal of *oness rachmana patrei* (that when one is forced to sin, he is not punished) to homosexual relations. While he writes that this concept does not mean that the homosexual act is halachically permitted, he also says, as mentioned before, that "no Orthodox rabbi should feel duty-bound to urge homosexual Jews to be celibate." He writes: [262]

> My own approach to the matter is that the Orthodox community should adopt the stance of *"oness rahmana patrei"* — the Merciful One overlooks what is out of a person's control. This was first suggested by R. Norman Lamm in the 1974 Encyclopedia Judaica Yearbook, and I believe that this principle should serve as a basis for formulating an Open Orthodox response to the many challenges of accepting and integrating homosexuals into our community.... Orthodox homosexual Jews really have no choice but to allow themselves to fulfill the intense desire for emotional and physical intimacy in the only way open to them.

Based on the halachic concept of *oness*, Farber attempts to legitimize homosexual relations. However it is clear after even a cursory study of the *sugya* that this position is absurd.

It is abundantly clear that the concept of *oness* does not apply to homosexual relations.

The Rambam writes in *Hilchos Yesodei ha-Torah* 5:6 that if a person is in danger of dying, and the only cure is one which

262. http://morethodoxy.org/2012/01/11/homosexuals-in-the-orthodox-community-by-rabbi-zev-farber. Retrieved July 24, 2015.

entails a Torah prohibition, he should violate the prohibition to save his life. However, if the prohibition involves idolatry, violating a sexual prohibition, or murder, one may *not* cure himself by committing one of these cardinal sins. The Rambam concludes that if one did cure himself by committing one of these three sins, the court should punish him accordingly.

In such a life-threatening situation, where the only way to survive is to violate one of the three cardinal sins, one must give up his life rather than violate the sin. Moreover, the court punishes him for violating the commandment. It is clear that the concept of *oness rachmana patrei* does not apply even in this situation. If *oness* would apply, he would not be punished for violating the Torah, since his act would have the status of coercion. Therefore to posit that *oness rachmana patrei* applies to a homosexual is clearly erroneous. In the Rambam's case where the person is going to die and his only hope for survival is to have relations with someone prohibited to him, *oness* does not apply; all the more so is the concept of *oness* inapplicable to a homosexual, no matter how strong his desire may be.

In a footnote—seemingly as an afterthought—Rabbi Farber writes that he is well aware of the Rambam's principle of *ein kishui elah la-daas*, meaning that male arousal is always with intent. Since male arousal is always with intent, it would mean by definition that the concept of *oness* does not apply as it does not have the status of coercion, thereby rendering Farber's argument moot. Interestingly, Farber neglects to quote the source of the Rambam, namely the explicit Talmudic passage (*Yevamos* 53b) which states unequivocally that *ein kishui elah la-daas*. Farber should be aware of this passage, as he does quote the Tosafos there. He claims that the idea of *ein kishui elah la-daas* is "vigorously questioned and debated by a number of *Rishonim* and *Aharonim*."[263] He cites Tosafos as one of these *Rishonim*.

Upon examining Tosafos, however, one notices that nowhere does it question or debate (vigorously or otherwise) the validity of the concept of *ein kishui elah la-daas*. As every novice student of the Talmud knows, Tosafos does not argue with an explicit Talmudic passage. Contrary to Farber's contention, Tosafos explains that even in a case where a man is forcibly held close to someone with whom he is forbidden to have relations, and becomes aroused, he is required to give up his life rather than commit the sin. This is because of the principle of *ein kishui elah la-daas*.

It comes as no surprise that Farber only mentions *ein kishui elah la-daas* briefly, in a footnote, for this concept undermines his entire argument. He attempts to mislead the reader by implying that this concept is subject to dispute amongst medieval commentators, when in fact it is an explicit Talmudic passage.

In conclusion, Farber offers a radical definition of *oness* which is both absurd and flatly rejected by the Rambam. In addition, he has invented a Tosafos and then claims that it disagrees with the Talmud. Also, he misleads the reader by implying that the concept of *ein kishui elah la-daas* was invented by the Rambam, when in fact it appears in an explicit passage in the Talmud.

In addition to the deficient scholarship which it displays, Farber's article stands as an example of the contempt which some Open Orthodox rabbis have for Torah scholars. He writes:

---

263. *Ibid.*

This may be one reason why, for centuries, a contemptuous, even belligerent, attitude towards homosexuals was the norm. An excellent, if sad, example of this is a letter by R. Moshe Feinstein written in 1976 (*Iggrot Moshe*, OH 4:115), where he treats homosexual activity like any other choice.

Rabbi Farber refers to Rabbi Feinstein's views as "contemptuous even belligerent" and "sad."[264] Rabbi Moshe Feinstein had the entire corpus of Jewish law at his fingertips. It is said that he never needed to check a reference because he knew it all by heart. In his 91 years, he dedicated every available moment to Torah study and was recognized as the leading American *posek* in his generation. Yet Rabbi Farber, who had only been ordained six years prior, and by an organization that might as well have the lowest entrance requirements of any Yeshiva in the world, treats Rabbi Feinstein's opinion with disdain and condescension. It appears that his brand of Orthodoxy is only "open" to those that share its views.

In conclusion, Open Orthodoxy's embrace of homosexuality as a legitimate lifestyle runs contrary to Orthodox Jewish belief. The full-fledged support of same-sex marriage, as well as the legitimization of same-sex relations, is in opposition to Jewish tradition. While portraying themselves as enlightened mavericks, they in fact worship at the shrine of popular culture. The true heroes are the genuinely Orthodox Jews who hold fast to the Torah's law despite enormous societal pressure to alter it.

---

264. See what Rabbeinu Yonah writes about denigrating Torah scholars: *Shaarei Teshuvah* (3:147).

7

Women's Issues

In 1963, Betty Friedan published *The Feminine Mystique* and launched the modern feminist movement. In the book, she said that women did not feel fulfilled in their traditional roles of wife and mother. These roles, she argued, were encouraged by men. She advocated that women seek fulfillment by pursuing goals and careers outside the home.[265]

Friedan's thesis is based on the underlying ideology of secular society that the individual has the right to do as he pleases. His goals in life are to seek money, power and the fulfillment of his desires. Only his personal autonomy is sacred. While men were pursuing these selfish goals, women were relegated to positions of housewife and mother. Feminism preaches that women should be given equal opportunity to pursue the same status and power as men and thereby gain fulfillment. While this movement is to be praised for its crusade for workplace protection, equal pay and an end of the exploitation of women, its intrinsic message is an extension of secular selfishness.

---

265. http://history1900s.about.com/od/1960s/qt/femininemystiq.htm. Retrieved August 27, 2015.

WHY OPEN ORTHODOXY IS NOT ORTHODOX

Unfortunately, secular feminist attitudes have penetrated Orthodoxy. Some in Orthodox circles believe that women will not feel spiritually fulfilled unless they perform the same spiritual roles as men. One can hardly blame these women for feeling this way, as the problem is rooted in some men's perverted view of Judaism. Many men view Judaism as an opportunity for self-aggrandizement. They do not view leading the prayer service as a chance to get close to God, but rather as an opportunity to display their singing talents. Speaking in front of the synagogue is not a chance to inspire, but rather an opportunity to impress the audience with their amazing oratorical skills. The rabbi is special not because he teaches Torah and guides the congregation, but because he sits next to the *Aron ha-Kodesh* and everyone stands up for him. Since men view Judaism as an opportunity for achieving honor, why should women be denied these same opportunities?

However, Judaism teaches that the purpose of life is not to gain power and honor, but rather to serve and come close to God by heeding His will.

In Judaism, different roles are assigned to different groups of people in the service of God. The *kohen* serves in the Temple, while the Levi assists and the *Yisrael* works the land. The tribe of Yisocher studies Torah full time while the tribe of Zevulun supports him. Just as different parts of the Jewish people serve different purposes, so too do men and women serve different roles.

Judaism has always believed that men and women are created for different roles in life according to their own unique strengths and abilities. The Torah has designated specific roles and commandments geared towards those strengths in the service of God. The roles of wife and mother, while denigrated by modern society, are exalted in Judaism as the means for creating and fostering a new generation firmly rooted in Torah and service of God.

Open Orthodoxy seeks to close the gender divide by equalizing the roles of men and women in Judaism. Many view the Sages as misogynists who sought to suppress women. They attempt to rectify this seeming sexist injustice by instituting new initiatives which cater to women who need to feel empowered.

In response to an article written about a Modern Orthodox high school that allowed some of its female students to don *tefillin*, a posting on Yeshivat Maharat's Facebook states:[266]

> This is the vision: "If the change agents within Orthodoxy become educators, role models and leaders of the next generation of modern Orthodox Jews, successfully pass on their commitment to both Halachah and egalitarianism, and continue to live a life committed to Jewish law, they could transform the face of modern Orthodoxy.

This sentiment is echoed by Dasi Fruchter, a student at Yeshivat Maharat,[267] "There we are, day in and day out, a group of feminist scholars and leaders, in a movement seeking to change the

---

266. https://www.facebook.com/Yeshivatmaharat?fref=ts. (January 24, 2014) Retrieved July 24, 2015.
267. http://www.yeshivatmaharat.org/class-of-2016. Retrieved January 29, 2016.

gender landscape of Orthodox Jewish leadership." [268] They view their egalitarian work as heroic. Rabbi Avi Weiss refers to Rabba Hurwitz, the first female rabbi he ordained, as his "Number 42"—a reference to Jackie Robinson, the man who broke the color barrier in baseball.[269] However, as will be shown, their accusations and proposed rectifications run vividly counter to Jewish law and Orthodox Judaism.

Sexist Sages

As we explained in Chapter 5, the Sages were objective elucidators of Torah whose only mission was to accurately transmit it to the next generation. The entire corpus of Jewish law speaks to their honesty, integrity and objectivity. The Rabbis of the Talmud did not have biases which influenced their interpretation of the Torah. This is the basis of our tradition.

Rabbi Josef B. Soloveitchik, in a 1975 lecture to rabbinic alumni, expressed the attitude one should have for the transmitters of Torah:[270]

> The act of *kabbalas haTorah* requires of us to revere, love and admire the words of the *chachmei hamesorah*, be they *Tanaim*, be they *Amoraim*, be they *Rishonim*, I don't care. This is our prime duty. They are the final authorities.

268. http://lilith.org/blog/2013/07/can-we-speak-for-ourselves/#sthash. wVyBd6IU.dpuf. Retrieved August 29, 2015.
269. https://www.youtube.com/watch?v=6DRXyGLJ4Rw. Retrieved July 26, 2015
270. Rabbi Moshe Meiselman, *Torah Chazal and Science* (Lakewood, New Jersey: Israel Bookshop Publications, 2013), p. 716.

Rabbi Soloveitchik also had harsh words for those who felt the Sages were biased in any way. He maintained that such a view constituted heresy. In the Rambam's classification of those who are "deniers of Torah" he includes one who "denies the teachers of Torah."[271] In the same 1975 lecture, Rabbi Soloveitchik said:[272]

> But moreover even those who admit the *Torah she-be'al Peh*, admit the truthfulness of *Torah shebeal Peh*, but they are critical of *chachmei Chazal* as personalities, they find fault with *chachmei Chazal*, fault in their character, *Rachmana litzlan*, or in their behavior, or in their conduct. They say that *chachmei Chazal* are prejudiced, which actually has no impact on the Halachah. Nevertheless needs to be considered a *kofer* (heretic). What means *vehamakchish maggideah*? He denies the perfection and the truthfulness of *chachmei Chazal*, not of the Torah again, but of the *chachmei Chazal* as personalities as real personae, as far as their character is concerned, their philosophy is concerned, their outlook of the world is concerned.

However, many Open Orthodox leaders claim that the rabbis of the Talmud were not unbiased transmitters of Torah, but rather were influenced by their times in their suppression of women.[273]

---

271. *Hilchos Yesodei ha-Torah* 3:8.
272. Rabbi Moshe Meiselman, *Torah Chazal and Science* (Lakewood, New Jersey: Israel Bookshop Publications, 2013), p. 716.
273. Contrary to the claims of Open Orthodoxy, the Sages had a positive view of women. As Rabbi Moshe Averick points out, "If the 'chauvinistic-male' Rabbis held women in such contempt, why then did they scrutinize the behavior of *Chanah,* the mother of Samuel,

In Chapter 4, we cited one such comment by Rabbi Ysoscher Katz. In a conversation on Facebook, he speaks about the long history of "misogyny" and "racism" in Jewish texts. He even states that the Bible itself is racist and misogynistic:[274]

> Chassidic and kabbalistic racism and misogyny is deeply problematic, and, of course, troubles me a lot, but, the problem is intrinsic to Jewish texts in general, not just to mystical texts. It's true for the *Tanach, Chazal, Rishonim* and *Achronim.*

This attitude is prevalent amongst YCT and Yeshivat Maharat graduates. Rabba Dr. Melanie Landau (Class of 2015), in an interview, recalls how deeply influenced she was by a feminist

---

to create our *entire model* of proper prayer before God? Why do they inform us that Sarah achieved a greater level of prophecy than Avraham? Why do they extol the heroic virtues of Rachel and Leah in raising the 12 tribes of the Israelite nation and that their merit stands by *Am Yisrael* throughout the generations? Why do they obligate a man to 'honor his wife more than himself?' Why do they teach that 'the Divine Presence only rests in the home because of the woman?' Why did they teach us that the entire redemption from Egypt—the seminal event in Jewish history—was due only to the righteous women of that generation? Why was the Torah offered first to the women and only then to the men? Why do the sages teach us that women did not participate in the sin of the Golden Calf or in that of the Spies? Where is there the slightest indication in our *mesorah* or in the teachings of our Sages that a woman cannot achieve the greatest levels of righteousness, holiness, and closeness to God, by fulfilling the obligations and commandments the Torah has placed upon her?" (http://www.algemeiner.com/2013/07/18/american-jewry-at-the-crossroads-isaac-mayer-wise-solomon-schechter-and-now-avi-weiss-and-sara-hurwitz. Retrieved July 28, 2015)

274. https://www.facebook.com/ysoscher?fref=ts. (June 9, 2015 comment to a June 1, 2015 post). Retrieved August 26, 2015.

professor when she attended the University of Melbourne. She relates how the teachings of this professor impacted her study of Jewish texts:[275]

> She was very black and white. She thought theology was part of the patriarchal structure. I was viscerally feeling pain in my body because of the repression, exclusion and marginalization of the feminine in Jewish texts.

Landau views the rabbis as suppressing femininity. However, she seeks to correct this injustice by fixing certain "sexist" Jewish practices. In 2012, she published a book entitled *Tradition and Equality in Jewish Marriage: Beyond the Sanctification of Subordination.* [276] In it, she describes traditional Jewish marriage, *Kiddushin*, as non-reciprocal in nature[277] and writes that, "… non-reciprocal marriage poses a moral problem." She even claims, "that marriage as an institution has supported women's subordination." [278] In order to rectify this injustice, she proposes new forms of marriage that are reciprocal in nature. Not only does she accuse the Rabbis of promoting gender inequality, she also does not view Jewish tradition as binding. As we mentioned in Chapter 5, she writes:[279]

---

275. http://www.jewishtelegraph.com/prof_191.html. Retrieved July 20, 2015.
276. Melanie Landau, *Tradition and Equality in Jewish Marriage: Beyond the Sanctification of Subordination* (New York: Bloomsbury Publishing, 2012).
277. *Ibid.* p. 7.
278. *Ibid.* p. 3.
279. *Ibid.*

In truth, this book also reflects my ambivalence about the binding nature of the tradition and the extent to which I would follow traditional norms where they conflict with other values that I hold. Through the process of researching this project, the claim of the authority that the rabbis held over me diminished somewhat. Even though I see the need for rabbinic authority for the continuation of that system in all of its shades, becoming intimate with rabbinic opinions and adjudications about marriage throughout the ages, particularly my sense of how rabbinic authority can be used as a channel for perpetuating gender inequality, undermined my capacity to accept rabbinic authority more than it had been undermined in the past.

Landau declares her ambivalence "about the binding nature of tradition" when it conflicts with her own values. She also states how her study of rabbinic opinions has shown her how their authority can be used to promote gender inequality. This in turn undermined her capacity to accept rabbinic authority.

It is surprising enough that an Orthodox Rabba does not view Jewish tradition as binding. What is more troubling is that Yeshivat Maharat seems to approve of her views. Landau's book was published three years before she received *semichah* from the yeshiva. It is even included in her biography on their webpage.[280] How can a supposed Orthodox institution grant rabbinic ordination to a woman who exhibits contempt for rabbinic authority? Either the staff at Yeshivat Maharat approves of her

280.http://www.yeshivatmaharat.org/class-of-2015. Retrieved July 20, 2015.

non-Orthodox views, or they never read her book. Remarkably, Rabba Landau is praised at the 2015 graduation as one who has a "deep understanding of our tradition."[281] It is possible, then, that she has a deep understanding of tradition, yet views it as non-binding and misogynistic.

Rabba Landau even accuses Biblical figures of sexism. On July 27, 2015, Yeshivat Maharat's Facebook page linked an article by her entitled, "Tisha B'Av, Tu B'Av and My Journey of Sexual Healing."[282] In it, she accuses the book of Lamentations, written by Jeremiah, and the Sages of engaging in misogyny:[283]

> This harsh imagery as well as motifs of women's unbounded sexuality are represented in connection to the destruction of Jerusalem as it appears in Lamentations—the biblical book read on Tisha B'Av— but also in other canonical and midrashic writings. We should resist relating to the metaphors of women as being humiliated and defiled as metaphors for the destruction of Jerusalem and instead of cringing because of their misogynous uses, we use them instead as a point of connection to violence against women of all types.

Landau takes issue with the Bible and Midrash's use of women to represent the destruction of the Temple. She labels them with the description of "misogynous." However her accusations are

---

281. http://www.yeshivatmaharat.org/graduation2015. Retrieved July 20, 2015.

282. https://www.facebook.com/yeshivatmaharat. (July 27, 2015)

283. http://forward.com/sisterhood/312327/tisha-bav-tu-bav-and-my-journey-of-sexual-healing. Retrieved July 31, 2015.

baseless. The Sages compared the "rape" of the Jewish people by the surrounding nations to that of a defiled woman. It is unclear why this is misogynistic and what it has to do with condoning violence against women.

The belief that Jewish texts suppress femininity is so widespread, that at Yeshivat Maharat, students have a procedure when they come across such a "sexist" passage. Dasi Fruchter, a current student relates:[284] A

> So we have a jar. In this jar we put a quarter, or a dollar, or whatever seems appropriate when a woman's voice seems egregiously absent from a conversation in the text.

Rabbi Ari Hart (YCT 2012) also accuses *Chazal* of promoting sexism. In a blog for the *Huffington Post*, he writes about the blessing *shelo asani isha*, "who has not made me a woman":[285]

> Written by male rabbis nearly 2,000 years ago, these words evoke for me the sexism too prevalent in the Orthodox world and beyond. These words have echoes of the religious misogynists who throw chairs at a woman for praying at the Western Wall or force women to sit at the back of Israeli buses. This blessing helps enable the religious sexism that silences women's voices, keeps them from positions of communal leadership, and denies them study of our sacred texts.

284. http://lilith.org/blog/2013/07/can-we-speak-for-ourselves. Retrieved February 27, 2016.
285. http://www.huffingtonpost.com/ari-hart/should-i-thank-god-for-not-making-me-a-woman_b_3197422.html. Retrieved July 21, 2015.

According to Hart, a blessing established by our Sages evokes sexism. He links these towering spiritual giants to the misogynists who abuse women by throwing chairs at them when they are trying to pray. Not only that, but by reciting this blessing one enables that sexism to continue.

This sentiment is echoed by Rabbi Yosef Kanefsky. He has stopped reciting the daily blessing of "*shelo asani isha*."[286] While we should not be critical of the Sages, he declares, their views were representative of their culture, which held women in lower standing:[287]

> One could also argue that we are religiously compelled to eliminate or adjust the *berakha* because it is a source of *Hilul Hashem*. Without in any way being critical of our Sages (who, like all of us, lived inside a set of contemporary intellectual and cultural assumptions), the *berakha* is a vestige of an understanding of women that is less morally developed than today's understanding.

Kanefsky contends that while the Sages are not to be blamed for their morally inferior attitudes, it still constitutes a desecration of God's name to recite this blessing. The possibility that the Sages possessed a tradition from God, and that they had access to greater divine wisdom, seems not to have occurred to him. Rabbi Kanefsky does not view the Sages as objective

---

286. Rabbi Yosef Kanefsky. "Follow-Up to the Blog Post: Adieu to 'Thou Hast Not Made Me a Woman'" *Keren* 2 (2014), p. 6.
287. *Ibid.* p. 8.

transmitters of Torah, but rather as being prejudiced by the views of their times.

Open Orthodox leaders consistently express the view that the Sages were unenlightened sexists, a far cry from being unbiased transmitters of Torah. Not only are these views not Orthodox, but according to the Rambam (as elucidated by Rabbi Soloveitchik), they are outside the parameters of accepted Jewish belief.

Remedies for a Sexist Tradition

Since, according to Open Orthodoxy, Jewish tradition was shaped by "misogynistic rabbis," it naturally follows that it needs to be reformed. Indeed, the members of the movement clearly seek to transform Orthodoxy. (This theme is pervasive in their writings).

In 2011, Rabba Sara Hurwitz was interviewed by Reform Rabbi Mark Golub on Shalom TV.[288] They discussed many issues affecting women in the Orthodox community. Rabbi Golub asks how she would respond to critics who might say that she is not fighting hard enough against a male-established Halacha which discounts women from counting in a *minyan* and disqualifies them from serving as a witness or leading the service. He asks, "What would you say to those who see themselves as championing the cause of women in the Jewish community if they would say you're not going far enough?" She responds, "That's a relevant point." While she could have gone

---

288. https://www.youtube.com/watch?v=mBabXl4NpB4. Retrieved July 20, 2015.

to HUC (Reform) or JTS (Conservative), where women are completely equal members of the rabbinate, she says that she loves the Orthodox community and that she is a traditionalist. She comments:[289]

> I do take Halacha very seriously. I grapple with it, I struggle with it, but I don't negate it and I don't want to get rid of it. And I think that if Halacha does change to allow women to be on a *beit din* [Jewish court], it's not going to be Sara Hurwitz making that change. It's going to take many many more years of serious thought and *teshuvot*, responsa, written by those who are even... more... *gedolei*... are more... are greater than me to make those changes.

According to Rabba Hurwitz, Halacha is a struggle which must be overcome. She struggles with it because it runs counter to her egalitarian values. While earlier in the interview she did say that as a woman she is ineligible to serve on a rabbinical court and that she is not trying to change the Halacha, she does entertain the possibility of the law changing over time to allow women to serve in this role. Unfortunately for her, the *Shulchan Aruch*, which states that, "a woman is disqualified from judging"[290] would seem to make such a change unlikely.

Her commitment to egalitarianism has caused her to make other disconcerting statements. Rabbi Golub comments that many Orthodox Jews in Israel find it offensive that some women wear *tefillin* at the Western Wall. Hurwitz responds, "You know

---

289. *Ibid.*
290. CM 7:4.

power is knowledge and there is no Halacha against women putting on *tefillin* and *tallis*." [291] It is extremely misleading for Rabba Hurwitz to unequivocally state that there is no such Halacha, since the Rema writes, "If a woman wants to be stringent and wear *tefillin*, we should protest."[292] She states that she does not "negate" Halacha while simultaneously ignoring rulings from the *Shulchan Aruch*.

Golub also asks Hurwitz about the plight of the *agunah*. She responds:

> It's such a painful issue. Seeing women who are suffering, seeing families who are suffering because they are going through so much turmoil and the added stress and tension of Jewish law being structured in the way that it is, is really, seems to be set against women. The irony is originally, when the *get* idea was orchestrated by the rabbis and the Talmud, it was meant to protect women, but it had the side effect that if a husband refuses to give his wife a *get*, they are chained.

Rabba Hurwitz laments that, while the Rabbis had good intentions in orchestrating the idea of a *get*, the system has actually caused women to remain trapped. It is unclear to what she is referring to, as the "*get* idea" was not orchestrated by the Rabbis but is an explicit verse in the Torah: *If a man will take a woman and have relations with her and if she does not find favor in his eyes, if he found in her a matter of immorality and he wrote*

---

291. *Ibid.*
292. OC 38:3

*for her **a book of separation** and sent her away from his house* (Deuteronomy 24:1). After making the baseless accusation that Jewish law "seems to be set against women" she falsely accuses the Rabbis of orchestrating the idea of *get* causing women to be trapped.

Rectifying a Halacha which "seems to be set against women" has prompted even more far-reaching innovations. Rabbi Golub asks Rabba Hurwitz about Rabbi Emanuel Rackman's solution to the *agunah* problem, which would allow a rabbinical court to annul a marriage when a woman cannot receive a *get*. He mentions how, even though his efforts were rejected by the greater Orthodox community, there have been rabbis who have adopted his reforms anyway. He asks, "So I'm wondering where you stand on that?" Hurwitz responds:

> I think you have to start somewhere and I think it would be a step in the right direction if there was a small group of rabbis sitting on a *Beit Din* and resolving this problem in the way you have suggested.[293]

Rabba Hurwitz supports innovations that have been firmly rejected by all Orthodox Torah scholars. Notably, in a 1975 lecture to rabbinic alumni, Rabbi Joseph B. Soloveitchik vehemently opposed these reforms.[294] Ignoring this opposition, Rabbi Asher Lopatin has also called for a "super-charged

---

293. She does mention that practically this would pose a problem because if one *beis din* would accept this idea and another would not, it would put the woman in an awkward position.

294. https://muse.jhu.edu/journals/mj/summary/v030/30.1.kaplan.html. Retrieved January 29, 2016.

Rackman model."[295] This position is also favored by Rabbi David Bigman,[296] a member of Yeshivat Maharat's advisory board.[297]

It is disconcerting that leaders of Open Orthodoxy enthusiastically endorse a method which was unanimously rejected by leading Torah scholars. The audacity of allowing a woman to remarry without a *get*, a halachic divorce, which would result in adultery and illegitimate children, is no less than breathtaking. And to support such a venture despite the opposition of recognized Torah scholars is unsettling, to say the least.

As mentioned earlier, some in Open Orthodoxy believe that the blessing *shelo asani isha* is sexist. Every morning, Orthodox males say this blessing, in which they thank God for not having made them a woman. In the morning prayers, thanks are given first for not having been created a non-Jew, who is only required to perform seven commandments. Then thanks are given for not having been created a slave or a woman, who are exempt from time-bound commandments. This litany of praise was designed incrementally to thank God for requiring men to fulfill all of the commandments. It was not designed to denigrate women.

In 2014, Yeshivat Maharat published the second volume of *Keren*, its Torah journal.[298] The entire publication deals with the blessing of "*shelo asani isha*." Ironically, the majority of the volume is taken up with articles written by men. It also includes

---

295. http://blogs.timesofisrael.com/reviving-the-rackman-agunah-beit-din. Retrieved July 23, 2015.

296. *Ibid.*

297. Rabbi Bigman serves on Yeshivat Maharat's advisory board. (http://www.Yeshivatmaharat.org/advisory-board.) Retrieved August 27, 2015.

298. *Keren* Volume 2. (2014).

a lengthy piece by Rabbi Zev Farber, who has expressed views stating that the Torah was not written by God.[299]

The journal's introductory piece is written by Rabbi Jeffery Fox, Rosh haYeshivah of Yeshivat Maharat, and Rabba Sara Hurwitz. They insist that it is important to acknowledge the women who have been "hurt" and "marginalized" by this blessing.[300]

As mentioned above, Rabbi Yosef Kanefsky also takes issue with this blessing. He writes, "I've stopped blessing God every morning for 'not having made me a woman.' [301] YCT's president, Rabbi Asher Lopatin, also encourages the removal of this blessing.[302] We have here Orthodox rabbis, charged with upholding a Jewish tradition, who have instead undertaken to alter a millennia-old practice. (It is interesting to note that some Christians maintain that Jesus enlightened the world by elevating women, as represented by the fact that Christians do not thank God for not making them women.)[303]

---

299. See Chapter 4.

300. Rabbi Jeffrey Fox and Rabba Sara Hurwitz. "Introduction" *Keren* 2 (2014), p. 1.

301. Cited by http://www.lukeford.net/blog/?p=35831. Retrieved July 26, 2015. See also Rabbi Yosef Kanefsky, "Follow-Up to the Blog Post: Adieu to 'Thou Hast Not Made Me a Woman'" *Keren* 2 (2014), p. 6.

302. http://morethodoxy.org/2009/06/29/goodbye-shelo-asani-god-did-nt-make-me-a-hello-sheasani-yisrael-god-made-me-a-yisrael-rabbi-asher-lopatin. Retrieved August 30, 2015.

303. James Gordon Bennet, editor of the New York Herald, observed in 1836, "...It was the author of Christianity that brought her out of this Egyptian bondage and put her on an equality with the other sex in civil and religious rights. Hence have sprung all the civilization, refinement, intelligence, and genius of Europe. The Hebrew prays, 'I thank thee, Lord, that I am not a woman' – the Christian – "I praise thee, Lord, that I and my wife are immortal" (David Hacket, *Religion and American Culture* [Psychology Press, 2003], p. 253).

Open Orthodox remedies to a "sexist" tradition seem endless. Rabba Hurwitz co-authored a gender-sensitive curriculum for studying Genesis, developed by the Jewish Orthodox feminist Alliance (JOFA). As JOFA's website states, it "...seeks to give our *Imahot* (Biblical matriarchs) a voice and encourages students to relate meaningfully to the *Imahot* as role models while challenging accepted gender stereotypes."[304]

Not only are biblical stories given a feminine twist, but Rabba Dr. Melanie Landau even refers to God as "She."[305]

Also, some feel that the synagogue itself contributes to women's oppression. Rabbi Zev Farber (YCT 2006) describes the way women are relegated to second class status by drawing a comparison from an all-male club which appeared in the popular cartoon *The Flintstones*.[306 B] He argues that this injustice must be rectified. He maintains that the halachic system itself relegates them to a lower status:[307]

> Other ways the second-class position of women in the synagogue is communicated are even more complex, as they appear hardwired into the halakhic system and changing or tinkering with them would be more than a little problematic for the halakhically observant.

He believes that the chauvinist nature of the synagogue was created by the halachic system (written by the rabbis). He has

---

304. http://www.jofa.org/Education/Bereishit. Retrieved July 20, 2015.

305. http://blogs.timesofisrael.com/reframing-god-as-judge. Retrieved August 31, 2015.

306. http://morethodoxy.org/2012/05/09/davening-among-the-loyal-order-of-water-buffaloes-by-rabbi-zev-farber. Retrieved July 26, 2015.

307. *Ibid.*

even proposed new blessings to be read by women when they are called up to the Torah.[308]

Maharat Rachel Kohl Finegold (Class of 2013) echoes Rabbi Farber's sentiment. She says that some women feel the synagogue is not an inviting place for them. Many women cannot comfortably sing in the musical key chosen by the *chazzan*. She writes:[309] C

> The choice of key is symbolic of the larger phenomenon— that the locus of control is elsewhere in the room. The decisions that are made as to how the service runs all come from a place to which we have no access.

For Maharat Finegold, the *shul* is yet another example of a male-dominated Orthodoxy which seeks to suppress even women's self-expression through song. Unfortunately, leading the prayers is not viewed as a chance to come close to God, but rather an opportunity for power and control.

In order to rectify these perceived injustices, Open Orthodox leaders have begun introducing new egalitarian reforms in the synagogue. For example, the National Synagogue in Washington, D.C., is led by and Rabbi Shmuel Herzfeld, a student of Rabbi Avi Weiss[310] and a member of YCT's Jewish leadership advisory board[311] and Maharat Ruth Balinsky

---

308. http://morethodoxy.org/2013/09/24/alternative-berakhot-for-wom ens-torah-reading-by-rabbi-zev-farber. Retrieved August 30, 2015.

309. http://morethodoxy.org/2014/07/18/why-dont-the-women-sing-in-shul. Retrieved July 26, 2015.

310. http://ostt.org/Rabbi_Herzfeld. Retrieved July 21, 2015.

311. http://www.yctorah.org/content/view/906/49. Retrieved August 21, 2015.

Friedman (Class of 2012).[312] Rabbi Herzfeld has initiated such reforms as women publicly reading the *megillah* (in front of men) and women serving as the *makreih* for *shofar* blowing.[313]

The Jewish wedding is another object of reform. Rabbi Dov Linzer offers a series of suggestions aimed at making the wedding more egalitarian. They include a *kallah's tisch*, consisting of the signing and reading of the pre-nuptial agreement, a bride putting a *tallis* over the groom at the *bedeken*, the groom circling around the bride under the *chuppah*, the groom asking permission to give the ring and the bride's verbal acceptance, having a woman read the *kesubah* under the *chuppah*, adding mothers' names to the *kesubah*, taking out the word "*besulta*" (virgin) from the *kesubah*, equalizing the financial obligations of the *kesubah* and women translating the seven blessings under the *chuppah*. He also entertains the possibility of women making the seven blessings at the wedding meal.[314] In another article, he discusses the best method of conducting a double-ring ceremony so as to circumvent Rabbi Moshe Feinstein's objection to the practice.[315]

Jorden Soffer, a student at YCT,[316] discusses several innovations that he and his wife made at their wedding to increase gender equality. As he puts it, "We sought a solution that would increase involvement of all of our guests." The language of solution is indicative of the belief that the wedding

---

312. While Maharat Balinsky Friedman did not serve on the clergy when these reforms were enacted, she presently leads the congregation as a Maharat, giving her implicit approval.

313. http://ostt.org/Gala_Video.php.

314. http://www.myjewishlearning.com/article/toward-a-more-balanced-wedding-ceremony. Retrieved July 21, 2015.

315. http://www.myjewishlearning.com/article/double-ring-ceremonies. Retrieved July 29, 2015.

316. http://www.yctorah.org/images//about%20our%20students%20 2014-2015%20email.pdf. Retrieved August 27, 2015.

customs, as they now stand, are problematic. To correct this problem, women sang at a *kallah's tisch*, the bride covered the groom's face, the bride was present at the *kesubah* signing, women signed the pre-nuptial agreement, and a female rabbi recited an eighth blessing under the *chuppah*.[317]

The agenda of Open Orthodoxy is clear. A Halacha which suffers from male bias must be fixed through radical reforms—rectifying what they view as millennia of oppression.

Yeshivat Maharat

Perhaps the most radical feminist innovation in Open Orthodoxy is the establishment of Yeshivat Maharat. Founded in 2009 by Rabbi Avi Weiss and Rabba Sara Hurwitz, the yeshiva grants *semichah* (rabbinic ordination) to women.[318]

Traditionally, women have never been trained as rabbis. It is interesting to note that some at Hebrew Union College have observed that the Conservative movement's break with Orthodoxy was solidified when the seminary began ordaining women:[319]

> The [Jewish Theological] Seminary—in deciding to ordain women as rabbis—broke dramatically with whatever remnant remained of its Orthodox roots.[320]

317. http://www.myjewishlearning.com/author/jordan-soffer. Retrieved July 29, 2015.

318. http://www.yeshivatmaharat.org/mission and history. Retrieved August 21, 2015.

319. *Tradition Renewed* Volume 2, p. 574. Cited by Rabbi Lawrence Kelemen (http://www.simpletoremember.com/articles/a/reformconservativeorthodox/#51).

320. Rabba Hurwitz has appeared in events with Rabbis Sandy Eisenberg Sasso (Recnstructionist) Sally Priesand (Reform), and Amy Eilberg

However, many in Open Orthodoxy have stated that there is no problem with women serving as rabbis. Rabba Hurwitz wants to "help the Orthodox community understand that it [ordaining women] is [halachically] permissible and something whose time has come."[321]

This section will show that, on the contrary, graduates of Yeshivat Maharat are not qualified to serve as rabbis.

The most significant reason why Yeshivat Maharat's graduates are not fit to serve as rabbis is the lack of halachic training they receive. One of a rabbi's major jobs is to serve as a *posek*, or decisor of Jewish law, for his community. A *posek* is a person who has gained a mastery over the Talmud and the accompanying halachic literature. Mere familiarity with the sources is insufficient, since in pondering each question one needs to examine its ramifications in all areas of Torah.

As Rabbi Weiss[322] conferred *semichah* upon one of Yeshivat Maharat's graduates in 2014, he said that she "has been found worthy and granted authority to teach and determine halachic

---

(Conservative) the first female Rabbis in their respective denominations. (http://njjewishnews.com/article/9471/pioneering-women-to-gather-for-historic-forum#.VeBjDPlViko. Retrieved August 28, 2015)

321. http://www.jewishjournal.com/membership/article/orthodox_shul_takes_first_step_to_hiring_female_clergy. Retrieved July 26, 2015.

322. Rabbi Moshe Averick points out that, when Rabbi Weiss appeared on the NY radio show, "Religion on the Line," he was asked if the move of ordaining women would create a schism in the Orthodox community. He responded that although there is a large rabbinic organization which opposes this move, the International Rabbinic Fellowship supports it. What he neglected to tell the radio host was that he co-founded the International Rabbinic Fellowship. (https://www.youtube.com/watch?v=6DRXyGLJ4Rw. Retrieved July 28, 2015.)

rulings for the Jewish people and has been ordained as a spiritual leader and decisor of Jewish law."[323]

The student application for Yeshivat Maharat similarly states:[324]

> Through a rigorous curriculum of Talmud, halakhic decision-making (*psak*), pastoral counseling, and leadership development, our graduates will assume the responsibility and authority to be *poskot* (legal arbiters) for the community.

Yeshivat Maharat seeks to provide *poskim* for Jewish communities. In addition, their website boasts that "upon graduation, students are experts in Jewish law, Talmud, Bible, and Jewish Thought."[325]

In Chapter 3, we discussed the vastness of the halachic corpus and the amount of time that is required to thoroughly master it. For example, we mentioned that in a classic yeshiva where students study halachic material for the entire day,[326] it takes about a year to cover only a fraction of the laws of *kashrus*. We also mentioned that yeshiva students who study for ordination have already been studying the Talmud for years in rigorous, full-time programs.

---

323. https://www.youtube.com/watch?v=AU7A-8Eo22c. Retrieved July 19, 2015.

324. http://www.yeshivatmaharat.org/admissions. Retrieved July 19, 2015.

325. http://www.yeshivatmaharat.org/four-year-program. Retrieved August 10, 2015.

326. This usually means at least 8.5 hours day fully immersed in Talmudic and halachic material. Also, most students spend much of their free time continuing their studies.

In this context, let us examine the academic standards at Yeshivat Maharat. Can its graduates be considered "experts in Jewish law, Talmud, Bible, and Jewish Thought" as well as "*poskot* for their communities?"

The standard program at Yeshivat Maharat is four years long. To be accepted into the yeshiva, students need only to "identify as Orthodox,[327] demonstrate a proficiency in Jewish text, and aspire to serve as spiritual leaders." [328] No previous yeshiva education or mastery of Talmud is required.

There is also a two-year track available for women who have already been involved in Jewish spiritual leadership for at least five years. While the two-year track does require candidates to pass an oral *Gemara* proficiency exam to gain admittance, in this program women receive ordination after a self-guided course of study.[329]

From the four-day sample schedule on their website, it is clear that the amount of time spent on the halachic material is significantly less than that of a classic yeshiva. Some days, only a fraction of the day is spent in the study of Halacha and Talmud. Moreover, while classic yeshiva programs have a study session every night, the schedule on this institution's website lists only one night session a week.[330] In addition, according to

---

327. Despite this requirement, an article in the *Australian Jewish News* describes Rabba Dr. Melanie Landau (Class of 2015) as "not identifying with any particular stream of Judaism," and quotes Landau as saying that her work "is beyond denominational lines." (http://www.jewishnews.net.au/aussie-first-for-rabbah-landau/48943. Retrieved July 22, 2015.)

328. http://www.yeshivatmaharat.org/admissions. July 19, 2015.

329. http://www.yeshivatmaharat.org/advanced-kollel-program. Retrieved August 28, 2015.

330. http://www.yeshivatmaharat.org/four-year-program. Retrieved July 19, 2015.

its website, several current students do not live anywhere near the yeshiva. Some live as far away as Maryland, Massachusetts, Illinois, California, England, and Israel.[331]

In addition to their halachic studies, students at Yeshivat Maharat also study Bible and Jewish thought and take classes in pastoral education, practical rabbinics and professional development. Furthermore, students participate in "programs in inter-denominational dialogue, inter-faith dialogue, and inclusiveness of marginalized groups within the Orthodox community."[332] They "are featured as Scholars-in-Residence at synagogues, participate in panel discussions, and engage in teaching opportunities." In addition, during their time at the yeshiva students serve as interns.[333]

It is quite astounding to hear the yeshiva claim that, in such a short time, its graduates are qualified to serve as *poskim* and are experts in Talmud, Bible, Jewish law and Jewish thought. Remarkably, all this is accomplished while taking time out to serve as interns and scholars-in-residence, to speak on panel discussions, to participate in interdenominational and interfaith programs and to take classes in practical rabbinics, pastoral education and professional development. With its varied course of study and all these extra-curricular activities,

---

331. http://www.ycshivatmaharat.org/class-of-2019-1. http://www.ycshivatmaharat.org/class-of-2020. http://www.yeshivatmaharat.org/class-of-2018. http://www.yeshivatmaharat.org/class-of-2017. http://www.thejc.com/news/uk-news/126348/feminist-group-founder-training-be-a-rabbi. Retrieved February 4, 2016.
332. *Ibid.*
333. *Ibid.*

we can assuredly state that it is simply impossible that Yeshivat Maharat's graduates are qualified to render halachic decisions.

Rabbi Ysoscher Katz said in a lecture:[334]

The success of female rabbinate will be dependent if they can produce serious scholarship.

Then according to Rabbi Katz, it would appear that the female rabbinate has not been successful.

Perhaps the biggest indictment of the yeshiva's level of scholarship is from its Dean herself. At a JOFA conference she relates that when the yeshiva sought writers for its first Halacha journal *Keren*, they received very few submissions from women. She says:[335]

...So we ended up publishing the first journal with very few *teshuvot* from women in it. [336] We got lambasted rightly so we actually had pulled it. We pulled the journal we dumped it. And we reinvested money into

---

334. Rabbi Ysoscher Katz, "Spiritual Explorers and their Discoveries," London, England. http://www.yeshivatmaharat.org/audio-and-video-links. Retrieved January 19, 2016.

335. Rabba Sara Hurwitz, "Spiritual Explorers and their Discoveries," London, England. http://www.yeshivatmaharat.org/audio-and-video-links. Retrieved January 19, 2016.

336. She claims that this was not because the women were not able to write, "We got very few responses from women, which is not surprising. It's not that there aren't women who are able to do it but what we discovered is that women tend to write at 3 AM in the morning, in the wee hours of the morning, whereas men tended to write as part of their jobs. So one of the training is to train women to write as part of their jobs."

finding women who would be able to write. Because I felt at first that people would understand that we are on a journey, on a journey to get more women to write on a high level. But then when it was actually published and you look at the table of contents and you see barely any women how could Yeshivat Maharat be putting out a journal like that. So we did rightly so pull it and republish it with other women's *teshuvot*....

Yeshivat Maharat's less-than-rigorous Halacha program is reason enough to render its graduates unqualified as rabbis and *poskim*. However, there are also technical halachic reasons why women do not serve as rabbis.

Throughout Jewish history, women have not been trained as halachic decisors, except in rare situations or in special circumstances.

Women are not eligible to serve as rabbis because it is a position of *serarah*, or authority and they are halachically excluded from serving in these roles. This is a view cited in the name of Rabbi Soloveitchik,[337] and for the same reason, Rabbi Moshe Feinstein felt that a woman should not even serve as a synagogue president.[338]

However, Dr. Erin Smokler, Yeshivat Maharat's Director of Spiritual Development and internship coordinator, declares that this opinion is incorrect:[339]

---

337. http://www.hakirah.org/Vol%2011%20Schachter.pdf. Retrieved July 30, 2015.
338. *Iggros Moshe* YD 2:45.
339. http://www.thedailybeast.com/articles/2013/06/17/a-historic-grad-uation-ceremony-for-orthodox-women.html. Retrieved July 20, 2015.

Halakha does not explicitly prohibit women from serving as religious leaders (*serrarah*); being authorities on law (*poskot*); or teaching religious text.

Dr. Smokler unequivocally states that women may serve in positions of *serarah,* contrary to the opinions of Rabbi Soloveitchik and Rabbi Feinstein. She has no previous yeshiva education listed in her biography,[340] yet she confidently offers an opinion which has been opposed by acknowledged Torah giants.

That Yeshivat Maharat is a product of secular feminist influences seems obvious. Yet, in an ironic effort to gain legitimacy, Rabbi Daniel Sperber in his remarks at the 2015 graduation of Yeshivat Maharat claims that it is actually a continuation of the Bais Yaakov movement—which, he points out, was approved by the Chofetz Chaim.[341]

In reality, Yeshivat Maharat could not be more ideologically removed from the Bais Yaakov movement. Bais Yaakov, the preeminent Orthodox women's educational institution, inspires Jewish women by emphasizing the beauty of Jewish womanhood and by strengthening the observance of commandments which are unique to them. This movement is directly responsible for thousands of Orthodox women who are proud and fulfilled Jews. All of this was accomplished without the influence of secular feminist ideals. On the other hand, Yeshivat Maharat

---

340. http://www.yeshivatmaharat.org/faculty-and-staff. Retrieved August 28, 2015.

341. http://www.yeshivatmaharat.org/graduation2015. Retrieved July 20, 2015.

and Open Orthodoxy seek to remake the Jewish woman in the feminist image, by sending the unfortunate message that only by imitating men will she be spiritually fulfilled.[342]

Modesty

Another reason women have not traditionally served as rabbis is this would require them to constantly be in front of men. This violates Jewish teachings of modesty. In fact Rabbi Moshe Feinstein wrote on this subject. He was once told about a synagogue where a woman would descend into the men's section and lead the congregation in an English prayer. Rabbi Feinstein said of the practice, "...it is obvious that it is prohibited and it is astonishing that an Orthodox rabbi would allow something like this."[343] In fact, Rabbi Feinstein even prohibits women from delivering *shiurim* to mixed groups in the synagogue.[344] It is interesting that, in ordaining women, Open Orthodox leaders do not acknowledge his stringent stance on this issue, yet are quick to cite his lenient opinions in other matters.[345]

The male sex drive is immense. While it is incumbent upon men to control their thoughts and actions, rules of feminine

---

342. For a Further discussion of the feminist influence on Orthodox Judaism, see Harav Aharon Feldman, *The Eye of the Storm.* (Jerusalem: Yad Yosef Publications, 2009, Chapter 12).

343. *Iggros Moshe* OH 4:70.

344. *Iggros Moshe* OH 5:12.

345. See Chapter 3 where we cite Rabbi Linzer who invokes Rabbi Feinstein's opinion in an effort to encourage people to donate to churches. Also see Rabbi Fox's claim that Rabbi Feinstein was lenient regarding conversion standards. (https://static.squarespace.com/static/5348363de4b-0531dce75bc53/t/546ce0d5e4b02e200e59ce8f/1416421589876/Male-BeitDinattheImmersionofaFemaleConvert1.pdf.)

modesty help facilitate this endeavor. These laws were not enacted to subjugate women, but were put in place because the Sages had a realistic understanding of the male sex drive. Laws include the prohibition to hear women sing, separation of the sexes during prayer, and the laws of seclusion with a woman. It is more than ironic that Open Orthodox congregations separate the sexes during prayer for this reason with a *mechitzah*, yet have no qualms about having a woman serving as rabbi where she will be constantly gazed at by men.

Rabbi Moshe Averick relates a poignant anecdote which demonstrates the wisdom behind these modesty laws: [346]

While I was living in Israel, a friend of mine told me he was looking forward to attending a Friday-night service at a particular synagogue in the *Nachlaot* section of Jerusalem. He had heard wonderful things about the Rabbi and the ecstatic and uplifting nature of the prayers. When I [later] inquired about his experience at this synagogue, the disappointment was all over his face. He said that the first half of the service, *Kabbalat Shabbat* [Welcoming the Sabbath], was incredibly uplifting. Then suddenly, before the beginning of the Evening Service, a beautiful young woman—modestly dressed, with her hair covered in the custom of married Orthodox women—stood up in front of the congregation at the podium and started reading a Chapter of Psalms out loud while everyone listened silently. At the conclusion of this reading she returned to her seat on the women's

---

346. http://blogs.timesofisrael.com/avi-weiss-and-neo-conservative-ju-daism. Retrieved July 25, 2015.

side and the Evening Service continued. It seems this is a regular occurrence on Friday night. He said, "That was the end of the spiritual experience. I simply could not get the image of this strikingly beautiful young woman out of my mind for the rest of the evening. Many of the other men told me the same thing." There is nothing strange or shocking about this story. His reaction was perfectly natural and normal. What would have been shocking is if he *did not* react that way.

In reality, many leaders of Open Orthodoxy do not exhibit such sensitivity to modesty. The notion of having women refrain from speaking in front of men is completely foreign to them.

In fact, in 2015, YCT hired its first female Rebbe.[347] That a woman will be teaching Talmud daily in front of men seems not to bother anyone at YCT.

Also, at the 2014 Graduation of Yeshivat Maharat, two women sang and others danced in front of the assemblage, which included many men. Among those present were Rabbis Avi Weiss, Asher Lopatin, Daniel Sperber, Dov Linzer, Jeffrey Fox and Ysoscher Katz.[348]

In another breach of the laws of modesty, one YCT graduate even invited immodest middle eastern style dancers to his synagogue in order to enhance the celebration of the Exodus from Egypt.[349]

---

347. http://www.yctorah.org/content/view/23/49. Retrieved August 28, 2015.

348. https://www.youtube.com/watch?v=AU7A-8Eo22c. Retrieved August 11, 2015.

349. http://www.redbankgreen.com/2009/12/red-bank-rabbi-injects-fun-into-customs.

The concept of modesty as a means of curbing the male sex drive is rejected by Open Orthodoxy. Rabbi Linzer strongly suggests that any religious demand for modesty derives from a desire to control women. He calls the idea that woman's modesty is actually meant to curb male sexual desire a "perversion."[350]

Linzer's attitude is echoed by Dasi Fruchter, a student at Yeshivat Maharat, whose image graced the yeshiva's website banner.[351] In a 2013 blog post for *Lilith*, entitled, "Rabbis in Red Lipstick" she writes:[352]

> The truth is I want to push back against centuries rife with the sentiment that men are unable to control themselves in the presence of beautiful women. I want to push back against the idea that there is anything deviant about a woman who is comfortable with her sexuality.

She pontificates if it is appropriate to dress in a provocative way:[353]

> ...I can't pretend that wearing red lipstick isn't provocative. But is that really a bad thing? I find the effort to deny the presence of sexuality usually only draws more attention, and makes that presence even

---

350. http://www.nytimes.com/2012/01/20/opinion/ultra-orthodox-jews-and-the-modesty-fight.html?_r=0. Retrieved July 21, 2015.

351. http://www.yeshivatmaharat.org. Retrieved August 28, 2015.

352. http://lilith.org/blog/2013/02/rabbis-in-red-lipstick. Retrieved July 21, 2015.

353. *Ibid.*

stronger. Being real about my sexuality and the ways I enjoy expressing it seems like a much better and more honest idea.

One of the most basic human instincts is to cover nakedness. Humans are ashamed of their sexual organs because they represent man's animalistic drives. The Torah views sexuality as a private affair between spouses which helps create a special bond between them. In Judaism, holiness is achieved by controlling these desires outside of marriage and behaving modestly.

So, to answer Ms. Fruchter's question: Yes, it *is* a bad thing for a female rabbi to wear sexually-provocative lipstick. This attitude epitomizes secular feminist ideology, in which a woman is empowered by expressing her sexuality openly. Ms. Fruchter advocates doing it while wielding the power of a rabbi. She writes about how she will feel with her lipstick in her pocket: "When I feel it there, I'll look forward to feeling empowered as opposed to tolerated."[354]

In another breach of the laws of modesty, many at YCT and Yeshivat Maharat discuss sexual topics publicly. While it is important to discuss these issues privately, the Talmud prohibits publicly teaching these subjects (*Chagigah* 11b), "Do not speak about sexual matters in groups of three."

Ignoring this Talmudic mandate, YCT and the Jewish Orthodox Feminist Alliance (JOFA) sponsor a series of podcasts called the "Joy of Text" about Judaism and Sexuality.[355] Sexual

---

354. *Ibid.*
355. http://jpmedia.co/podcasts/joy-of-text. Retrieved August 20, 2015.

topics are discussed in graphic detail by Rabbi Dov Linzer and Dr. Bat Sheva Marcus, Clinical Director at the Medical Center for Female Sexuality[356] and a founding member of JOFA.[357] She has been hailed as an "Orthodox Sex Guru."[358]

In one live co-ed podcast, women were encouraged to engage in deviant sexual behavior which is included under the prohibition of, *Do not perform the practices of the land of Egypt which you dwelled* (Leviticus 18:3). Rabbi Linzer and Dr. Marcus also describe in detail activities which are usually not discussed publicly in polite company. They are too inappropriate to mention here.[359] In another episode, Dr. Marcus mentions that to earn her degree she was required to watch "hours and hours" of pornography.[360]

Yeshivat Chovevei Torah, Yeshivat Maharat, and the Jewish Orthodox Feminist Alliance also sponsored a four day long co-ed course on sexual education. Besides speaking about the act of intimacy in great detail, participants were shown graphic photographs and models.[361]

Yeshivat Maharat's Facebook page[362] touts an article written by Rabba Dr. Melanie Landau (Class of 2015). In the article,

356. https://www.linkedin.com/in/bat-sheva-marcus-9a420b13. Retrieved February 21, 2016.

357. *Ibid.*

358. http://www.nytimes.com/2015/01/25/magazine/the-orthodox-sex-guru.html?_r=0. Retrieved August 20, 2015.

359. http://jpmedia.co/does-sexting-lead-to-mixed-dancing-and-more. Retrieved August 19, 2015. http://jpmedia.co/the-common-problems-episode. Retrieved February 21, 2016.

360. http://jpmedia.co/the-pornography-episode. Retrieved January 21, 2016

361. http://www.thejewishweek.com/news/new-york/joy-sex-ed. Retrieved January 21, 2016.

362. https://www.facebook.com/Yeshivatmaharat. (July 27, 2015)

she relates comments she made while sitting on a panel about Judaism and sexuality. In the article she describes her personal intimate experiences.

Even the most holy topics are sexualized. A YCT Facebook post describes a Yom Kippur *shiur* given by Rabbi Linzer:[363]

> Rabbi Dov Linzer's *shiur* today explored the topic of the erotic imagery surrounding the Kohen Gadol's entering the Holy of Holies on Yom Kippur, and how this intimate encounter was made available to the entire people. Listen to Rabbi Linzer's *shiur* to hear more on this topic!

While some display a total lack of modesty, others actually blame the halachic system itself for creating a sexually-exploitive environment. Rabbi Yosef Kanefsky reacts to a rabbi who was caught in an act of sexual immorality:[364]

> I could blame no one for reacting to this unseemly spectacle by disparaging religion generally, and Orthodox Judaism in particular. Religion generally, for the hypocrisy that regularly percolates to its loftiest levels, and Orthodox Judaism in particular for its halachic policies that potentially place women into the hands of powerful men who might take advantage of them.

363. https://www.facebook.com/YCTRabbinicalSchool/posts/ 10152810067498274. (October 2, 2014) Retrieved July 29, 2015.

364. http://morethodoxy.org/2014/10/24/and-the-lord-god-said-youre- not-about-sex-by-yosef-kanefsky. Retrieved July 28, 2015.

He blames halachic policies for this rabbi's misdeeds—when, in fact, it was because this rabbi did *not* follow established halachic procedure that he erred. The Halacha creates boundaries between men and women precisely to prevent such temptation. It is doubtful that this rabbi began with his sexually-deviant behavior at the outset of his career. Rather, he first became lax in other areas of Halacha which were designed to regulate the male sex drive. [365]

---

365. Harav Aharon Feldman, in his book, *The Eye of the Storm* (p. 105) describes a similar situation. An article in the feminist magazine *Lilith* praised a charismatic Orthodox rabbi who relaxed the halachic boundaries between the sexes. However the article laments, that this leader also used his power to sexually exploit women. The article states that a committee has been formed to:

...explore ethical and moral guidelines for rabbis and people in positions of lay spiritual leadership, to bring into focus the power imbalances between someone in a position of spiritual leadership and the person he or she is serving.

Rabbi Feldman observes that these ethical and moral guidelines were actually created by Judaism:

Remarkably, such guidelines have been in place for thousands of years in Jewish society. These are the laws designed to curb the male sexual appetite. Foremost among them are the laws of *yichud*, which forbid a man to seclude himself with a woman other than his wife and family. ("Seclusion" means remaining in a closed area where it is not likely that someone will enter within a short time.) Then there are the laws of *negiah*, which forbid kissing or otherwise coming into affectionate physical contact with any woman except for one's wife and family. Most halachic authorities hold that this extends even to innocuous touching such as shaking hands. Finally there are the general practices of *tzeniyus* by which sexually provocative behavior is forbidden and the social contact between men and women is reduced to a minimum. Among the Orthodox, for example, at weddings men and woman dance in separate areas and their

Open Orthodox rabbis protest against the sexual improprieties of men in power, while at the same time actively work to relax the very safeguards meant to curb such abuse.

Open Orthodoxy's attitude towards women's issues is a microcosm of their view of Torah in general. An imperfect halachic system created by sexist rabbis must be rectified in order to fit in with modern egalitarian ideals. This approach has given birth to radical innovations and ventures which are doomed to failure.

---

schools are segregated by gender.... The laws stem from a wisdom which teaches that male sexuality must be contained before its passions are aroused, not afterwards when its control becomes nigh impossible. Had the subject of the *Lilith* article kept them, none of the improprieties described there could have ever occurred. And if they would be adopted by all Jews everywhere, there would be no need for seeking methods for curbing persons in power.

He observes the irony that those who seek solutions to the male abuse of power actually favor removing those safeguards which have already been set in place by Judaism:

...I found it highly ironic to read several of the comments in the *Lilith* article praising this charismatic teacher of Judaism, juxtaposed to its earnest quest to curb the sexual appetites of those in power. The article praises him for having been a pioneer in cutting down the barriers between the sexes. He allegedly removed the *mechitzah* between men and women in the synagogue. He hugged every man, woman and child he met, even "kissing them on their lips." The article notes how he was ostracized by the Orthodox community for such behavior who, it is implied, were a reactionary force holding back the liberation of Jewish women (and, one might add, of Jewish men). These accounts are then followed by an account of his sexual misbehaviors, deploring the sad fact that the same person who brought so much light to Jewish society was so inconsistent in his personal life.

8

Ecumenicalism

Interfaith

Judaism has always sought to create boundaries between Jews and non-Jews. God prohibits intermarriage with these words:[366]

> You shall not intermarry with them, you shall not give your daughter to his son and you shall not take his daughter for your son. For he will cause your child to turn away from after Me and they will worship the gods of others, then God's wrath will burn against you, and He will destroy you quickly.

Also, the Rabbis instituted laws to prevent the sort of friendly mingling that could lead to intermarriage, such as the prohibition of eating food cooked by non-Jews and of consuming non-Jewish wine and bread.[367]

---

366. Deuteronomy 7:3.
367. See the Mishnah, *Avodah Zarah* 35b, with Rashi's commentary.

Jews have traditionally not joined with Gentiles in religious events for the obvious reason that their beliefs are diametrically opposed to those of Judaism. For example, Christianity believes that Jesus "fulfilled" the Torah and that its commandments are no longer obligatory. They preach that God rejected the Jews for not accepting Jesus and are now despised. Jews, on the other hand, believe that they are the Chosen People to carry out God's will in the world, and that the Torah is eternal. While it is important to be kind and respectful to non-Jews, joining with them in religious matters is another story.

Eminent halachic authorities such as Rabbi Moshe Feinstein and Rabbi Joseph B. Soloveitchik forbade interfaith dialogue. Rabbi Feinstein forbids participation in interfaith committees and dialogue for any reason:[368]

> ... We are making it known that there is a clear and total prohibition to make joint committees with rabbis and priests or to participate in any such convention, not the one which will be held in Boston nor any place, not in this country or any other, and also for matters not related to faith and religion, without any exceptions....

Rabbi Soloveitchik similarly forbids interfaith dialogue, except regarding matters of humanitarian and cultural necessity.[369]

Yet Open Orthodox rabbis do participate in interfaith religious events, imply that there is validity to all religions, and propose radical egalitarian reforms.

---

368. *Iggros Moshe* YD 3:43.
369. Rabbi David Hartman, *Love and Terror in the God Encounter: The Theological Legacy of Rabbi Joseph B. Soloveitchik* (Woodstock, Vermont: Jewish Lights, 2001) pp. 161-162.

As mentioned earlier, the egalitarian ideal is so sacred at YCT that its Rosh haYeshivah questions whether Halacha should be bent in order to justify egalitarian beliefs.[370] Also, mentioned earlier in Chapter 3, Rabbi Linzer puts this attitude into practice by encouraging Jews to help rebuild churches. Traditionally, Jews have bent their views to fit the Halacha. Linzer favors the opposite.

On June 17, 2015, a horrific mass shooting occurred at the Emanuel African Methodist Episcopal Church in Charleston, South Carolina. Parishioners were gunned down by a young white supremacist while in the midst of Bible study.

Every decent human being deplores such acts. Rabbis Avi Weiss, Shmuel Herzfeld, and Etan Mintz (Member of YCT's Jewish Leadership Advisory Board[371] and honorary alumnus[372]) went further. They traveled to Charleston to participate in the church's Bible study class. Rabbi Weiss said of the experience:[373]

> The class began. At times I felt uneasy. The theology espoused was not ours. These ambivalent feelings, however, were eclipsed by the recognition that we were in a holy place—a place where people were murdered simply because of the color of their skin.

370. Rabbi Dov Linzer, "On the *Mitzvot* of Non-Jews: An Analysis of *Avodah Zarah* 2b-3a." *Beloved Words Milin Havivin* 1 (2006), p. 36.

371. http://www.yctorah.org/content/view/906/49. Retrieved January 21, 2016.

372. http://www.yctorah.org/index2.php?option=com_content&do_pdf=1&id=30. Retrieved August 30, 2015.

373. http://www.postandcourier.com/article/20150707/PC1002/150709580/1021/. Retrieved July 22, 2015.

While it is important to show solidarity with those who have experienced tragedy, it is unnecessary to join in the study of their texts, which reject the Jewish faith, or to call their house of worship a "holy place."

YCT also participates in events which advance the egalitarian ideal. They co-sponsored the *Elijah Interfaith Institute* summer program, where participants studied the tenets of Christianity, Islam, Hinduism and Buddhism.[374]

Not only is the study of other religions encouraged; some in Open Orthodoxy even embrace the teachings of other religions. YCT's July 2015 Newsletter features a student profile. The student's interests are listed as "Aggadah, Zen Buddhism, and Chassidut."[375]

Rabbi Hanan Shlesinger is a member of the International Rabbinic Fellowship[376] and serves on the advisory board of Yeshivat Maharat.[377] In an article, entitled, "What Tisha B'Av Can Learn From Ramadan," he describes the beauty of the Muslim holiday of Ramadan. He discusses lessons he has learned from it and writes that he participated in many *iftar*, or breakfasts,

374. http://www.elijah-interfaith.org/fileadmin/pictures/Summer_School.pdf. http://elijah-interfaith.org/about-elijah/our-history/history-more. http://webcache.googleusercontent.com/search?q=-cache:xh7Gatdnk78J:www.elijah-interfaith.org/fileadmin/pictures/Summer_School.pdf+&cd=4&hl=en&ct=clnk&gl=us. Retrieved September 11, 2015.
375. http://files.ctctcdn.com/49c02d16001/c642ff23-f2d2-4a76-82ef-2924dd5e17eb.pdf. Retrieved July 30, 2015.
376. http://jewishstudiesinitiative.org/rabbis/our-rabbis. Retrieved August 19, 2015.
377. http://www.Yeshivatmaharat.org/advisory-board. Retrieved August 19, 2015.

with his Muslim neighbors. He writes how lessons learned from this Muslim holiday have influenced his views on the Israeli-Palestinian conflict:[378]

> I ask myself: Will my Ramadan affect my Tisha B'Av? Has enough empathy with my Muslim/Palestinian neighbors taken root in my heart to realize the challenge that the insights of our tradition present to the current political status quo? Is my Jewish self-understanding and honest enough to see that the moral iniquity that our prophets and Sages spoke up against is still dancing among us in the way that we relate to and behave towards the Palestinian people? And will I have the courage and fortitude to do something about it?

It is not uncommon for YCT rabbis to participate in religious events with Christian clergy and church groups. Rabbi Weiss's synagogue hosts Baptist choirs (which include women).[379] Rabbi Etan Mintz invited a reverend to his synagogue where he led the congregation in song during his sermon.[380] Other joint religious events are actually carried out in churches. The City Road Chapel United Methodist Church's blog invites its congregants to a Passover *seder* in the church led by Rabbi Saul Strosberg. In addition to being a 2005 graduate of YCT, Strosberg is also a

---

378. http://www.myjewishlearning.com/rabbis-without-borders/what-tisha-bav-can-learn-from-ramadan. Retrieved July 28, 2015.

379. http://images.shulcloud.com/111/uploads/Flyers/MLK-2013-flyer.pdf. Retrieved July 21, 2015.

380. http://www.jta.org/2015/05/05/news-opinion/united-states/etan-mintz-reflections-baltimore. Retrieved January 23, 2016.

member of the board of the International Rabbinic Fellowship[381] and a member of Yeshivat Maharat's advisory board.[382] The Church's webpage states:[383]

> What if our family's collection of thankful stories started in Egypt about 3,500 years ago? It is now known in the Jewish community as the Seder Meal. It is a Jewish feast celebrating the beginning of Passover. This year on April 9, at 6:00 p.m. we will be blessed to share this special feast in our Welcome Center. Rabbi Saul Strosberg, of Congregation Sherith/Israel, Nashville, Tennessee, will be our host as we gather to worship and learn about the meal Jesus shared with his disciples.

In another expression of joint religious cooperation, Rabbis Asher Lopatin, Jason Herman (YCT 2005 and Executive Director of the International Rabbinic Fellowship[384]) and Nissan Antine (YCT 2006 and President of the International Rabbinic Fellowship[385]) participated in the Jewish-Catholic Neocatechumenal Way conference.[386] The Neocatechumenal

381. http://www.internationalrabbinicfellowship.org/leadership.   Retrieved August 19, 2015.
382. http://www.yeshivatmaharat.org/advisory-board. Retrieved August 19, 2015.
383. https://www.facebook.com/cityroadchapel/posts/688619657870837. Retrieved August 12, 2015.
384. http://www.internationalrabbinicfellowship.org/leadership.   Retrieved August 19, 2015.
385. Ibid.
386. https://www.facebook.com/asher.lopatin. (May 8, 2015) Retrieved July 29, 2015.

Way is "a faith-based educational group that operates under the auspices of the Catholic Church."[387] It engages in missionary activity and is dedicated to Christian renewal.[388] Participants at the conference were serenaded to "The Suffering of the Innocents: A Symphonic Homage and Prayer," a piece of music which "was inspired by the death camp's gate, alongside Jesus's suffering on the cross, with his mother Mary crying for him, like all mothers of children slaughtered."[389] They also engaged in vespers, or Catholic prayers, led by a rabbi.[390]

At the conference, Rabbi Asher Lopatin, along with 120 Catholic Cardinals, participated in a Lag B'omer celebration. Participants danced around a bonfire overshadowed by a gigantic golden statue of Pope John Paul II.[391]

Christian Clergy are even invited into the rabbinical school itself. Rabbi Andrew Kaplan, a 2009 graduate of YCT, describes how, in 2006, Catholic Cardinals and Bishops visited the yeshiva. They addressed the students and then jointly studied Tractate *Berachos* with them.[392]

387. http://jewishexponent.com/headlines/2015/05/philly-area-rabbis-travel-to-israel-as-guests-of-catholic-church. Retrieved July 29, 2015.

388. http://w2.vatican.va/content/benedict-xvi/en/speeches/2006/january/documents/hf_ben-xvi_spe_20060112_neocatecumenali.html. Retrieved July 29, 2015.

389. http://www.timesofisrael.com/where-cardinals-and-rabbis-go-to-forgive-and-pray. Retrieved July 29, 2015.

390. For a detailed description of the conference and the roots of the Neocatechumenal Way, see Rabbi Avraham Gordimer's article at http://www.israelnationalnews.com/Articles/Article.aspx/16936#.VblC3PlVikp.

391. https://www.facebook.com/asher.lopatin. (Post and comment, May 7, 2015) Retrieved July 29, 2015.

392. http://yctchevre.blogspot.co.il/2006/03/cardinals-and-bishops-visit.html. Retrieved July 21, 2015.

Among the speakers was Cardinal Jean-Marie Lustiger, the late archbishop of Paris. Lustiger, a born Jew who converted to Catholicism during the Holocaust, is reported to have previously said that as a Catholic he is a "fulfilled Jew."[393] Former Chief Rabbi Yisroel Meir Lau had a different take on this. He declared that Lustiger "betrayed his people and his faith during the most difficult and darkest of periods."[394]

Some Open Orthodox rabbis even suggest changing the Haggadah to reflect their egalitarian views. Rabbi Shmuly Yanklowitz (YCT 2010) writes:[395] A

> Friends, please consider omitting the passage שְׁפֹךְ חֲמָתְךָ אֶל הַגּוֹיִם (asking God to pour wrath upon the nations of the world) in the Haggadah this year. This was a justifiable addition in the past (added during the oppressive Crusades) & anti-Semitism is certainly still alive today, but our prayers today need to focus on peace, justice, love, & healing.

Rabbi Yanklowitz seeks to alter a prayer whose source is the Bible (Psalms 79 and 69 and Lamentations 3). He continues that it is laden with "anger and hate." His reasoning is foggy at best. At this point in history, is it appropriate to remove this passage? The world stands idly by as Iran openly calls for the destruction of Israel and builds a nuclear bomb to do so. Antisemitism

393. http://www.jta.org/2007/08/06/news-opinion/united-states/lustiger-a-friend-and-puzzle-to-jews Retrieved August 28, 2015.

394. http://www.nytimes.com/2007/08/06/world/europe/06lustiger.html?pagewanted=all&_r=0. Retrieved August 28, 2015.

395. https://www.facebook.com/rshmuly.yanklowitz/posts/10152612745941307?pnref=story. (April 2, 2015)

has reached levels not seen since the Holocaust, as Jews are slaughtered in French supermarkets while those near Gaza are in constant fear of rocket attacks. There has never a more appropriate time to fervently pray, *Spill your wrath upon the nations which do not know you and the kingdoms which do not call out in your name. For they have devoured Jacob and destroyed His habitation. Pour your anger upon them and let Your fiery wrath overtake them. Pursue them with wrath and annihilate them from beneath the heavens of Hashem.*[396]

A statement by Rabbi Jefferey Fox best summarizes the views of Open Orthodoxy. In a Facebook post, he writes:[397]

Spirituality is like water and religion is like tea. Without water we simply cannot live. It is the tea that adds the flavor to life. All people have their favorite tea, often inherited from their family of origin. If you like a different kind of tea, I see no reason to try and change your mind.

---

396. Yanklowitz also takes issue with the term "non-Jew." He writes on Facebook, "I'd like to suggest we stop referring to a category of people as "non-Jews." There is no such group of collective identity consisting of "them," "the goyim." Each group has its own unique dignity. They are called Christians, Hindus, Muslims, atheists, Americans, nurses, neighbors, friends, etc. Furthermore I'm not a non-Christian or a non-Muslim." (https://www.facebook.com/rshmuly.yanklowitz/posts/10152869916766307?pnref=story. (August 5, 2015) Retrieved August 5, 2015.)

397. https://www.facebook.com/jeffreysfox/posts/10153470471869948?pnref=story. (July 14, 2015). Retrieved July 29, 2015.

In Fox's eyes, Judaism is not absolute, God given truth, but rather one flavor in an array of legitimate religious beliefs.

Interdenominational

Throughout Jewish history, movements have arisen which seek to re-create the Jew in a new image. Among the more popular movements have been the Sadducees and Karaites. These groups—which have all but vanished today—rejected the Oral Torah and rabbinic authority. In modern times, as well, the Reform, Conservative and Reconstructionist branches of Judaism preach similar views.

The Reform movement, which first gained a stronghold in Germany in the nineteenth century, denied the divinity of Torah. As Abraham Geiger, a founder of the movement, said, "The Talmud must go, the Bible, that collection of mostly so beautiful and exalted human books, as a divine work must also go."[398] The Conservative movement is an offshoot of the Reform Movement. Many Conservative Jews do not believe that the Torah was literally dictated by God. As one JTS Professor put it: "The biblical account of revelation is classic myth.... Torah then represents the canonical statement of our myth."[399] The Reconstructionist movement, an offshoot of Conservative, rejects the notion of God as a being.[400]

---

398. Michael A. Meyer, *Response to Modernity: A History of the Reform Movement in Judaism* (New York: Oxford University Press, 1988), p. 91. Cited by Rabbi Lawrence Kelemen http://www.simpletoremember.com/articles/a/reformconservativeorthodox/#9.

399. Neil Gillman, "What American Jews Believe" symposium, *Commentary* (August 1996), p. 23. Cited by Rabbi Lawrence Kelemen, *ibid.*

400. http://jewishrecon.org/resource/faqs-reconstructionist-approaches-jewish-ideas-and-practices. Retrieved July 22, 2015.

These movements champion beliefs that are antithetical to Torah Judaism. Orthodox Jews fervently believe that the Torah is both divine and eternal.

The opinion of Orthodoxy, as expressed by its leaders, has been to refrain from joining with non-Orthodox Jewish clergy. To do so would be to grant them legitimacy as representatives of authentic Judaism. Rabbi Joseph B. Soloveitchik expressed his view as follows: [401]

> It is my opinion that Orthodoxy cannot and should not unite with such groups which deny the fundamentals of our *weltanschauung*. It is impossible for me to comprehend, for example, how Orthodox rabbis, who spent their best years in *yeshivos* and absorbed the spirit of *Torah Shebaal Peh* and its tradition, for whom Rabbi Akiva, the Rambam, the Rema, the Gra, Rav Chaim Brisker and other Jewish Sages are the pillars upon which their spiritual world rests, can join with spiritual leaders for whom all this is worthless.... From the point of view of the Torah, we find the difference between Orthodox and Reform Judaism much greater than that which separated the *Perushim* and the *Tzedukim* in the days of *Bayis Sheini*, and between the *Kara'im* and traditionalists in the *Gaonic* era. Has Jewish history ever recorded an instance of a joint community council that consisted of *Kara'im* and Torah-true Jews?

401. From 1954 Yiddish article by Rabbi Soloveitchik in Der Tog Morgen Journal. Cited by Rabbi Avraham Gordimer. http://www.scribd.com/doc/233645350/Open-Orthodoxy-Outright-Heresy-and-the-Orthodox-Rebirth-of-the-Conservative-Movement#scribd, (p. 26). Retrieved July 22, 2015.

Open Orthodoxy does not share Rabbi Soloveitchik's view. As we will show, in some cases they seek the expansion of non-Torah Judaism and go as far as to praise non-Orthodox movements. They also provide platforms for their leaders to teach Torah. They embrace non-Orthodox denominations and grant these movements legitimacy as representatives of authentic Torah Judaism. The most sacred duty of an Orthodox rabbi is to faithfully teach and transmit the divine Torah. How can Orthodox leaders promulgate the teachings of movements which reject this most basic belief?

Rabbi Lopatin himself seeks the expansion of non-Orthodox forms of Judaism:[402]

> But my dream is to have Hebrew Union College, the Jewish Theological Seminary, Hadar, and Chovevei on one campus, to move in together. We'd each daven in our own ways, but it could transform the Upper West Side. I'm not talking about closing down campuses, because I want more Torah, not less. I want to hear different opinions. Disagreement is OK—I don't care if we come to a consensus, but put it all out there and continue the conversation.

He expresses his desire that Torah study, as taught by Reform and Conservative institutions, be expanded. Although the Reform and Conservative movements generally reject the eternal and divine nature of the Torah, Rabbi Lopatin inexplicably wishes for the growth of these movements.

---

402. http://www.tabletmag.com/jewish-life-and-religion/130760/the-new-morethodox-rabbi. Retrieved July 26, 2015.

Open Orthodox rabbis have gone even further in granting non-halachic movements legitimacy by encouraging the expansion of non-Orthodox practices. Rabbi Avi Weiss believes that the Reform and Conservative movements should be granted rights to perform conversions and wedding ceremonies in Israel:[403]

> Spiritual striving and religious growth can only be nourished in a spirit of openness. For this reason, Israel as a state should give equal opportunities to the Conservative and Reform movements. Their rabbis should be able to conduct weddings and conversions.

Not only does recognizing non-halachic weddings and conversions grant these movements legitimacy, it validates practices which the Torah does not recognize. Weddings and conversions are two of the most fundamental building blocks of Jewish identity. Anything but a halachically sound ceremony for each of these things can lead to terrible spiritual disarray within the community. Yet Open Orthodoxy is a proponent of granting Conservative and Reform officials this very right.

YCT graduates share the views of their leaders. They even go as far as to praise aspects of the Reform movement. Rabbeinu Yonah in *Shaarei Teshuvah* (3:148) explains, based on a verse in Proverbs (27:21), that a person's value system can be ascertained by seeing what he praises.

---

403. http://blogs.timesofisrael.com/end-the-chief-rabbinates-monopoly. Retrieved July 29, 2015.

Rabbi Saul Strosberg a YCT (Class of 2005) rabbi in Nashville, Tennessee, invited Reform Rabbis Mark Schiftan and Shana Goldstein Mackler to speak at his synagogue. Moreover, Rabbi Goldstein Mackler, who is Rabbi Strosberg's *chavrusa* (Torah-study partner), taught a class at the synagogue about the High Holy Days. A synagogue rabbi is responsible to accurately transmit Jewish tradition to his congregants. How could a Reform rabbi, who disagrees with the fundamentals of that tradition, be invited to share her perspective?

In addition, Rabbi Strosberg attended services at the Rabbis' Reform synagogue and delivered a sermon praising the rabbis as "colleagues" and "mentors."[404] In his sermon, he told the congregants that he wants "...to share with you some of the elements of Reform Judaism which I find appealing."[405] B

Strosberg continues by contrasting Orthodox Judaism's obligatory view of the commandments to Reform's opinion that they are voluntary. He praises the Reform perspective:[406]

But in Reform Judaism, the relationship seems different. One has the autonomy to choose those mitzvoth which one finds meaningful and compelling. Though I have a way of life integrated by Jewish law and tradition, there are many beautiful practices that I take for granted, that I don't think about much, that I perform by rote. On the other hand, given the autonomy to choose my commandments, and to integrate them in a way that

404. http://www.sherithisrael.com/events_messages.asp. "Friday Night at the Temple." Retrieved July 22, 2015.
405. *Ibid.*
406. *Ibid.*

is specifically meaningful to me, I have an incredible opportunity to feel connected, to become inspired, and to want grow.

Not only does Strosberg imply that the Reform approach is legitimate, he offers reasons why it is actually superior! How can an Orthodox rabbi praise an approach which views the Torah as non-authoritative?

Some have praised other aspects of the Reform movement. Rabbi Chai Posner, a 2010 graduate of YCT and the Alumni Representative to YCT's Board of Directors,[407] stated that the Orthodox "could learn a thing or two" from the new Reform prayer book. While he states that he is not advocating changing the *machzor*, he says the Reform prayer book is being heralded as the most "inclusive" prayer book yet. Examples he cites of its inclusivity are: referring to God in the feminine and replacing the phrase "bride and groom" with the word "couple."[408] C

Rabbi Shmuly Yanklowitz (YCT 2010) feels that one should learn from all denominations and that Orthodox Judaism has made some "stubborn mistakes." He writes:[409]

Reform Judaism grew by distancing itself from Orthodoxy's stubborn mistakes. Orthodoxy grew by distancing itself from Reform's radical mistakes. All

407. http://www.yctorah.org/content/view/22/49. Retrieved January 26, 2016.

408. http://www.bethtfiloh.com/ftpimages/230/download/download_1640332.pdf. Retrieved January 23, 2015.

409. https://www.facebook.com/rshmuly.yanklowitz?fref=ts. (July 23, 2015). Retrieved July 24, 2015.

denominations will thrive when they start learning from each other's strengths and not just their weaknesses! Do we all have the humility to fulfill the rabbinic teaching: "Who is Wise? One who can learn from everyone!"

It is unclear which "mistakes" Yanklowitz is referring to. The Reform movement has distanced itself from the profoundly Jewish belief in a divinely-given Torah. Does Rabbi Yanklowitz, ostensibly an Orthodox rabbi, consider this belief mistaken?

In July 2015, Rabbi Yanklowitz posted a picture of himself on Facebook with the first female Conservative Rabbi, Amy Eilberg. He writes:[410]

With my wonderful chavrusah, Rabbi Amy Eilberg (the courageous first woman ordained in the Conservative movement, a talmidah chachamah, a peace activist, educator, & just an ehrlicher Yid)!

He praises her as a *talmidah chachamah*, a Torah scholar. The praise of non-Orthodox rabbis is echoed by Rabbi Avram Mlotek (Class of 2015). He describes his feelings after being ordained, "I feel humbled in light of the great rabbis whose title I share with sincere trepidation."[411] Among the great rabbis he lists are Heschel (Former Professor at HUC and JTS-DR),[412] Kaplan, Shachter-Shalomi (Jewish Renewal-

---

410. https://www.facebook.com/rshmuly.yanklowitz?fref=ts. (July 23, 2015). Retrieved August 28, 2015.

411. http://www.thejewishweek.com/news/new-york/what-we-talk-about-when-we-talk-about-rabbis. Retrieved August 4, 2015.

412. https://www.jewishvirtuallibrary.org/jsource/biography/AHeschel2.html. Retrieved August 28, 2015.

DR), and Mychal Springer (Director of the Center of Pastoral Education JTS-DR).ᴰ He does not specify, but one suspects that he is referring also to Rabbi Mordechai Kaplan, founder of the Reconstructionist movement.[413] Shachter-Shalomi was known to praise the spiritual value of certain illegal drugs as well as Buddhism. He was also among the first rabbis to ordain women and accept homosexuals into his congregation.[414]

If these are the idols of Open Orthodox rabbis, is it surprising that they share similar views? And it is no less surprising that Open Orthodoxy's views, like those of these figures that they venerate, have moved beyond the pale of Orthodoxy.

Open Orthodox leaders also provide non-Orthodox rabbis with platforms to teach Torah. How can Orthodoxy encourage the teaching of non-Orthodox ideas? What significance is there to a Reform rabbi lecturing about the Jewish tradition if he believes that it is not ordained by God? This kind of thing is reminiscent of the world that Alice in Wonderland found when she fell down the rabbit hole: strange, illogical and intellectually topsy-turvey.

YCT and Yeshivat Maharat co-sponsored a community *beit midrash* program together with the Jewish Theological Seminary (Conservative), HUC-JIR (Reform), Pardes Institute, Drisha, and Mechon Hadar. The event's location rotated between the participating institutions.[415] Speakers at the program included

413. https://www.jewishvirtuallibrary.org/jsource/biography/kaplan. html. Retrieved August 28, 2015.

414. http://www.nytimes.com/2014/07/09/us/zalman-schachter-shalo- mi-jewish-pioneer-dies-at-89.html Retieved August 4, 2015.

415. http://www.yctorah.org/content/view/926/17/. Retrieved July 22, 2015. http://www.jtsa.edu/News/Press_Releases/JTS_to_Host_Com- munity_Night_Study_Sessions.xml. Retrieved January 29, 2016.

many non-Orthodox rabbis. Rabbi Mordechai Shwartz, a JTS ordained assistant Professor of Talmud and Rabbinics, delivered a lecture.[416] Other lecturers included, Noah Bickhart, a JTS adjunct professor of Talmud and Rabbinics, who spoke about "Sex and Freedom." Also, Amy Kalmanofsky, an associate professor of Bible at JTS, delivered a lecture entitled, "The Dangerous Sisters of the Torah."[417] At the Seminary, Kalmanofsky teaches a feminist interpretation of the Torah. As her bio on JTS's webpage states, "Feminist interpretation, she believes, enables the Bible to remain relevant and continues to open up the text to new interpretation and meaning."[418]

YCT also partnered with the Reconstructionist Rabbinical College, Interfaith Power and Light, and other institutions at the Sixth annual Pearlstone Beit Midrash retreat. Topics discussed at the retreat included "an in-depth exploration of Creation, one day at a time, using traditional texts to uncover contemporary issues and values."[419]

Graduates of YCT actively promote the teaching of non-Orthodox forms of Judaism. The Valley Beit Midrash is an organization which seeks to bring Jewish programming to the Phoenix, Arizona area. They aim to improve the "quality of Jewish Life" by, among other things, "teaching, modeling, and inspiring the value of pluralism."[420] It is led by Rabbi Shmuly Yanklowitz

416. http://www.yctorah.org/content/view/926/17/. Retrieved July 22, 2015.
417. http://www.jtsa.edu/News/Press_Releases/JTS_to_Host_Community_Night_Study_Sessions.xml. Retrieved January 29, 2016.
418. http://www.jtsa.edu/Academics/Faculty_Profiles/Amy_Kalmanofsky_Bio.xml?ID_NUM=13137. Retrieved July 22, 2015.
419. https://www.facebook.com/events/567842649976842.
420. https://www.valleybeitmidrash.org/about-us. Retrieved August 25, 2015.

(YCT 2010), its Executive Director. It has the approval of Open Orthodoxy's leadership as Rabbis Avi Weiss and Asher Lopatin serve on its advisory board. [421] On Facebook, Yanklowitz proudly boasts the diversity of the Beit Midrash's lecturers:[422]

> Thrilled about our amazing lineup at Valley Beit Midrash this year! We have more than doubled our intellectual pluralistic Jewish education program for the coming year! Higher & Higher!

Several Open Orthodox rabbis are featured as lecturers, such as Rabbi Avi Weiss, Rabbi Daniel Sperber, Rabbi Haggai Resnikoff (YCT 2014 and rebbe at YCT),[423] and Rabbi Steven Exler (YCT 2009). However, several Reform and Conservative rabbis also are scheduled to deliver lectures,[424] including the President of

---

421. https://www.valleybeitmidrash.org/about-us/leadership. Retrieved August 25, 2015.

422. https://www.facebook.com/rshmuly.yanklowitz?fref=ts (August 25, 2015). Retrieved August 25, 2015.

423. http://www.yctorah.org/content/view/23/49. Retrieved August 25, 2015.

424. Some of the speakers include:

- Rabbi Dovid Wolpe, Conservative (http://sinaitemple.org/about_us/index.php. Retrieved August 25, 2015.)
- Rabbi Ellie Spitz, Conservative (http://www.cbi18.org/about/clergy/rabbi. Retrieved August 25, 2015.)
- Rabbi Sherre Hirsch, Conservative (http://www.sherrehirsch.com/about-sherre-hirsch. Retrieved August 25, 2015.)
- Rabbi Aaron Panken, Reform (http://huc.edu/about/presidents-office/rabbi-aaron-d-panken-phd. Retrieved August 25, 2015.)
- Rabbi Rami Shapiro, Reform (http://www.rabbirami.com/bio. Retrieved August 25, 2015.)
- Rabbi Lawrence Kushner, Reform (http://www.spiritualityandpractice.com/explorations/teachers/view/72. Retrieved August 25, 2015.)

Hebrew Union College.[425] One Conservative Rabbi is speaking about "Jewish Views on the Afterlife: Does the Soul Survive?"[426] That someone who belongs to a movement that does not share the Orthodox view of Torah is given a platform to lecture about such a serious topic is troubling, to say the least.

Such pluralistic organizations are not unique in the world of Open Orthodoxy. In their September 2014 newsletter, YCT proudly touts "an impressive new initiative" started by an alumnus:[427]

> OpenSinai.com, a unique online Jewish learning resource founded by Rabbi Ben Greenberg (YCT 2009), has launched. Read more about this impressive new initiative and Rabbi Greenberg's goal to make Jewish learning more readily available around the world.

According to their website, OpenSinai.com seeks to "empower Jews throughout the world with access to real-time pluralistic Jewish learning."[428] It was jointly founded by Rabbi Greenberg, his wife, and Conservative Rabbi Rebecca Wolitz Sirbu. In addition to the seven Open Orthodox-affiliated spiritual leaders, educators include several Reform and Conservative Rabbis.[429]

---

425. http://huc.edu/about/presidents-office/rabbi-aaron-d-panken-phd. Retrieved August 25, 2015.

426. https://www.facebook.com/rshmuly.yanklowitz?fref=ts (August 25, 2015). Retrieved August 25, 2015.

427. http://myemail.constantcontact.com/News-from-YCT.html?-soid=1101152783508&aid=ifefSmYFWHg

428. http://www.opensinai.com/about.html. Retrieved July 22, 2015.

429. http://www.opensinai.com/meet-our-educators.html. Retrieved August 25, 2015. https://www.facebook.com/opensinai/photos_stream. Retrieved January 29, 2016.

The holidays are a special time for interdenominational events. For Tisha B'Av 2015, Rabbis Nissan Antine (YCT 2006 and President of the International Rabbinic Fellowship), Uri Topolosky (YCT 2005 and member of Yeshivat Maharat's advisory board),[430] and Shmuel Herzfeld (student of Rabbi Avi Weiss)[431] participated in a rabbinic panel with an Orthodox Sefardi rabbi, Conservative Rabbi Adam Raskin, and Reform Rabbi Susan Shankman.[432] For *Shavuos* 2015, Rabbi Ysoscher Katz participated in an interdenominational learning program at a Reform Synagogue.[433]

Interdenominational events are also routinely held on the synagogue level. Rabbi Zachary Truboff, a 2010 YCT graduate, serves as rabbi of the Cedar Road Synagoge in Cleveland, Ohio, and is the Secretary of the International Rabbinic Fellowship.[434] Rabbi Truboff invited Reform and Conservative rabbis to his synagogue to discuss the holiday of *Sukkos* and had each rabbi deliver a *dvar Torah*. At the event's conclusion Truboff declared, "The beauty of a sukkah is its inclusiveness."[435] Again, Judaism is all about unity. But when certain Jews break with some of the most sacred tenets of the Divinely-given Torah, this kind of inclusiveness gives them an undeserved stamp of legitimacy.

430. http://www.yeshivatmaharat.org/advisory-board. Retrieved August 19, 2015.

431. http://ostt.org/Rabbi_Herzfeld. Retrieved July 28, 2015.

432. https://www.facebook.com/photo.php?fbid=10153087385552613&set=a.10150119821532613.284712.530542612&type=1&theater. Retrieved July 28, 2015.

433. http://congregationbethelohim.org/shavuot2015 . Retrieved July 30, 2015.

434. http://www.internationalrabbinicfellowship.org/leadership. Retrieved February 1, 2016.

435. http://www.yctorah.org/component/option,com_docman/task,doc_view/gid,1424/

A 2009 Jewish Telegraph Agency article describes the collaboration of Rabbi Uri Topolosky, a 2005 YCT graduate, and Rabbi Robert Loewy of the Reform Gates of Prayer temple in New Orleans. It details how Rabbi Topolosky attended Reform services and joined in song with the congregation, and how the two rabbis study together and "bounce sermon ideas off each other."[436]

A YCT rabbi has even invited a Reform female rabbi to lead the prayers in his synagogue. A 2013 article in the *Forward* details how Rabbi Alice Goldfinger's career as a Reform rabbi ended when she suffered a traumatic brain injury. It goes on to describe how Rabbi Akiva Herzfeld, a 2007 graduate of YCT, invited her to help him lead the Friday night services. Herzfeld also praised her as a "religious leader."[437] However, he does admit that his actions go against tradition:

> They might say I'm not doing a good job preserving tradition, but it's more important to stand up for someone who needs you to stand up for them.

The article also records Rabbi Avi Weiss's reaction when told about his student's actions:

> As you speak, I am filled with pride and tears. You have given me one of my proudest moments. Judaism is not

---

436. http://www.jta.org/2009/08/31/life-religion/unusual-reform-orthodox-partnership-born-of-katrina-blossoms. Retrieved August 7, 2015.
437. http://forward.com/news/174706/maine-rabbis-injury-forges-remarkable-partnership. Retrieved, July 22, 2015.

just a system of the head, but a system of the heart. It's a balance, and Akiva gets it.

This is not a question of "head" versus "heart." This break with tradition for no compelling reason is certainly not a matter for pride. While it is imperative to help all Jews who are suffering, providing an ego boost for someone is insufficient reason to have a Reform female rabbi lead the services.

Not only do Open Orthodox rabbis seem to favor other denominations, some even display negative attitudes towards Orthodoxy. Rabbi Lopatin appeared on a panel sponsored by the Hartman Institute. He was asked about the challenges he faces in advancing an agenda within a community that is resistant to it. Lopatin responded that Orthodoxy is currently not a "moral beacon" and that the Orthodox community must champion certain "counter currents" and turn them into "currents." He spoke about advancements regarding the *agunah* issue and new policies towards homosexuals.[438 E] According to Rabbi Lopatin, Orthodox Judaism, which seeks to carry out the will of God, does not presently serve as a beacon of morality. By instituting liberal reforms, he mistakenly believes, Orthodoxy will regain its moral stature.

Non-Orthodox leaders seem to understand the significance of their acceptance by Open Orthodoxy. At Rabbi Asher Lopatin's installation as President of YCT, a rabbinic panel was convened featuring Rabbi David Ellison the Chancellor of Hebrew Union College (Reform), Rabbi Arnold Eisen Chancellor of the Jewish

---

438. https://www.youtube.com/watch?v=znehRqrAsTA. Retrieved August 7, 2015.

Theological Seminary (Consevative), Rabbi Elka Abrahamson, President, the Wexner Foundation and Rabbi Arthur Green, Ph.D., Rector of Hebrew College (Pluralistic). It appears that the significance of the event was not lost on the panelists. Rabbi Green commented:[439]

> We are all, I think, deeply honored by your invitation to us and the strong statement you make by having this panel here at this occasion. We are all very aware of it and very grateful to you.[440]

While all Jews should be respected and loved, it would be dishonest to claim that Orthodox Judaism does not have serious theological problems with the Reform, Conservative, and Reconstructionist movements. These differences are so basic to our core beliefs as Torah Jews that they must prevent us from joining and teaching with them. Open Orthodoxy's embrace, approval and encouragement of these movements does not strengthen Orthodoxy, but rather undermines it.

Open to Orthodoxy?

From its relations with non-Jews and non-Orthodox Jews, it would appear that Open Orthodoxy is living up to its goal of openness and inclusivity. YCT's website states that it is deeply committed to:[441]

439. https://www.youtube.com/watch?v=lu_0lP59Kyc. Retrieved July 26, 2015.
440. At the gathering, Rabbi Ellison quoted someone who said, "The Jews may have done better than God did in relation to the Holocaust."
441. http://www.yctorah.org/content/view/1/49. Retrieved August 7, 2015.

Affirming the shared covenantal bond between all Jews, promoting love of all Jews (*ahavat Yisrael*) and actively pursuing the positive and respectful interaction of all Jewish movements.

It seems, however, that YCT's "love of all Jews" does not extend to other Orthodox movements.

In a spirit which cannot be described as open or inclusive, Rabbi Ysoscher Katz denigrates an entire segment within the Orthodox community:[442 F]

The Kohanic leadership (the ultra-Orthodox of their time) were a quick-shoot, gun ready at any hint of dogmatic deviation. The Rabbis (the MO of their time), it seems, advocate a more gun-shy judiciary. Ultimately the Rabbis won, relegating Kohanic extremism to the dustbin of Jewish history. The moderate, gun-shy voice will prevail again, today.

According to him the "ultra-Orthodox" will inevitably be written out of existence because of their "quick-shoot" and "gun ready" attitudes.

In another such example of Open Orthodox inclusiveness, Rabbi Linzer compares a certain group of Orthodox Jews to the Biblical spies.[443] He begins his piece by contrasting leadership based on fear to leadership based on faith. He applies this concept to current groups within the Orthodox community:[444]

---

442. https://www.facebook.com/ysoscher?fref=ufi&pnref=story. (July 13, 2015) Retrieved July 30, 2015.

443. Numbers Chapter 13.

444. http://files.ctctcdn.com/49c02d16001/738edf3c-07f4-423d-91de-b6e03a280e62.pdf. Retrieved July 24, 2015.

This is one of the things that distinguishes Modern Orthodoxy. Orthodoxy has in many ways become a religion of fear....

He continues that the fear in the Orthodox world has caused some to rely on the guidance of "a *Gadol* and his *da'as Torah*." He compares this approach to that of the spies whose fear made them want to return to Egypt:

> For some, the answer to this is to have communal issues decided by a *Gadol* and his *da'as Torah*, to say: "Is it not better for us to return to Egypt? Perhaps we were slaves in Egypt, but everything was secure and predictable. In Egypt, someone else did the thinking for us." This is leadership of fear, a *Yiddishkeit* destined to stay in the desert and never go into the Promised Land.

While Open Orthodoxy embraces non-Orthodox Jews, other groups within Orthodoxy are identified with one of the most tragic stories in the Torah. He claims that seeking advice from a *Gadol*, or great Torah sage, is an attitude based on fear. *Da'as Torah* means seeking guidance from Torah scholars who have spent their lives dedicated to the service of God and learning His will. For someone who lives his life based on Torah values and may be unsure if the Torah has a view on a certain issue, the logical thing to do is to seek the counsel of a sage who is an expert in the field. According to Linzer this is "leadership of fear" and is a slave mentality. Is it a slave mentality for someone with a medical issue to seek out a specialist?

Earlier we mentioned that Rabbi Lopatin seeks the expansion of non-Orthodox rabbinical schools. While he seeks the expansion of these institutions, others actually criticize Orthodox *yeshivos*. On YCT's promotional video, Rabbi Linzer says:[445]

> It is almost nonexistent where in a traditional yeshiva they are asking: How does this relate to my religious life? How is this meaningful to me? How is this meaningful to others?

According to Linzer, students of classical *yeshivos*, which have sustained Judaism for 200 years, do not apply what they learn to their daily lives. As anyone who has studied in a classical yeshiva can attest, this claim is totally baseless. The discourse in *yeshivos* is absolutely geared toward relating one's learning to one's life. *Yeshivos* are not ivory towers filled with airy intellectuals debating theories for intellectual stimulation. Rather, yeshiva students devote themselves energetically to seeking out the meaning and relevancy of every page of Talmud and every line of *mussar* that they learn.

Rabbi Katz goes so far as to accuse an entire yeshiva of being unsophisticated. He claims that the Brisk yeshiva is unsophisticated when it comes to theology. He continues that "Litvish" theology is "simplistic" and "impersonal." When his life hit a bump he says, "all that Torah was useless."[446] [G] Remarkably, such criticism is only reserved for the "ultra Orthodox"

---

445. https://www.youtube.com/watch?v=j2o8oKMrtUw.
446. https://www.facebook.com/ysoscher?fref=ufi&pnref=story. (July 28, 2015). Retrieved August 28, 2015.

population. Does Rabbi Katz ever speak publicly about the Reform and Conservative movements in such negative terms?

In summary, Open Orthodoxy wholeheartedly embraces non-Jewish and non-Orthodox movements, while denigrating other forms of Orthodoxy. While it is good to engage in constructive criticism, it is hypocritical to flaunt an openness that is not open to all. By their choice of whom to support and whom to criticize, proponents of Open Orthodoxy have made their loyalties all too clear.

9

Biblical Interpretation

As has been shown, personal and societal values impact the way Open Orthodox rabbis see Judaism. It clouds their interpretation of Jewish law and perception of Biblical commandments,[447] and has prompted many of them to criticize the Sages of the Talmud of immorality, particularly of misogyny.[448]

The fealty to external values also impacts the way they interpret Biblical stories. While Orthodox Jews have always understood the Bible in the context of the Oral Tradition as transmitted through the Sages, many Open Orthodox leaders interpret the Bible with their own definition of values and morality. This approach has produced some novel interpretations. Abraham is accused of failing the test of the *Akeidah*[449] while Korach[450] and the spies are deemed to have

---

447. See Chapter 5.
448. See Chapter 7.
449. http://morethodoxy.org/2010/10/12/did-abraham-fail-his-final-test-by-rabbi-hyim-shafner. Retrieved July 25, 2015.
450. https://www.facebook.com/ysoscher?fref=ts. (June 20, 2014). Retrieved August 31, 2015.

been correct.[451] That this approach is not Orthodox is an understatement.

Not only do Open Orthodox rabbis treat the Sages of the Talmud with disrespect, they even venture to criticize the Torah's most revered figures. Using modern notions of ethics and morality as their yardstick, Open Orthodox rabbis attribute major character flaws and errors to Torah personalities. Traditionally, as with any part of the written Torah, Jews have understood the lives of these angelic individuals through the interpretation of the Sages and the Oral Torah. When the Sages speak about shortcomings of Torah figures, it is only that they did not a attain perfection of some elevated trait.[452] However many Open Orthodox rabbis claim that Biblical figures suffered emotional and social problems or were harsh and unfeeling persons.

Moses and the Desert Experience

Moses is described in the Torah as the humblest of all men. As the verse testifies, *And the man Moses was exceedingly humble, more than any man on the face of the earth* (Numbers 12:3). The Rambam describes Moses' special relationship with God as a connection which no other human in the history of mankind has ever experienced. He achieved greater knowledge of God

---

451. https://www.facebook.com/ysoscher?fref=ts. (July 31, 2014). Retrieved September 1, 2015.

452. For instance Joseph remained in jail two extra years for asking the cupbearer to remember him; see Rashi to Genesis (40:23). His offense was only that he did not obtain an elevated level of faith in God.

than any other person who ever lived. It is even counted as an article of faith that every Jew (must) believe in this unique relationship.[453] A

However, Open Orthodox leaders manage to find fault with Moses' character and leadership. With regard to his sin of hitting the rock,[454] Rabbi Linzer claims:[455] B

> For each one of these things shows that Moshe is still the leader of old and is not able to adapt to the changes ahead.... If after all this time Moshe still sees the people as incorrigible rebels who can only be beaten into submission, then it is time that Moshe step back and allow a new leader to take over.

According to Linzer, Moses was morally deficient, a visionary whose vision had failed. (For examples of accurate explanations of this episode see the commentaries of the Rambam[456] and Ramban *ad loc.*) [457]

Linzer also criticizes Moses's leadership skills in the handling of Korach's rebellion. Moses' failure as a leader seems to be a common theme in Linzer's writings. After describing mistakes Moses made in his dealings with the rebellion he writes:[458] C

---

453. Rambam, Comentary to the Mishnah, *Sanhedrin*, Chapter 10.
454. Numbers, Chapter 20.
455. http://origin.library.constantcontact.com/download/get/file/1101152783508-960/Section1-NL0004-Parasha-REV.pdf
456. Chapter 4 in his introduction to *Avos*.
457. Numbers (20:8).
458. http://rabbidovlinzer.blogspot.com/search/label/Parshat%20Korach. Retrieved August 29, 2015.

In the end, he demands a showdown with one ultimate winner and one ultimate loser. And the consequences were drastic and deadly—truth won out, but at the expense of completely destroying the other side. This is one way of approaching conflict, but it is not the only way, and it is not necessarily the way that will lead to the best results. Such an approach focuses on a narrow, abstract, truth, but not on the deeper truth of human beings, of human emotions and motivations, of societal realities and of inter-personal relationships. Such an approach can at times even be quite counter-productive.

According to Linzer, Moses did not handle the conflict with Korach in the best way possible—a way to which God Himself acceded—but rather in a way that Linzer deems "counter-productive." Linzer even validates the position of Korach, "It is hard not to hear an echo of Korach's claim that 'All the people are holy and the Lord is in their midst' (16:3)."

As any beginner student of the Bible knows, Moses was victorious and Korach and his followers descended into the depths. Rabbi Ysoscher Katz, however, maintains that the battle still rages on:[459] D

Over 3,000 years later and we still haven't solved the debate between Moshe and Korach. Moshe advocated

---

459. https://www.facebook.com/ysoscher?fref=ts. (June 20, 2014). Retrieved August 31, 2015.

a centralized model of leadership, while Korach advocated an egalitarian, lay-led model: *Ki kol ha'eidah kulam kedoshim, u'be'tocham Hashem....*

Katz goes on to claim that Korach's vision is actually the correct one, and that in the World to Come his vision will be embraced. This shocking claim is questioned by someone on his Facebook page, "Well, Korach got swallowed up into the bowels of the earth, so not sure how anyone can say his approach was better...." Katz responds, "...one gets punished for espousing the right idea prematurely."[460]

Katz maintains that Korach's position—an egalitarian approach congruous to the position championed by Open Orthodoxy—is "the right idea."[461] It speaks volumes that one of Open Orthodoxy's most vocal leaders equates the movement's own egalitarian mission with that of Korach.

Not only are Moses's leadership skills called into question, but Rabbi Ysoscher Katz goes a step further. He claims that the Sages criticized Moses's views and portrayed him as "confused." Under a picture of Michelangelo's statue of Moses, Katz writes on Facebook that the Rabbis viewed Moses as a "confused and

---

460. *Ibid.* (Comment to the same post.)
461. This book has shown in great detail Open Orthodoxy's commitment to egalitarianism in its practices regarding women and its relations with non-Orthodox and non-Jewish movements (see Chapter 8). As mentioned in Chapter 7, a post on Yeshivat Maharat's Facbook page reads, "This is the vision – "If the change agents within Orthodoxy become educators, role models and leaders of the next generation of modern Orthodox Jews, successfully pass on their commitment to both Halacha and egalitarianism, and continue to live a life committed to Jewish law, they could transform the face of modern Orthodoxy (https://www.facebook.com/Yeshivatmaharat?fref=ts. (January 24, 2014, retrieved July 24, 2015).

flummoxed philosopher" and that they categorized his views as "conservative" and "archaic." This approach, as irreverent and erroneous as it is, is the one which he says he prefers. [462 E]

A contrasting post (the very next one) serves to highlight Rabbi Katz's views. In it, Katz is considerably more charitable toward Leonard Nimoy, a famous Jewish actor, than he is toward Moses. Nimoy created controversy in 2002 when he published a book of his artistic photographs called *Shekinah*.[463] His pictures included nude women wearing *tallis* and *tefillin*. Katz praises him as an artist.[464 F] In a truly remarkable confusion of values, Rabbi Katz views the greatest Jew of all time as confused and outdated, while he praises the artistry of a man who published perverse photographs and defiled religious objects.

In a similar expression of these sentiments, Rabba Hurwitz blames Moses for the sin of the blasphemer (Leviticus 24):[465]

Even though the *ben isha Yisraelit* clearly saw himself as Jewish, others were unwilling to accept him. The *ben isha Yisraelit* takes his case to Moshe, seeking out empathy from another Jew who also grew up as an outsider in Egypt. However, Moshe ruled in favor of Dan, and the *ben isha Yisraelit*, angry and dejected, responds by blaspheming God's name.

462. https://www.facebook.com/ysoscher?fref=ts. (February 25, 2015) Retrieved July 24, 2015.

463. https://celebrity.yahoo.com/blogs/celeb-news/leonard-nimoy-photography-legacy-controversy-191709616.html. Retrieved September 16, 2015.

464. https://www.facebook.com/ysoscher?fref=ts (February 27, 2015).

465. http://hosted-p0.vresp.com/1015677/52ed4e64e1/ARCHIVE. Retrieved July 24, 2015.

Moses is portrayed as insensitive and callous. While she's at it, Rabba Hurwitz also finds fault with the Jewish people:[466]

> Perhaps if the community had embraced the *ben isha Yisraelit,* rather than pushed him away—if they had welcomed him, sat next to him in *shul,* shown him the correct place in the *siddur*—he might not have been compelled to blaspheme God's name.

She also posits that the blasphemer's stoning was actually an atonement for the people's sin in not accepting him into the community. (While she admits that it is hard to read this interpretation into the text, she suggests that there was a holy aspect to the stoning since it is comparable to the scapegoat of Yom Kippur.)[467] Hurwitz blames Moses and the Jewish people for their lack of openness and inclusiveness. This is not surprising as these values are the sacred cows of Open Orthodoxy. Hurwitz is a prime example of someone interpreting Torah through the lens of her own values.

Rabbi Herzl Hefter goes as far to say that the Sages believed that Moses and the Sanhedrin were the "oppressors" and "villains" of the story.[468] [G]

Rabbi Katz also has novel interpretations of other Biblical stories. He maintains that, because of recent tragedies in Israel, the spies were correct in not wanting to enter the land of Israel.

---

466. *Ibid.*
467. https://www.youtube.com/watch?v=19HS4H3pje8. Retrieved July 26, 2015.
468. http://blogs.timesofisrael.com/a-way-forward-and-what-does-the-lord-ask-of-you. Retrieved January 22, 2015.

He begins by asking. "Was Middle Eastern geopolitics Moses' blind spot?" He continues:[469]

> For me, the dialogue between Moses and the spies has now become more difficult to understand. Given what has been transpiring here the last couple of weeks (and years), one wonders why Moses, the "loving shepherd," was so angry at the spies' reportage. It turns out that their description of Israel as a land which is אוכלת יושביה was correct; this land indeed has an insatiable cannibalistic appetite, voraciously consuming its inhabitants. Turns out their prognosis was indeed true; why then did Moses condemn them? This land's cadaver lust appears insatiable, its blood thirst unquenchable. The poet pleads ארץ אל תכסי דמם!

Katz affirms that the report of the spies was correct. The fact that, the Jewish people were condemned by God to wander the desert for 40 years after believing this report seems not to bother him at all. God's wrath is rendered irrelevant. For Katz, apparently, his view on current events supersedes the Written Torah.

The *Avos*

Open Orthodox criticism is not only reserved for Moses, but for our forefathers as well. In this regard there seem to be two types of Open Orthodox rabbis. Some believe that the *avos* did

---

469. https://www.facebook.com/ysoscher?fref=ts. (July 31, 2014). Retrieved September 1, 2015.

not exist,[470] while others believe that they existed but made critical mistakes.

It is in the merit of the forefathers that the Jewish People exists today. Their outstanding character traits and their individual approaches to serving God form the foundation of our own national temperament. None of this, however, prevents Open Orthodox rabbis from presenting these giants as misfits who suffered from a host of psychological and emotional problems.

For example, Jewish tradition teaches that Abraham displayed ultimate obedience to God by attempting to sacrifice his son, Isaac. Much of Jewish liturgy revolves around our plea for God to have mercy on His people in the merit of Abraham's success in passing this formidable test.

Rabbi Hyim Shafner, who sits on the board of the International Rabbinic Fellowship[471] and the advisory board of Yeshivat Maharat,[472] apparently fails to see Abraham's accomplishment as a success at all. He questions whether Abraham was correct in attempting to sacrifice his innocent son. In a post entitled, "Did Abraham Fail his Final Test?" he concludes:[473]

> Perhaps, on some level in the narrative of the *Akeidah*, Abraham failed the test. I would suggest this is why God never speaks to Abraham after commanding him to take Isaac as a burnt offering.

---

470. See Chapter 4.

471. http://www.internationalrabbinicfellowship.org/leadership. Retrieved August 19, 2015.

472. http://www.Yeshivatmaharat.org/advisory-board. Retrieved August 19, 2015.

473. http://morethodoxy.org/2010/10/12/did-abraham-fail-his-final-test-by-rabbi-hyim-shafner. Retrieved July 25, 2015.

The Torah contradicts Shafner's claim. After Abraham demonstrates that he is prepared to sacrifice his son if that is God's wish, an angel of God stops him and says: *For now I know you are a God fearing man, since you have not withheld your son, your only one, from Me* (Genesis 22:12). According to the verse and Jewish tradition, Abraham passed this test with flying colors. This attribute of self-sacrifice was transmitted to his descendants for eternity, giving them the strength to sacrifice their lives for God. But Shafner concludes that the message of the story is that perhaps the world would be a better place if we would disobey God's command and protect an innocent child. The real test was for Abraham to say "no" to God.[474]

Rabba Sara Hurwitz echoes Shafner's sentiments about the *Akeidah*:[475]

The sacrifice of Isaac, however, I would like to suggest, is sacrifice without purpose. Avraham's willingness to sacrifice Yitzchak went too far, and therefore could not be a sacrifice with the intent to bring about change.... Avraham hasn't just changed his name, as Rambam may have suggested he should do. Rather, he has become utterly unrecognizable, losing his essence, his moral intuition. Avraham was willing to sacrifice. But he transcended the normative expectations for giving something up. He went too far.

474. *Ibid.*

475. http://static1.squarespace.com/static/5348363de4b0531dce75bc53/
t/537e1dade4b0a676a00c4fc7/1400774061504/Rabba-Sara-
Hurwitz-Rosh-Hashana-2013-final.pdf. Retrieved August 29, 2015.

She continues that we should not learn from Abraham's example, and echoes Rabbi Shafner's contention that because of Abraham's mistake, God does not speak to him again:[476]

> We must make a sacrifice that brought us *"tefillat* Chana" the prayer of Chana whose formulation evolved into the *amidah*, the *Shemoneh Esrai* that we recite today. Not the sacrifice of Avraham that resulted in God's silence, in a God that did not speak directly to Avraham again.

She confidently asserts—in glaring contradiction to an explicit verse and millennia-old Jewish tradition—that Abraham was wrong and went "too far" in attempting to sacrifice Isaac, and insists that we not learn from his example.

One member of Yeshivat Mahrat's administration goes even further, illogically claiming that it was God who failed the test of the *Akeidah*. During a panel discussion, Dr. Erin Smokler, Yeshivat Maharat's Director of Spiritual Development,[477] presented her view of this episode:[478]

> ...While this was a test for Avraham, there was a learning curve for God as well. So there seems to me in my read that God set out to test, assuming success, but it turned out that God has to learn along the way that there are actual dangers in this kind of universe.

476. *Ibid.*

477. http://www.yeshivatmaharat.org/faculty-and-staff.

478. Dr. Erin Smokler, "Reading and Rereading the Akedah: Ethics, Submission and Serving God," October 15, 2013. http://www.yctorah.org/component/option,com_docman/task,cat_view/gid,201/Itemid,13/. Retrieved February 26, 2016.

So why would God test at all? Maybe it was a sport that God used to be into. It seems to me that God has to learn that it wasn't the best sport at all. So when you ask the question did Avraham fail the test back there. I think that in a sense you'll forgive the irreverence here for those who find this blasphemous. I think in a sense it was God who failed the test here....

She absurdly suggests that God tested Abraham for "sport" and that he has to "learn that it wasn't the best sport at all." [479] These views, which can only be termed blasphemous, elicited no condemnation from Rabbi Dov Linzer who was also present.

Apart from taking issue with the *Akeidah*, some Open Orthodox rabbis also call into question Abraham's parenting skills. Rabbi Linzer writes:[480]

When Avraham was out calling in the name of God and building alliances, he wasn't spending much time at home....

He maintains that the *Akeidah* was a metaphor for Abraham sacrificing his parental duties:

Every day, Avraham sacrificed his paternal responsibilities to Yitzchak fro his mission, for his calling.

---

479. See Chapter 4 where we cite Smokler's statement that "Moshe taught God (whom he had only just met) a profound lesson about humanity...."

480. http://rabbidovlinzer.blogspot.com/search/label/Parshat%20Toldot. Retrieved August 29, 2015.

He writes that some would argue that he should have been a "better father" and that, "we never see his love for Yitzchok." Rabbi Linzer's insight into Abraham's parenting abilities have not a shred of basis in the Torah. They are a total invention. Linzer denigrates the founder of our faith with baseless conjecture grafting his own bias onto the Biblical story.

A father ignoring his son seems to be another popular theme in Rabbi Linzer's writings. According to him, not only was Abraham a neglectful parent, it seems that this trait was passed down to Isaac. He says that Jacob was "unloved" by his father and was a "loner."[481] [H] He proceeds to psychoanalyze Jacob and posits that he overcompensated for his shortcomings through his mode of dress:[482]

> Yaakov never lets anyone see his vulnerabilities. He has cloaked himself in Esav's clothes—the clothes of the strong, independent, fearless hunter—so that no one can see the Yaakov, the not-always strong, not-always confident, herder of sheep who lies underneath.

It is amazing that Linzer is able to muster such unbased insights into the inner psyche of Jacob. As if this is not enough, he adds that this emotional immaturity caused him to be callous to his wife. Eschewing the interpretations of the classic commentators,

---

481. http://rabbidovlinzer.blogspot.com/search/label/Parshat%20 VaYishlach. Retrieved August 29, 2015.
482. *Ibid.*

he calls into question Jacob's ability to relate to others.[483] Rabbi Linzer goes on to claim that, while Jacob was able to handle life when things went well, he could not handle adversity:[484]

> To project such strength is great when everything works out, like it does in the beginning of our *parashah*—it is Yaakov's strategy, Yaakov's coordinating, his actions and no one else's that save them from Esav. But what about the times when he can't handle it all himself? At those times, he is unable to turn to others and he is paralyzed.

He goes on to say that Jacob could not let others see his vulnerabilities, that he lashed out, was unfeeling and "paralyzed." It is unclear where Rabbi Linzer has gained such insight into the mind of our forefather Jacob. Where are the *midrashim* and teachings of *Chazal* to back up his claims? Apart from the disrespect with which he treats the subject matter, he lays little or no foundation of proof for any of his opinions.

Not only do they ignore the explanations given by the classic commentators, some even treat their explanations with disdain. The Torah says, *Dinah the daughter of Leah whom she had borne to Jacob went out to see the daughters of the land* (Genesis 34:1). Rashi comments that she is called the daughter of Leah since she is also one who "goes out" as it says, *And Leah went out to greet him* (Genesis 30:16). Maharat Rori Picker Neiss (Yeshivat Maharat 2014) comments that "In no uncertain terms, Rashi is saying that Dinah bears, at the very least, some of the blame

---

483. *Ibid.*
484. *Ibid.*

for her attack." With no basis, she claims that Rashi is blaming Dinah for her abduction. Picker Neiss also calls his comments "incredibly troubling and deeply painful." [485] She portrays Rashi as a sexist with a blame-the-victim mentality.

Rashi is not the only one portrayed as a sexist. In an article posted on Yeshivat Maharat's website, a current student even accuses Abraham of exploiting Sarah's sexuality. Such an interpretation belies an ignorance of the simple meaning of the verse.[486]

Open Orthodox rabbis write about biblical figures as though they were mentally or morally deficient people with emotional issues. That Orthodox Jews have always displayed the utmost reverence for them, and have only understood them through the lens of the Sages, seems not to matter to the leaders of this movement. They interpret Biblical stories with a jaundiced eye, ascribing their own values and deficiencies to the holiest of people and outdoing each other with outrageous interpretations.

485. http://www.myjewishlearning.com/the-torch/the-violation-of-di-nah-the-violation-of-our-society/#. Retrieved August 31, 2015.
486. http://static.squarespace.com/static/5348363de4b0531dce75b-c53/t/5453ac44e4b024a86e8b5d17/1414769732248/Parshat-LechLechaHagarandSaraiAbuseDvar.pdf. Retrieved February 27, 2016.

10

Conclusion

Deviant movements are not new to the Jewish people. Many have arisen throughout our history, seeking to reshape the Jew in the modern image by replacing the morals of Torah with those of society. At the time, these groups appeared to be Judaism's future—yet, as history has shown repeatedly, those unfaithful to true Torah never endure.

Open Orthodoxy is merely the most recent of these movements. Its adherents reject core Jewish beliefs and embrace whatever happens to be popular at the moment in the secular world. Torah and Jewish Law are viewed as obstacles which must be overcome in order to advance their agenda. However, while Open Orthodoxy's predecessors clearly stated who they were, this movement has a fraudulent name. It is perhaps the first movement to call itself "Orthodox" while simultaneously rejecting Orthodox beliefs. With their dishonest name, this wolf in sheep's clothing is poised to dupe well-meaning Jews into following in its misguided ways.

The Rambam lists beliefs which are outside the pale of Torah Judaism. Unfortunately, as we have shown, many Open Orthodox leaders champion these views and beliefs.

The Rambam writes that someone who claims that even one letter of the Torah is not from God is considered a *kofer*, or denier of Torah. In Chapter 4, we showed that Rabbi Zev Farber has expressed the view that the Torah has multiple authors and that Biblical characters are "folkloristic." He writes that the stories of Creation, Adam and Eve, Noah's Flood, the Tower of Babel, the Exodus, the journey through the desert and Joshua's conquest of Israel were all fictional. These comments elicited no condemnation from YCT.

Rabbi Ysoscher Katz writes that whether God "factually" wrote the Torah is immaterial, and declares that the story of the Exodus "happened in the Torah," implying that whether it factually happened is irrelevant. Also, after accusing the Bible of racism and misogyny, he writes that he favors "excising or updating" troublesome parts of the Jewish texts. Rabbi David Almog writes that whether or not the Revelation at Sinai happened does not impact his experience of "the sweetness and goodness of Torah". Daniel Goodman, a student at YCT, claims that the Bible had multiple writers. Rabbi Lopatin cites an article by Rabbi Herzl Hefter which posits that "we do not have access to certainty or objective truth," and that "refined moral convictions and religious sensibilities may be considered a form of divine revelation." Lopatin, rather than condemn this view, goes so far as to praise the writer as a "first-rate *talmid chacham*" and a "great man."

The Rambam also declares that the Torah cannot be added to or subtracted from, yet in Chapter 4 we cited Rabbi Linzer's bold claim that, "We have erased not Amalek, but the mitzvah to destroy them."

According to the Rambam, one who does not believe in the validity of the Oral Law is a *kofer*. In Chapter 4 we quoted Rabbi Linzer, who affirms a belief that the Talmud should not be taught as objective truth, and Rabbi Katz, who questions the Talmud's relevance. In Chapter 7 we showed that Rabba Melanie Landau writes in her book—which is touted on Yeshivat Maharat's webpage—that she experiences "ambivalence about the binding nature of the tradition."

Also, rejected is the entire idea of the Oral Law. As opposed to unbiased transmitters of Torah, the Sages are viewed as reflecting the archaic values of their times. In Chapter 7 we cited many Open Orthodox leaders who claim that the Sages were male chauvinists seeking to promote a sexist agenda. Rabba Melanie Landau describes feeling pain in her body over the marginalization of the feminine in Jewish texts, and views the use of defiled women as metaphors for the Temple's Destruction in Lamentations as misogynistic. Rabbi Katz believes misogyny is intrinsic to Jewish texts, including *Tanach*. The blessing established by the Rabbis of "*shelo asani isha*" according to Rabbi Ari Hart, evokes "sexism"; Rabbi Yosef Kanefsky declares that reciting it constitutes a desecration of God's name. Rabbi Zev Farber also claims that the Rabbis relegated women to second-class status in the synagogue.

In addition to being critical of the Sages, Open Orthodox leaders are also critical of Torah personalities. In Chapter 9 we discussed several troublesome statements made by Open Orthodox leaders. Rabbi Katz claims that the Rabbis viewed Moses as "confused" and "flummoxed" and his legal views as "conservative" and "archaic." Rabbi Hyim Shafner and Rabba Hurwitz criticize Abraham for binding Isaac, while Dr. Smokler claims that God failed the test. Rabbi Linzer criticizes Abraham and Isaac for their parenting abilities and accuses Jacob of having emotional issues. Rabba Hurwitz also implicitly blames Moses for the sin of the blasphemer.

The Rambam writes that the twelfth principal of faith is to believe that the Messiah will come and that one who belittles this fact is a *kofer*. In Chapter 4 we quoted Rabbi Shmuly Yanklowitz, who rejects the notion of the Messiah as a person, affirms the position that the rebuilding of the Temple is of little importance, and says that the Jews are better off in exile.

The Rambam also writes that God does not have human attributes. In Chapter 4 we cited Rabbi David Kalb, who claims that God "has issues" and is lonely. Also, Dr. Smokler makes the illogical claim that Moses taught God.

In addition to holding views which are considered beyond the pale of accepted belief, other troublesome views are also being preached by proponents of Open Orthodoxy.

In Chapter 5 we showed that, following in the footsteps of the Reform and Conservative movements, Open Orthodoxy views Jewish Law as an obstacle which must be overcome and reconciled with modern values. Rabbi Linzer asks if "we should be bending the halakha to conform to our modern notions of egalitarianism." This view has prompted him to encourage Jews to help rebuild churches. Rabbi Akiva Herzfeld speaks disparagingly of the "wall of religious textual evidence," and Rabbi Ysoscher Katz refers to the "terror of religiosity" and the need to "cajole the tradition to reconcile itself with our modern sensibilities."

We have also shown the antipathy towards the Torah itself. Rabbi Katz labels the commandment of Sotah "capricious and patriarchal" and deems the Torah's view of divorcees insulting. Rabbi Linzer feels the commandment to destroy Amalek is immoral, while Rabbi Zev Farber says several commandments are "ethically problematic." Rabbi Hart claims that the Sages viewed certain commandments as "morally challenging," while Rabbi Yanklowitz even decries parts of Jewish tradition as "evil."

A hallmark of Orthodoxy is its faithfulness to its tradition and its customs. In Chapter 7 we described innovations suggested by Rabbi Linzer to make the Jewish wedding more egalitarian, Rabba Dr. Landau's proposal of new forms of egalitarian marriage, the ordaining of women and the erasure of the blessing "*shelo asani isha*."

In Chapter 6 we discussed Open Orthodoxy's widespread approval of same-sex marriage, with Rabbi Sperber even entertaining the possibility of Orthodox rabbis performing such ceremonies. Rabbi Katz and Rabbi Farber have gone on to legitimize certain same-sex relations.

In Chapter 8, we demonstrated Open Orthodoxy's embrace of non-Jewish and non-Orthodox movements. Rabbi Avi Weiss refers to a church as a "holy place" and has Christian choirs perform in his synagogue. Rabbis Lopatin, Herman, and Antine attended a conference where rabbis and cardinals danced in front of a golden statue of the Pope. Rabbi Hanan Shlesinger ponders how his Ramadan will affect his Tisha B'Av, and a YCT student lists "Zen Buddism" as one of his interests. YCT and Open Orthodox rabbis regularly participate in interdenominational events. Rabbi Lopatin wishes for an expansion of non-Orthodox rabbinic institutions. Open Orthodox rabbis consistently provide forums for Reform and Conservative clergy to teach Torah. In addition, Rabbi Saul Strosberg praises Reform Judaism and invites Reform rabbis to teach in his synagogue.

In Chapters 3 and 7, we highlighted the sub-par *semichah* programs at Yeshivat Chovevei Torah and Yeshivat Maharat. We pointed out the lack of scholarship and dishonesty displayed in their leaders' halachic writings. In Rabbi Fox's responsum, he cites portions of Rabbi Ovadia Yosef's opinion yet neglects to quote him when Rabbi Yosef's opinions are different from his own. Rabbi Linzer also misrepresents the view of Rabbi Moshe Feinstein in order to advance his own agenda. Rabbi Katz went so far as to invent an opinion out of thin air to achieve his halachic goal. In Chapter 6 we demonstrated how Rabbi Farber erroneously claims that the concept of *ein kishui elah la-daas* is a dispute amongst the medieval commentators, when it is actually an explicit Talmudic passage. Rabba Hurwitz believes that Jews should not discourage converts, a view opposed by the Talmud. She also states that "there is no Halacha against women putting on *tefillin* and *tallis*," though the Rema says we should protest this practice. She even accuses the Rabbis of orchestrating the idea of *get*, which oppresses women, even though it is a verse in Deuteronomy.

Therefore, we are forced to conclude that the beliefs and practices of Open Orthodoxy are, in fact, not Orthodox. One who seeks to live by the Orthodox tradition should not follow their leaders, but seek guidance elsewhere.

The influence that this movement is having on Orthodox Jewry cannot be overlooked. Open Orthodox leaders serve as synagogue rabbis across the country, many of them in towns with small Jewish communities, where there are few if any other Orthodox synagogues, making them the sole representatives of Torah Judaism in those areas.

Perhaps even more unsettling are the educational positions held by Open Orthodox rabbis. Many are teachers in Orthodox schools where they transmit Torah to the next generation. They are also the representatives of Torah Judaism on college campuses.[487] Members of a movement which rejects basic Torah beliefs are charged with educating potentially thousands of impressionable young Jews. That this movement could potentially transmit a distorted Judaism to the next generation is alarming, to say the least.

While many Jews throughout the ages have fallen prey to the onslaught of assimilation and been led astray by various movements, the Jewish people as a nation has always endured. As the chosen nation of God, we are charged with the mission of bringing His message to the world and, as such, we will never be destroyed. Jews have remained faithful to that message against all odds and it is certain that they will ultimately recognize

---

487. http://www.yctorah.org/images/yct%20bragflyer%20layout%20 frontback%20final%207-23-14%20%283%29.pdf. Retrieved August 28, 2015.

Open Orthodoxy for what it is. May we all continue to follow Hashem in observance of authentic Torah tenets, and may our lives be a sanctification of the Name of God always.

Endnotes

Chapter 3

A. Originally cited on p. 61:

In the end of the day the reason I could write that *teshuvah* and I'd like to say its hard work, and in some ways it is hard work. But it isn't. I mean I've been trained since I was... I mean I'm 47. You know I went to Satmar. We obviously skipped *Tanach* because *Tanach* is for *Maskilim*. Mishnah is for lightweights. So we just get to *Gemara* right away. So when I was seven, I started learning *Gemara* and here I am 40 years later not doing anything else because I can't do anything else. So In some ways it's pretty easy for me to write a *teshuvah*. I can think of that of that Rosh I can think of that Rema, you know, and frankly if you read my *teshuvah* I kind of knock a Rema and you know I have the *pai'ess* and I have the tradition so I can get away with it. Women could do the same thing but only if we can commit the resources....

B. Originally cited on p. 64:

I wish I could go back to Borough Park this Shabbos. I would love to have another apparition, similar to the one I had last time I was there. This time though, I would like to meet God. Perhaps he could explain Himself to me. Why does a relationship with him have to be so volatile? While in the end of Shemot/beginning of Va'Yikra He was desperately pursuing intimacy with humanity, by mid Devarim (particularly in this week's parsha) He acts like a jilted lover, ferociously angry, and cursing uncontrollably. It's a bit erratic. The rationalist's attempt to make sense of such erratic behavior stopped speaking to me the day my religiosity left the rationalist arena. I long ago stopped looking to the rationalists for religious meaning. Being a rationalist believer is an oxymoron, a complete contradiction in terms. Religion and theological belief operate on a plane all by themselves, roughly midpoint between our minds and our hearts. That's the realm in which such aggressive Divine behavior has to make sense. So far it doesn't. The best attempt at dealing with this challenge is Jack Mile's book: God A Biography. Check it out. He's a real theological lamdan.

C. Originally cited on p. 64:

A MUST read-if you are infatuated with the Book of Job as much as I am. "This is without doubt due, in part, to the Book's amorality. I believe that if you woke a lot of people in the middle of the night, and asked them why they cared about the Book of Job, they would name the most troubling, least sympathetic character in that document: God. He, not Job, is the star of the Book, and though he is not loving or fair, that seems to be part of the attraction. Once God appears and speaks, you are almost blown to the ground... "

D. Originally cited on p. 65:

R. I. P. Moshe Rabbainu was destroyed in last week's parsha, his spiritual quest squashed. After pursuing God for many years, he was, so to speak, finally ready to move in. Drooling over the topographical beauty of Israel, he beseeches God to let him enter, to be close and intimate. God harshly rejects Moshe's courtship. All He offers him is a peek. Moshe, like Icarus, gets burned once he attempts to get too close. God, abhors intimacy. He, like the sun, burns those who get too intimate. כי ה' אלקיך אש אוכלה הוא. His spiritual quest crushed, Moshe experienced a spiritual death. From here on in he was merely a dead man walking, his life's pursuit denied and rejected. Exaggerated piety is the flip side of extreme evil, God abhors both. Humanity's task is to find a balance, not to veer too far from the Divine path, but, at the same time, also not to get too close. Intimacy is not His thing. As Ecclesiastes warns, אל תהי רשע הרבה, but at the same time also אל תהי צדיק הרבה. Abundant spiritually burns and annihilates. Below: Sun, or the Fall of Icarus (1819) by Merry-Joseph Blondel, in the Rotunda of Apollo at the Louvre.

E. Originally cited on p. 68:

Rashi got it wrong. Misled by the way things are ordered in the Bible, where the narrative precedes the laws, he assumes (as he says explicitly in his first comment on the Torah) that the narrational section of the Torah is the preamble and the legal part the climax. Au contraire! As he himself repeatedly points out, the Torah is not a linear text. In this case the order is actually inverted, the law is the introduction and the narrative the content. For Rashi, observance is the essence of religion, but that is not necessarily true. Religion is theology, not jurisprudence. Halacha is the mechanical means which allows religion to achieve its vibrant spiritual end. Laws do not have intrinsic religious value. They are there to provide the framework in which our spiritual narrative can grow and blossom. As this week's Torah portion switches from story telling to commanding, do not let the shift obscure your focus. We indulge in these laws so that we are better equipped, personally and communally, to further perpetuate our transformative religious narrative.

Chapter 4

A. Originally cited on p. 82:

…With what [e.g., Why] do we believe in him [Moses]? Standing at Sinai, that our eyes saw and not another's. Our ears heard and not another's, the fire, the sounds, the lightning. He went into the clouds and the Voice said to him, *Moses, Moses, say to them, this and this.* Also it says, *Face to face Hashem spoke to them* (Deuteronomy 5:4). And it says, *not with your fathers did I seal this covenant* (Deuteronomy 5:3). And how do we know that the event of Mount Sinai alone is proof that his prophecy is true beyond a doubt? It says, *Behold I come before you in a thick cloud so that the people will hear me speaking to you, so that they will believe in you forever* (Exodus 19:9). It implies: before this, they did not believe with complete faith, but rather with a faith that had thought after it [i.e., doubt].

B. Originally cited on p. 86:

Our new model should be: BELIEF in a God you doubt or believe no longer exists; and, along those lines, BELIEF in a Mamad Har Sinai moment that you no longer accept as factual. We can do this by categorically shifting our conception of faith. We need to take belief out of the logical arena and put it where it belongs, in the psycho/spiritual realm. Belief is a religious mantra, not an intellectual conviction. A Religious faith-statement is dogmatic, not scientific. This understating of our religious charge could perhaps be our new and reconstituted Luchot.

C. Originally cited on p. 87:

Poor rationalists, they spend their lives feeding an insatiable theology which constantly craves new "proofs." Today it is the website Mosaic's turn to bring an offering of "evidence" to placate the Gods of science. See link below for a confection of scientific morsels which attempt, once again, to "prove" the validity of the Exodus story. Time to crush that misconception about Jewish theology and return to our pre-Maimonidean A- rational roots. The Exodus story definitely and irrefutably happened—in the Torah.

D. Originally cited on p. 88:

God (talk) needs a tune-up. Our religious discourse is outdated, stuck in medieval paradigms. We still talk about "ought" when "ought" language no longer resonates with your average 21st-century intellectual. We need to update it! "Should" needs to be replaced with "could". I long ago made that change. I don't believe in God merely because I have to, I believe in Him because

I want to, because belief in a transcendent Being adds meaning to life. Likewise, I don't accept the Divinity of the Torah because of Maimonides' Eighth Principle. As a matter of fact, I sometimes have trouble with Maimonides' arguments, I don't always find them compelling or convincing. Instead, I believe that the Torah is Divine because I chose to believe that; because believing in the Divinity of the Torah adds a spiritual dimension to my moral and religious pursuits, something it otherwise would not have. In other words, I WILL myself to believe. My beliefs are volitional, not obligatory; a mental choice, not necessarily an intellectual conviction. And, that is the plane in which we need to conduct our religious discourse. We should set aside language of "obligation," "ought," or "required," and replace it with language of "will," "choice," and "meaning." The questions we need to ask are: 1) Does the choice to believe add meaning to life? And 2) could one will themselves to believe? I think the answer is YES on both: a life of belief is more meaningful, and, ANYONE can will themselves to believe if they so choose--even an atheist!"

E. Originally cited on p. 94:

As an Orthodox Rabbinical School, Yeshivat Chovevei Torah is committed to the classic, Torah-true *mesoret* of *Torah Min Hashamyim,* a basic tenet of Jewish belief. That is what we teach. As Rav Nati Helfgot, Chair of our Philosophy Department (*Machshava*) wrote, the yeshiva teaches in a classical and traditional way that both the oral and written Torah were revealed to Moshe at Sinai and in the wilderness. At the same time, as Rav Ysoscher Katz wrote, since we are an Open Orthodox rabbinical school, we want our students to struggle openly throughout their lives as they integrate the *mesoret* into their own hearts and souls. Our *talmidim* are exposed to a range of views on *Torah Min Hashamayim* from our classic commentaries and thinkers, and students will embrace different views along this traditional spectrum. Some *talmidim* are in the midst of theological work to uphold Orthodoxy in a way they find intellectually honest. One recent example is Rav Zev Farber, whose journey has taken him to the outer boundaries of Orthodox thinking on this subject. Rav Zev is thinking honestly and personally, but his ideas are different from, and in some ways contradictory to, what we teach and ask our students to believe at YCT. He discusses his struggle in more detail here. Rav Zev is a big enough *talmid chacham* to defend his Orthodoxy from all his critics. We support his honesty and speaking his mind, but he speaks for himself, not YCT. His beliefs on this matter are his own and far from the broad classical views of *Torah Min Hashamayim* that we at the Yeshiva believe in. Yeshivat Chovevei Torah Rabbinical School actively encourages diversity of thought—all anchored within our students' passion for their Orthodoxy. I invite you to become part of the conversation, part of a dynamic Orthodoxy that is open and contemporary, but, most important, an integral part of the unfolding of *Hashem's* holy Torah, given to us all so long ago at Sinai.

F. Originally cited on p. 96:

It is the task of contemporary Modern Orthodox *poskim* to determine halachically-appropriate responses to twenty-first-century expressions of heresy. Modern Orthodoxy is charting new territory in this arena. Never before have we been tasked with adjudicating something of such magnitude and complexity, nor do we have precedents on which to build. While ultra-Orthodoxy did condemn heretics over the years, contra Dr. Berger, those decisions cannot be replicated in the Modern Orthodox context, a milieu entirely different than theirs. Their decisions are, therefore, informative but not dispositive. YCT will, of course, make a judicial decision about those students who have unfortunately espoused heretical views, but that decision will be distinct from its predecessors. It will also take time to produce. Those who clamor for resolution will have to wait.

G. Originally cited on p. 96:

There is no doubt that one can raise legitimate critiques of YCT. (I'm the first one to admit that there are many.) Addressing them, however, requires knowledge, nuance and sophistication, something that's sorely missing in these columns and blog posts. Heresy is one of the most complex questions in Halacha, something we at Chovevei have been debating for years. Pat and simplistic approaches might work for the Chareidi community, but we are not Chareidi, we are modern. A Modern Orthodox *posek* needs time to resolve questions of such monumental significance. Issues like women's Talmud study, bat mitzvah and the like, which pits tradition against modernity, took a long time to sort out. Heresy is no different. It poses huge challenges to a religious Jew who is committed to Halacha and to modernity. Erring on these matters, one way or another, is extremely consequential and detrimental to people's lives. נצחיות התורה makes us confident that we will eventually figure this out, but it will take time, nuance, knowledge and sophistication, not loud voiced newspaper columns, to get there.

H. Originally cited on p. 102:

We live in a post-modern world where objective truth is rejected and absolute claims are frowned upon. I would go as far as to say that rationalism (in the general and colloquial sense) as a source for *Emunah* is bankrupt, it increasingly speaks to fewer people. It, therefore, behooves us to come up with alternative models. Chassidut could very well be that alternative model. Facts and empirical truth is not Chassidut's primary currency. While it does a priori accept the biblical theological faith statements, its goal is not to argue or prove the scientific veracity of the Bible's claims. Truth is not of primary concern for these thinkers. Chassidic theology has two main features. It is a-rational and a-historical. It is apathetic about Jewish historicity as a proactive theological stance. The Torah for Chassidim is there to teach us how to live life and serve God, the narrative qua narrative (the origin story) is mere background music. The narration parts of the Torah are, therefore, not of much theological significance to them, they are a-historical. However, during those rare occasions when they do pay attention to the biblical "stories," their orientation is a-rational. They absolutely "believe" those stories, but their belief is internal: it is true because it happened in the Torah. That is where these events transpire and that is where these stories matter. Asking about their historicity is, as far as they are concerned, foolish and missing the point. At the same time, to the extent that the biblical narratives have religious and theological significance, they read those stories through the Rabbinic lens. So, for example, while Moshe's historicity is not historically relevant to them, his persona carries theological and ethical significance.

I. Originally cited on pp. 105-106:

Aside from the basic Halakhic question-is there a way to exempt a female convert from having to tovel (dunk) in the presence of the three men of the Beit Din?-the issue raises larger philosophical questions:

1) How do we deal with a halakhic requirement that no longer conforms with contemporary notions of ethics and morality?
2) What are the rules for reinterpreting halakhic idioms (terms like be'dieved and the like)?
3) What is the role of the Talmud in MO pesika; does it have legal weight and halakhic authority, or did chasimas ha'talmud rob it of halakhic significance? Feel free to share, disseminate, and distribute.

J. Originally cited on p. 106:

We believe that this Oneness is neither a body nor a bodily force, nor is He subject to any bodily characteristics—movement, rest, or dwelling—be they inherent or by chance. Therefore, the Sages repudiated [the possibility of any] cohesion or separation [concerning Him], as they said: "Above there is no sitting, standing, division, or 'cohesion'" (a usage based on Isaiah 11:14). As the prophet (*ibid.*, 40:18-25) said: "Who is comparable to the Almighty...?" For if He had a body, He could be compared to other bodies. All the corporeal terms used in the Scriptures to describe Him—such as walking, standing, sitting, speaking, and so on—are metaphorical. As the Sages have said: "The Torah speaks in the language of man." This is the Third Principle, as affirmed by the verse (Deuteronomy 4:15) *You have not seen any image.* That is to say, you cannot conceive of Him as having any form because, as stated, He is neither a body nor a bodily force. (Translation from http://www.aish.com/jl/p/mp/48924072.html.)

K. Originally cited on p. 107:

And since it has been clarified that He has no body, it is clear that no aspect of physicality can be ascribed to Him.... He has no death and no life like the life of a physical being, and no foolishness or wisdom like the wisdom of a wise man; he has neither sleep nor wakefulness, neither anger, nor laughter, neither happiness nor sadness, neither quietness or speech like the speech of people. The Rabbis said, "Above, there is no sitting or standing, no combination or separation."

L. Originally cited on p. 108:

We believe and affirm that the Messiah will come. One should not think he is detained. [Rather,] *If he should tarry, await him* (Habakkuk 2:3). One is not to assign him a specific time of arrival, nor should one use Scripture to deduce when he is coming. For the Sages have said, "The souls of those who calculate the end will be shattered." [One must also] believe that [the Messiah] will surpass all the kings who have ever ruled in terms of his grandeur, his greatness, and his honor. [Man should] exalt, love, and pray for him according to the prophecies prophesied about him by all the prophets from Moshe Rabbeinu to Malachi. He who doubts or belittles [the Messiah's arrival] denies [the authority of the Torah, which explicitly promises his arrival] in the story of Bilaam and in Deuteronomy 30. Included within this Principle is [the idea] that the king of Israel must come from the House of David and the seed of Solomon. Anyone who opposes this dynasty defies the Almighty and the words of His prophets. (Translation from http://www.aish.com/jl/p/mp/48929482.html).

Chapter 5

A. Originally cited on p. 120:

Chazal were the R. Riskin's of their time. They too were committed to creating a Yiddishkeit which is in constant dialogue with their ethical sensibilities. They read Torah with a critical lens and whenever they encountered a perceived injustice they did whatever they could (within legitimate boundaries) to undo the challenging misread. This week's *parsha* is a perfect example. Simply read, the biblical sotah procedure seems capricious and patriarchal. The rabbis, incorporating Divinely ordained hermeneutics, drastically revised the procedure. The result: a process that is sensitive and somewhat egalitarian. They were the progressives of their time, and, relative to their milieu, quite radical. They too were vilified, but in the end they prevailed. Ultimately their enterprise received the divine imprimatur. It is because of their courage that Rabbinic Judaism is still around today. Their interpretations allowed Judaism to survive, thrive and ultimately triumph.

B. Originally cited on p. 121:

While *Chazal* tempered the laws and used various maneuvers in avoiding any untoward consequences of the laws existing on the books, they don't deal with the intent and the meaning of the laws that go to the heart of the ethical problems. In other words, *Chazal* avoided the problem by reinterpreting the laws and presenting their interpretation as the Torah's original intent. This does not solve the problem for those of us who believe that laws developed over time, and that the rabbinic interpretation is anachronistic. Thus, we have little choice but to try to uncover the moral underpinnings of the Torah's legislation and deal honestly with its limitations. How are we to do this?

C. Originally cited on p. 127:

Colleagues, and "friends," I wrote a *teshuvah* (in Hebrew), in which I argue for a more *tzanuah* approach toward female conversions,* especially in light of the inappropriate allegations coming out of Washington, D. C. (Please click on link embedded in the link below.) Aside from the basic Halakhic question—is there a way to exempt a female convert from having to *tovel* (dunk) in the presence of the three men of the Beit Din?—the issue raises larger philosophical questions: 1) How do we deal with a halakhic requirement that no longer conforms with contemporary notions of ethics and morality? 2) What are the rules for reinterpreting halakhic idioms (terms like *be'dieved* and the like)? 3) What is the role of the Talmud in MO *pesikah*; does it have legal weight and halakhic authority, or did *chasimas ha'Talmud* rob it of halakhic significance?

Chapter 6

A. Originally cited on p. 136:

Many of my Orthodox co-religionist obviously understand this danger, yet they insist that homosexuality is so perverse that it should override the church/state consideration, for it threatens the very moral fabric of our society. It is here that I take strong exception. Over the years, I have met countless gay people and gay couples who live loving, exemplary lives. I know this firsthand as some are members of my synagogue. Of course, there are gay people who live unethical lives; this fact, however, is a reflection of their humanness, not their sexual orientation. The same is true for heterosexuals. I did not always see things this way. I grew up being taught that the Bible regarded homosexuality as an abomination. This is the most common translation of the word "to'evah" used by the Bible to proscribe homosexual intercourse. To'evah, however, is a biblical term that has no exact English equivalent. The Talmud interprets it as a composite of three words: to'eh atah bah – "you have gone astray" in engaging in this kind of relationship. That is a far cry from an "abomination." Still, as an Orthodox Jew, I submit to the Biblical prohibition. But as an open Orthodox rabbi, I refuse to reject the person who seeks to lead a life of same sex love. If I welcome with open arms those who do not observe Sabbath, Kashrut or family purity laws, I must welcome, even more so, homosexual Jews, as they are born with their orientation. In fact, many heterosexual improprieties are called to'evah, in addition to violations of laws wholly outside the realm of sexuality such as cheating in business. To single out homosexuality from other biblical proscriptions is unfair and smacks of a double standard.

B. Originally cited on p. 139:

Religious Freedom and Marriage Fairness Act: As rabbis, parents, and citizens of Illinois, we want to offer all loving and committed couples in our community the support and protections of having the state recognize their marriage. The best way to offer these protections is through the passage of the marriage bill in the Illinois legislature as it not only supports loving couples, but allows clergy to make their own decisions about whether to officiate. The words of Psalm 89 resonate deeply with us: "This world will be built on love... Righteousness and justice are the foundation of God's throne, compassion and truth go forth from it." We find compassion in our tradition as the Torah commands us to treat everyone with dignity for humankind was created in God's image. We find truth in our tradition as Rabbi Hillel advised: "That which is hateful unto yourself, do it not unto your neighbor. That is the whole of Torah. The rest is commentary. Now go and learn." We find righteousness in our tradition as it commands us to not discriminate against anyone including couples who deserve the rights and protections of a marriage recognized by the state. We find justice in our tradition as it urges us to create communities of people striving to become more holy, inclusive, integrated and whole. We believe that we are obligated to build this world on love. There is no better way to strengthen the love of family and support all loving families than to insure that all loving couples are able to obtain an Illinois marriage license. Some clergy will officiate at all weddings and some will not, yet we know that supporting full marriage equality through the Illinois legislature is our opportunity and sacred obligation to work with God to create a world of love and justice, compassion, peace, and pride.

Rabbi Shoshanah Conover, Temple Sholom of Chicago
   (Reform)
Rabbi Asher Lopatin, Anshe Sholom B'nai Israel Congregation
   (Orthodox)
Rabbi Michael Siegel, Anshe Emet Synagogue (Conservative).

C. Originally cited on p. 142:

I like to not talk about *Vayikra* actually, because I feel like it narrows the conversation like it's a dead end. Like where do we go from there it's an abomination it's over. But to me what we know about being lesbian, gay, bisexual, transgender, queer, you know gender neutral, like this is the way people are, right, like this is life. The psychiatric community knows that this is life and the Rabbis will eventually get it and they will stop focusing on that *pasuk*, I believe.

D. Originally cited on p. 149:

Glad to see this progress in a venerated American institution! It is inevitable that we will reach a societal pinnacle where all will indeed be treated equally! Halleluyah, Boy Scouts of America!

Chapter 7

A. Originally cited on p. 168:

While, like in many parallel Orthodox Yeshivot, we struggle with understanding Halachic (Jewish law) nuances between great Talmudic sages, we also battle with the very nature of the text itself. There we are, day in and day out, a group of feminist scholars and leaders, in a movement seeking to change the gender landscape of Orthodox Jewish leadership. Yet we sit at our tables in front of books where the voices of women barely appear. When they do, it is certainly not as serious partners in the development of the Halachic discourse. So we have a jar. In this jar we put a quarter, or a dollar, or whatever seems appropriate when a woman's voice seems egregiously absent from a conversation in the text. For example, you can walk into our classroom one afternoon as we explore passages where Rabbis discuss the nature of what was likely the uterus. One Rabbi proposes that it resembles a bag of coins with an opening at the top. No, another Rabbi exclaims, what about a home with a door? You'll certainly find me tossing quarters into the jar during that conversation.

B. Originally cited on p. 176:

Watching the Flintstones with my children one day, it struck me that our synagogues have an uncanny resemblance to Lodge No. 26 of the Loyal Order of Water Buffaloes, where Fred and Barney go to have a men's night out. I say this in jest, but it is illustrative. The men of the LOWB wear a special garb, they have a special code and gestures which they use, and there are no women. Although our synagogues are a step advanced from the Stone Age lodge—we let our women watch—the resemblances are worth noting; only the men have the special garb, only the men know the secret handshake, and when the Grand Poobah speaks, his podium faces only men.

C. Originally cited on p. 177:

> Of course, there is more than a simple a choice of musical key that can cause some women to diminish their voice in *shul*. Some feel that the synagogue is not an atmosphere that is open and inviting to women. The choice of key is symbolic of the larger phenomenon—that the locus of control is elsewhere in the room. The decisions that are made as to how the service runs all come from a place to which we have no access. While it's true that all the men in the room are also at the mercy of the *baal tefillah*'s choice in music and the *gabbai*'s choice in aliyah, we women know that these positions will never be open to us. I cannot simply wait until next week to choose my favorite tunes for *Kedusha* at *Mussaf*. I might indirectly influence the choice when my husband leads *davening*, and he chooses tunes he knows I'll enjoy. Thus, it is only when I have an emissary on the other side that I feel I can have a voice. And even then…. Well, let's just say my husband has a lovely tenor voice which does not jive well with my alto.

Chapter 8

A. Originally cited on p. 203:

> Friends, please consider omitting the passage שְׁפֹךְ חֲמָתְךָ אֶל הַגּוֹיִם (asking G-d to pour wrath upon the nations of the world) in the Haggadah this year. This was a justifiable addition in the past (added during the oppressive Crusades) & anti-Semitism is certainly still alive today, but our prayers today need to focus on peace, justice, love, & healing. This is a powerful moment in the Haggadah to feel a little pain, pray for strength, and meditate

on our crucial moral leadership role in our un-redeemed world. We are to take the high road & not hide behind prayers of old laden with anger & hate, justifiable then (in powerlessness & isolation) but potentially dangerous today (in an era of power & inter-dependence). Rabbi David Hartman wisely advised: "A sacred text is a text that haunts me all the time—but it doesn't paralyze me."

B. Originally cited on p. 209:

For the record, I'm not an expert in anything. I am passionate about Judaism and I love the Jewish people with all my heart—but I am not an expert. And for sure, I do not know a lot about Reform Judaism. Having said that, tonight, I wanted to share with you some of the elements of Reform Judaism which I find appealing… and in order for an Orthodox Jew to speak this way, I obviously feel a sense of comfort with who I am, a commitment to true openness, genuine and heartfelt respect, no hard feelings, and a passionate desire to connect the Jewish people with our tradition and to bring unity to the Jewish nation.

C. Originally cited on p. 210:

You know, we Orthodox Jews could learn a thing or two from the new prayer book published by the Reform movement this year. It is being heralded as the most inclusive prayer book yet. They've substituted phrases like bride and groom with the word couple. They refer to God in the feminine in some cases. While I am not advocating changing our Machzor, I am arguing that we should be more careful with our language. We should always be attempting to maximally include and minimally exclude.

D. Originally cited on p. 212:

Last month I was ordained as a rabbi. I joined the ranks of those far more learned, wise and experienced than I, and in so doing I am linked to a chain that connects me to the sages of old and the sages of now. Their names fill my bookshelves: Heschel, Soloveitchik, Kaplan. Their ethos permeates my spirituality: Carlebach, Schachter-Shalomi, Schneerson. Their presence in my life directs mine: Rabbi Yitz Greenberg, Rabbi Avi Weiss, Rabbi Mychal Springer. I am indebted to these men and women who believe in the timeless truth of our Torah and brought me to where I am today.

E. Originally cited on p. 218:

...and I do think that if halachic, traditional Judaism can some how get back to being a moral beacon. And Rav Daniel, that challenge of why aren't we a moral beacon for the world. But if we can become a moral beacon than I think we can, Orthodoxy can have a great message for the entire Jewish world and beyond. And many people do work in Jewish farming and in treatment of animals and in all sorts of areas but we have to get back to that current of morality that frequently maybe usually is a counter current and that's what we are trying to look for.

F. Originally cited on p. 220:

Au contraire! To react zealously to heresy is a chillul HaShem. A kiddush HaShem is to act God like (yoma 69B), methodically and with restraint. Chazal rued the day they impulsively rejected a heretical student outright (Sanhedrin 107b), implicitly blaming the disintegration of the Jewish community on an absolutist judiciary. As we now know, the Rabbi's absolutist approach to a student who did not conform to the expected norms caused long term damage to our physical and spiritual wellbeing. It was a tragic mistake. Judging heresy, they teach us, needs to be done deliberately and methodically. Heresy, like every capital crime, may take five, ten, or maybe even up to seventy years to adjudicate. One suspects that Brachot 32B (כהן שהרג את הנפש) is a veiled critique of leadership which kowtows to the bloodthirstiness of the masses. The Kohanic leadership (the ultra-orthodox of their time) were a quick-shoot, gun ready at any hint of dogmatic deviation. The Rabbis (the MO of their time), it seems, advocate a more gun shy judiciary. Ultimately the Rabbis won, relegating Kohanic extremism to the dustbin of Jewish history. The moderate, gun-shy voice will prevail again, today. While condemnation and pat answers placates some people, many find them hurtful and insulting. They are looking for courageous leadership, one which consoles rather than condemns. They want Rabbis who honor their theological struggles, and address these complex questions with the sophistication that they deserve.

G. Originally cited on p. 222:

My disillusionment with Brisk came when I realized that all that Brisker sophistication stops when it comes to theology. Litvish theology tends to be simplistic and impersonal. When my life hit a bump, all that torah was useless, I was looking for a language that would allow me to express my pain and anger to Him in real and personal language. That is what brought me back אל חיק החסידות. Their theology is personal, deeply psychological and incredibly sophisticated.

Chapter 9

A. Originally cited on p. 226:

We believe that [Moshe Rabbeinu] is the father of all the prophets before and after him, all of whom were beneath him in stature. He was chosen above all mankind, achieving a greater knowledge of the Almighty than anyone before or since. Moshe Rabbeinu reached a level that surpasses human attainment and approximates the angelic. There was no barrier that he did not penetrate, no physical limitation that hindered him and no imperfection, large or small, [to impede him]. In achieving this [level], he lost his sensual and imaginative faculties; his drives and desires ceased, leaving only his pure intellect. Concerning this, it is said that Moshe communicated with God without any angelic intermediary. (Translation from http://www.aish.com/jl/p/mp/48925042.html. Retrieved August 20, 2015.)

B. Originally cited on p. 226:

The answer might be that their sin is all of those and none. It lays not in the acts themselves, but in what they demonstrate. For each one of these things shows that Moshe is still the leader of old and is not able to adapt to the changes ahead. Think of what he could have done differently: He could have engaged the people rather than running to the Tent of Meeting and calling on God to help. God even told him to break the old patterns and commanded him to speak to the rock, not to hit it, but he couldn't do it. Instead, he fell back into what was familiar, hitting the rock rather than speaking to it. There is a lot of symbolism in the choice of whether to speak or to hit. Does one speak, trying to engage, thinking that there can be a meaningful connection with the other side, believing oneself and the other are open to the change that can emerge when two sides are in open and reflective conversation? Or does one hit, believing that no true conversation can take place and that behavior can only be modified by brute force from above? If after all this time Moshe still sees the people as incorrigible rebels who can only be beaten into submission, then it is time that Moshe step back and allow a new leader to take over.

C. Originally cited on p. 226-227:

Moshe's response is all about proving who is right and who is wrong. He speaks to, or more accurately, *at*, Korach but not with him. He summons Datan and Aviram but does not go to them. He makes no attempt to genuinely engage his opposition, to listen to them and try to understand their complaints or their motivations. He points out Korach's hypocrisy, noting that he is not after equality for the people but leadership for himself. And while Moshe may be completely correct in this point, revealing this truth will hardly win Korach - or even the people - over. Moshe may be rightfully hurt that the people are shifting the blame for their failures and their current predicament onto him, but calling out to God and focusing on the wrongness of that claim rather than the people's reality gets him nowhere. In the end, Moshe demands a showdown with one ultimate winner and one ultimate loser, and the consequences are drastic and deadly: truth wins out, but its price is the complete destruction of the other side. This is one way of approaching conflict, but it will not necessarily lead to the best results. Here, the focus is on a narrow, abstract truth, not the deeper truth of human beings, human emotions and motivations, societal realities, or interpersonal relationships. An approach such as this can even be quite counter-productive. What is the aftermath of Moshe's proofs? Are the people satisfied now that they know he was right and Korach was wrong? Quite the contrary: "But on the morrow all the congregation of the children of Israel murmured against Moshe and against Aharon, saying, 'You have killed the people of the Lord'" (Bamidbar, 16:41). The people do not see justice in Moshe's actions; his response was too violent, even if he was right.

D. Originally cited on p. 227:

Over 3,000 years later and we still haven't solved the debate between Moshe and Korach. Moshe advocated a centralized model of leadership, while Korach advocated an egalitarian, lay led model-Ki kol ha'eidah kulam kedoshim, u'be'tocham Hashem... While a simple read would suggest that Moses was right and Korach wrong, some commentators don't accept that narrative. The Yismach Moshe (1759-1841) said that had he been around during the fight between Moshe and Korach he wouldn't have necessarily sided with Moshe. At best, he would have remained neutral. The Arizal goes even further. According to him, Moses' victory was temporary. He believes that in the world to come Korach's approach would be triumphant. Korach's nuanced formulation, Ki kol ha'eidah kulam "kedoshim," upped the ante. Not only did he disagree with Moshe's politics, he thought that the centralized model also shortchanged the community's religiosity. The way he saw it, his model isn't just politically prudent, it is also more conducive to creating sacredness. Kedusha (the spirit of the Torah, קדושים תהיו) is generated by the community, not by its leaders."כשהלכה רופפת בידך, פוק חזי מאי עמא דבר; communal sentiment is a significant factor in determining Halakhic norms (Yerushalmi, Pesachim, ch. 4) And the debate rages on ...(Below, Botticelli-The Punishment of the Rebels)

E. Originally cited on p. 229:

Moses Transformed. (In honor of his Hebrew *yahrtzeit* tonight, the seventh of Adar) The Biblical Moses is presented as a jurist; the "law" animates and inspires him. *Chazal* completely rewrite his character. The Rabbis reject his judicial views as conservative and archaic. They also downplay his jurisprudential significance, emphasizing instead a different aspect of his personality. The Talmudic Moses is less of a jurist and more of a theologian. They portray him as a confused and flummoxed philosopher who wrangles with God and authors theological treatises. Personally, I prefer the Talmudic version. Judicially, his legal philosophy has been supplanted by Rabbinic jurisprudence; biblical "law" has little significance for the contemporary jurists. His theology, on the other hand, is as relevant today as it was during the time of the Exodus. The things that perplexed him then still confound us today, many centuries later. יהא זכרו ברוך*

F. Originally cited on p. 229:

Leonard Nimoy died this morning. Nimoy was more than just "Spock," he was also an artist and noted photographer. His photography forced you to take a walk in the garden of uncertainty (עץ הדעת טוב ורע), they left you inspired and repulsed. You were left wondering if he was a boundary-pushing mystic, or merely a perverse opportunist. Thankfully, we will never know the answer. And, that is precisely what made him a good artist. He did exactly what artists are supposed to do: shake our world and rattle our complacency. *Lecha Dodi Likrat Kallah Shabbat Malkata*! May your soul soar upwards to unite with the *Shekhina*, the aspect of God that simulated your imagination, allowing you to create art that left your admirers inspired and perplexed.

G. Originally cited on p. 230:

Our sages extended understanding and compassion toward the one who cursed God and actually cast Moshe and the Sanhedrin in the role of the oppressors. Moshe and the Sanhedrin are agents of the Torah of the Mind and God's voice in this midrash is that of the Torah of the Heart. There is no practical resolution to the conflict offered here. I believe that our Sages, by boldly casting Moshe and the Sanhedrin as the villains, and bringing in the poignant proof texts from *Kohelet*, intended to shock us into grappling with the issue.

H. Originally cited on p. 236:

Yaakov, unloved by his father, driven away from his home and homeland at an early age, was a loner. He always had to do everything, and he would do it alone. Yaakov never learns to reach out to others for help. Sure, he calls Rachel and Leah to the field. But he didn't consult with them. He just needed them to acquiesce to a decision he had already made. Yaakov never lets anyone see his vulnerabilities. He has cloaked himself in Esav's clothes—the clothes of the strong, independent, fearless hunter—so that no one can see the Yaakov, the not-always strong, not always confident, herder of sheep who lies underneath. Consider his unfeeling response to Rachel when she complains to him about her barrenness: "Am I in God's stead, who has withheld from you the fruit of the womb?" (Breishit 30:2). The Rabbis were rightfully shocked: "Is this how you respond to those in distress?!" (Breishit Rabbah). But what made him respond this way? It was his inability to be present for another person when she was weak, when she was feeling vulnerable. He could never expose this part of himself, so he could not relate when others exposed themselves this way to him. "You have to be strong. If you have any issues—talk to God like I do—don't turn to others for help." To project such strength is great when everything works out, like it does in the beginning of our *parashah*—it is Yaakov's strategy, Yaakov's coordinating, his actions and no one else's that save them from Esav. But what about the times when he can't handle it all himself? At those times, he is unable to turn to others and he is paralyzed. His daughter is raped by Shechem—he does nothing. He hears, and he is silent. He waits for his sons to return—not to consult with them, but because he is paralyzed. They then take over and tragedy ensues. And all he can then do is lash out. Where was his voice earlier when it was needed? Reuven sleeps with Bilhah after Rachel dies. What does the verse say: "And Israel heard." And then nothing. He is not able to handle this alone. Does he turn to anyone for help? No. Just silence and paralysis. Yosef is presumed to be dead, and his whole family attempts to console him. But they have nothing to offer him. He is committed to being alone in his suffering. Better to suffer alone than to let people see you weak, to let people see that you need them. This was Yaakov. *Va'yivater Yaakov livado.* At the end of the day, with all his wives, children, and sheep, he is left alone. He has chosen to be alone. He must be strong. He must do it all himself.

I. Originally cited on p. 238:

The Rabbis connect these stories. Why did Leah go out? She went out to bring Jacob back to her tent. Why did Dinah go out? As her mother's daughter, she, too, must have gone out to entice a man back to her tent. This Rashi is incredibly troubling and deeply painful. In no uncertain terms, Rashi is saying that Dinah bears, at the very least, some of the blame for her attack.

J. Originally cited on p. 238:

Regardless of exactly what transpired, it's clear that Abram employs Sarai's sexuality as a tool and, to some extent, abandons her to the possibility of sexual assault in Pharaoh's harem. We might read Sarai's explosive, violent anger towards Hagar in light of the incident in Egypt. Just as Sarai was used and abandoned in Egypt, so she uses and abuses Hagar sexually/tactically/ reproductively/physically. In treating Hagar as she does, Sarai acts from deep rage, just as a victim of abuse might behave.

About the Author

David Rosenthal is a *musmach* of Ner Israel Rabbinical College where he has been a *talmid* for the past ten years. He holds a BS degree from Johns Hopkins University and is from Manalapan, NJ.

www.ingramcontent.com/pod-product-compliance
Lightning Source LLC
Chambersburg PA
CBHW051821040426
42447CB00006B/302